RED SPIES IN THE U.S.

OTHER BOOKS BY THE AUTHOR:

The Brigitte Bardot Story
Marilyn Monroe: Her Own Story
Clark Gable
Let's Twist
Vince Edwards
Red Spies in the U.N.
The Hidden Side of Jacqueline Kennedy
The Chicago Nurse Murders
Red Spies in Washington
Jackie and Ari: For Love or Money?
The Gary Cooper Story
Johnny Cash
Ordeal by Trial: The Alice Crimmins Case
The John Wayne Story
The Bobby Sherman Story
Three Picassos Before Breakfast

RED SPIES IN THE U.S.

George Carpozi Jr.

Arlington House   New Rochelle, New York

Library of Congress Catalog Card Number 73-9818

Manufactured in the United States of America

Library of Congress Cataloging in Publication Data

Carpozi, George.
    Red spies in the U. S.

    1. Espionage, Russian—United States.
2. Subversive activities—United States.
3. United States. Federal Bureau of Investigation.
I. Title.
E743.5.C289   327'.12   73-9818
ISBN 0-87000-223-6

Contents

A Lesson To Be Learned . . .

This book, my third on Soviet espionage and my twentieth in the field of documentary reporting, is respectfully dedicated to L. Patrick Gray III, the short-term Acting Director of the Federal Bureau of Investigation, who declined the Bureau's assistance and cooperation to the author—contrary to the gracious aid and collaboration granted by his predecessor, the late J. Edgar Hoover, in the preparation of the earlier spy books.

It is the author's sincere hope that Mr. Gray will come to recognize that curtains of secrecy cannot be lowered on a free press, and that there is no way of preventing penetration by enterprising and inquisitive reporters determined to gather facts in the possession of the Bureau that rightfully belong in the public domain.

GEORGE CARPOZI JR.□

Sorry, But The FBI Can't Help You Anymore . . .

Back in October of 1963, when I was Chief Assistant City Editor on Hearst's *New York Journal-American*, I had the germ of an idea about writing a book on Communist espionage. I was motivated by the increasing number of stories we were processing on the City Desk about Soviet spy activities involving Kremlin diplomats assigned to the United Nations.

I believed that a book which catalogued the many cases and cited chapter and verse of Soviet subversion was warranted.

I spoke with Pierre J. Huss, Hearst's chief correspondent at the UN, who agreed that the subject was not only topical but one which begged to be told, to alert the American people to the peril we faced from a country that had been accelerating its espionage activities against us in the decade since the Rosenbergs were executed for passing our atomic secrets to the Soviet Union.

Huss agreed to work with me on the book and his first order of priority was to discuss our project with Henry Cabot Lodge, the U.S. Ambassador at the UN. Lodge agreed that the book must be written. He also promised Pete full cooperation on any matters dwelling on espionage that reposed in the files of the American Delegation to the UN—provided disclosure did not interfere with current investigations or hamper the work of the Federal Bureau of Investigation, which was conducting on-going probes into Soviet subversion at the time.

Before we made any appreciable headway in assembling information for our book, Pete and I encountered an offer of cooperation and assistance from one of the most unexpected sources—the FBI.

That offer came about quite by accident, for neither Pete nor I had dreamed that J. Edgar Hoover's Bureau would entertain any willingness to provide information about cases beyond the meager and terse press releases usually issued after the smashing of each spy escapade.

All of that information, of course, was already in our newspaper libraries and we didn't require the FBI's assistance to conduct that research.

It was on an October day in 1963 that Guy Richards, an Assistant City Editor on the *J-A*, called me away from my slot on the City Desk and asked me to meet Cartha "Deke" DeLoach, the chief of the FBI's Public Information Bureau in Washington, and John F. Malone, who only recently had taken over the New York City FBI office as Agent-in-Charge. DeLoach and Malone had dropped into our City Room to discuss a story that Richards was working on.

After exchanging amenities, I turned to Malone and said that Huss and I were preparing to write a book about Soviet espionage. Then, almost kiddingly, I said, "And, of course, we expect that you'll cooperate fully with us since most of the cases we're interested in were handled by your office."

Before Malone could reply, DeLoach said:

"George, I don't think you should write a single word about any of the cases . . . "

He paused briefly before continuing. I was startled. Tearing through my mind in that instant was the distressing thought that the FBI was brazenly suggesting that we not write the book on espionage. But then DeLoach went on to finish what he had begun to say.

" . . . until you have come down to Washington and talked

with us. We have files on all the cases and I'm sure we can steer you right with facts that are not available to you. I think the book you want to do can be a great one if it has the documentation that we are in a position to provide."

DeLoach asked me to phone him in Washington at the first opportunity to schedule a day when I could drop into the Justice Department Building and set the wheels in motion for the writing project.

I called DeLoach in mid-December but he apologized that he could not possibly help me at that time. The Bureau, he said, was "up to its neck in work" in the wake of President John F. Kennedy's assassination.

But in February, 1964, when I called DeLoach again, he was ready to see me. I went to Washington and DeLoach immediately brought me to meet an agent named Fern C. Stukenbroeker, who was to supervise the FBI's research of cases that Huss and I were interested in and to provide us with all the details and data that the Bureau could release without endangering investigations of current or unsolved cases.

Stukenbroeker broke out a file on just one of the cases bearing on espionage, that of Judith Coplon, the American government-girl, and Valentin Gubitchev, the first UN spy unmasked by the FBI in an attempt to steal secrets from the Justice Department in Washington.

"Just glance at the size of this file," Stukenbroeker said to me. "It's enormous. Of course there is no way that I can allow you to leaf through it. That will have to be our job—to cull it and give you a comprehensive writeup on the case."

The file was more than a foot thick. It was a monumental task and I couldn't help but feel elation over the generous assistance and cooperation that the FBI was prepared to give Huss and me in our endeavor to write the first authentic account of espionage emanating from the Soviet Delegation at the UN.

Every file was not as thick as the Coplon-Gubitchev case. But each one was voluminous nevertheless.

In a few weeks, I received the first writeup on a case from Stukenbroeker, and in the weeks and months following, the mailman periodically dropped off envelopes from the FBI in Washington containing other cases. By year's end, all the cases that Huss and I had planned on covering in our book—and a number of others that we knew nothing about but which the FBI saw fit to make available to us—were in our hands. The book was written and published under the title *Red Spies in the U.N.* On the jacket back was this endorsement from Henry Cabot Lodge:

> In this book, Mr. Huss and Mr. Carpozi give chapter and verse on instances of attempts by Soviet spies to penetrate official American secrets and thus directly to endanger the security of the United States . . . I applaud their putting this sinister and unsavory record between two covers.

Publication was in 1965. Reviewers were extremely generous in their praise of the work. Huss and I decided to write a sequel, a book about espionage directed from the Soviet Embassy in Washington.

Again as before, the FBI leaned over backwards to help gather cases for us. But just as this work was begun, Pete Huss collapsed in the corridors of the UN and died of a heart attack. I carried on the work myself and in 1968 the book was published under the title of *Red Spies in Washington.*

In the early part of 1972, while I was visiting my editor at Arlington House Publishers in New Rochelle, New York, our discussion turned to espionage.

"Have you another factual spy book in you?" the editor wanted to know. "I've been reading newspaper accounts about continuing Soviet espionage in this country and I believe an in-depth book-length reporting job is warranted."

I agreed that there were many cases which had not been covered, mainly because the concentration and focus of the earlier books were primarily the United Nations and Washington. But there were instances of Soviet espionage in other cities, which had been ignored in the earlier volumes because of the geographical limitations that Huss and I, and later myself, had placed on cases we would cover.

And there were additional instances of Kremlin subversion that had occurred since 1968.

I was then commissioned to write the third book in the series, to be entitled *Red Spies in the U.S.*

The very next morning, as I prepared to make my phone call to the FBI in Washington to determine its readiness to help in assembling the new cases for me, the radio clarioned the bulletin that J. Edgar Hoover was dead. This was no time, I decided, to bother the Bureau with a request for research into spy cases. I decided to give them a decent interval to recover from the shock of Hoover's death and to overcome the predictable turmoil that would follow the demise of the man who had run the Bureau virtually single-handed for the past half-century.

Soon, President Richard M. Nixon appointed a new head to take over the Bureau for what then was ostensibly a temporary period, perhaps until after the 1972 Presidential election. The man he chose was Louis Patrick Gray III, who had no experience in law enforcement per se. He had spent twenty years in the Navy, practiced law, saw a bit of service as an executive assistant in Health, Education and Welfare, then briefly ran the Civil Division of the Justice Department. His tenure in that post ended when the President appointed him Acting Director of the FBI.

What was heartening to me about Gray's elevation to the director's job—despite criticism in many quarters that he was bringing the Bureau perilously close to the political arena and risking involvements that Hoover had sedulously avoided—was a statement he made in a *Life* magazine interview concerning the "Red Menace."

Hoover had always given total priority to subversives and potential subversives as well as to radicals. Gray indicated quite clearly that such attention in the past was justified because grand juries had returned indictments against the accused, though many of the cases ultimately failed in court.

"Our job is not to determine whether they should be prosecuted," Gray was quoted in the article. "But when any individual breaks the law of the U.S. and the FBI has jurisdiction, we're going to investigate."

Gray went on to say that surveillance of radical groups was justified even if they only threatened to break the law.

"The potential is there, the motivation is there," Gray said. "These people are virulently opposed to our constitutional society. Whether they have the capability or not is not for us to judge. We have to provide the intelligence about them."

At that juncture, I felt that the Bureau's policy toward lending cooperation and assistance to an author writing about espionage, a far more heinous crime than radicalism, had remained unchanged

13

and that help would be forthcoming in the same willing manner as on those two prior occasions during Hoover's lifetime.

In my awareness, of course, was the unmistakable trend the Nixon Administration was following in its relations with the world's two leading Communist nations—the Soviet Union and Red China. President Nixon's historic journeys to those countries clearly left no question that our nation's goal was a lessening of the tensions of the long-running Cold War.

Thus, despite Gray's published views, I had to stop and wonder whether this new Administration policy might not reflect itself in the hierarchy of the FBI and its attitude toward opening its files on Communist espionage activity to a writer. Would the FBI, I asked myself, perhaps prefer to remain silent on this subject and display no desire to publicize what has always been one of the sore points in America's relations with the Soviet Union?

I telephoned my contact at the Bureau—Agent Fern Stukenbroeker—and advised him of my commitment to write *Red Spies in the United States*. Could he help me once again? I wanted to know.

His response surprised me, but it didn't startle me. I'd half-expected what he had to say.

"Things have changed in the Bureau," he told me. "We have new policies here now . . . "

He suggested that I make my request directly to the new Director.

On September 6, 1972, I composed the following letter:

> *Dear Mr. Gray:*
>
> I'm writing to you at the suggestion of Fern C. Stukenbroeker to enlist the Bureau's cooperation and assistance in my next writing project—a sequel to my earlier books, *Red Spies in the U.N.*, published by Coward-McCann in 1965, and *Red Spies in Washington*, published by Trident Press, a division of Simon & Schuster, in 1968.
>
> The target of my new book is all significant cases of espionage in the United States that were not reported in my earlier works, as well as all those the FBI investigated since publication of *Spies in Washington*.
>
> It is of course understood that I shall not request material under current investigation nor that which is not in the public domain. That was the arrangement under which write-ups

and/or resumes were provided to me by the Bureau when I gathered material for the first two books.

Again as before I intend to abide by the ground rules guiding discretion and good taste in writing about this sensitive subject. And as a prologue of my good intentions I submit what is past and which stands as my record—the two earlier books which were written with the indispensable assistance of the Bureau.

May I again count on that valued cooperation?

My best wishes.

Very sincerely yours . . .

A little more than two weeks later I received the following response from Gray:

Dear Mr. Carpozi:

Your letter of September 26, 1972, with enclosures, has been received and I appreciate the thought which prompted you to write.

In regard to your inquiry, I regret that the current pressure of the official work of the FBI makes it impossible for us to cooperate with you in your proposed book. I hope that you will understand our position in this regard.

Sincerely yours . . .

The author then proceeded to carry on his investigation of cases despite the FBI Director's polite but implacable rejection of the request for assistance and cooperation.

The results of that investigation into Soviet espionage activity in the United States are reflected in the pages of this book.

Part I

How The Soviet Spy Network
Got Its First Foothold in the United States

Chapter 1

The Strange Double-Life of the Hollywood Producer

A steady hand with neatly manicured, highly buffed fingernails opened the cablegram delivered to the door of the hotel room in Munich. But when the short, pudgy, perfumed man with the bald head and sunlamp tan ripped open the envelope, unfolded the wire, and read the cryptic one-word message, his hands began trembling, his face paled.

"CINERAMA"

That's all there was to the cable.

The man walked uneasily to the telephone on the night table beside the bed and nervously dialed the switchboard.

"Please," he said in a quivering caviar accent, "I want to check out immediately. Would you prepare my bill."

Then he phoned the airport for a reservation on the next flight to London, leaving two hours hence.

Boris Mihailovitch Morros had reacted instinctively to the unsigned transatlantic communication. Decoded it meant:

"Come home. Your life is in danger."

The time had arrived for the sixty-two-year-old Hollywood

producer and music director to leave Europe as hurriedly as he could.

What peril faced him now after more than twenty long years in espionage?

It had been a very long road and a very long career, which even at this moment, as he frantically packed his luggage for his urgent departure, Morros couldn't escape remembering. He'd been involved in some of the century's most sprawling cloak-and-dagger thrillers, entailing virtually every trick in the spy's handbook—coded messages, ambulating international agents, furtive conferences in Prague, Paris, Munich, Berlin, London, Moscow, and most other European capitals, not to overlook New York, Washington, and Hollywood.

Not to overlook New York, Washington, and Hollywood because those cities were the festering hotbeds for the clique of spies that Morros worked with.

There'd been hairbreadth escapes so numerous he couldn't remember half of them; even at this very second, as he opened the door for the bellhop he'd summoned to carry his luggage downstairs, Morros was wondering if he'd make it safely out of the country.

What information had the sender of the cablegram unearthed that showed Morros' life was in peril?

Morros couldn't even begin to guess. All he could do was get out of Bavaria and get out fast. That was how it had been prearranged. When the message came, no matter where he was, he'd have to go.

Rankling his mind right now—as it had for some time—was the peril that had been cast by a prominent American woman who deliberately had almost given Boris Morros away. It was her intuition—a woman's intuition—that enabled her to see through his own motives as an operative in the Soviet Union's worldwide spy network.

She was a remarkable woman. For the moment it will suffice merely to identify her—Martha Dodd, daughter of the one-time United States Ambassador to Germany, Dr. William E. Dodd, and a woman who, wittingly or otherwise, became enmeshed in Soviet espionage while her father was serving his country in the Third Reich during the turbulent 1930s.

After paying his bill and making it safely into a taxi with his luggage, Morros still couldn't help but feel the breath of danger he'd been warned about as the cab sped him over the deserted dark streets of Munich toward the airport for the 11:30 P.M. flight to England. His nervousness may or may not have been apparent to the hack driver, but it was frighteningly real to Morros, who turned repeatedly to steal glimpses out the rear window to assure himself he wasn't being tailed.

Not until he was on the plane and airborne did Morros relax, and even then not fully. He still felt gnawings of apprehension, and was beset with uncertain fears that one or more of the thirteen passengers on the flight might be aboard solely to assassinate him.

There'd been other times on such flights that Morros had felt the tingling, hairbreadth electricity now pulsating through his body, but it had never been quite like this. No one had told him before that his life was so unequivocally in danger.

Even when he'd switched planes in London and was winging his way across the Atlantic, Morros still felt the awful burden of fear and danger. Was this going to be his end, he wondered? After twenty years, why now? Twenty years . . . that was so long ago. That was the beginning . . .

The beginning could be traced back by Boris Morros to the early 1930s, when he blandly started serving the Soviet Union with small, seemingly innocent favors in exchange for guarantees that food packages would be expedited to his parents in Russia.

To Morros it seemed harmless, for at the time he was caught up in the whirling make-believe world of Hollywood, whose tinseled glamour removed the sense of reality from those who were part of that madness. He had no clear head for much else than the multitude of productions in which he was involved. He couldn't consign any great measure of thought to other matters. Directing at Paramount Pictures was his all-consuming interest.

He compromised himself with officials at the Soviet Embassy in Washington because he was too preoccupied with his work to see the folly of his ways. Moreover, he felt that hardly any concession would be excessive if his parents got their food parcels.

Since he had come from Russia himself, Morros might have

been expected to know what he was getting into. The Russia he left in 1916 was not the Russia of the 1930s. Yet somehow he always retained the image of his birthplace as he knew it once upon a time.

Morros was born in 1895 to a family of musicians in St. Petersburg, now Leningrad, and he was a prodigy. At the age of four he could play the cello. By the time he was eight he had appeared in his first concert, and even before he attained his twelfth birthday he had mastered almost every musical instrument.

His talent was so considerable that the composer Rimsky-Korsakov agreed to coach him at the Imperial Conservatory of Music in St. Petersburg. He did a masterful job on young Boris, who was graduated at fourteen. By the time he was seventeen, he had become assistant musical director of the 108-piece Imperial Symphony Orchestra, succeeding his father.

In 1913, when only eighteen, Morros was moved by Czar Nicholas into the royal palace to supervise all musical events there. During his stay, Morros met every Russian of any importance, including the eccentric and diabolical mad monk, Rasputin, the most influential individual member of the Russian hierarchy.

One night while Morros was leading the orchestra for the Czar, Rasputin came along. The musician and the monk had words. Rasputin flew into a rage. Then calming, he whispered to Morros:

"If you didn't play so good I would kill you. But as it is, I give you these beads."

He handed the trembling musical conductor a string of birch-colored beads. "They will bring you luck," Rasputin smiled.

When the Russian Revolution came, Morros thought it was a minor disturbance that would soon blow over. He was more interested in Mozart than Marx, and to get away from the noise of the upheaval, he and nineteen friends took off for Turkey. Among them were the actors Akim Tamiroff and Mischa Auer.

Together they produced a show called *Chauve Souris*, or, as it was known in English, *Flying Bats*. Morros composed one of the songs for the production. The number was called "Parade of the Wooden Soldiers."

During its run, Morros fell in love with the prima donna of the revue, Katherine Modin, and they were married. Shortly afterward, in 1920, *Chauve Souris* was brought to New York City where it became an instant hit.

Morros quickly applied for naturalization. Not long afterward, he met Adolph Zukor, head of Paramount Pictures, who installed him as conductor of the orchestra in the pit of Broadway's famed Rivoli Theater.

Although a long-hair, Morros showed his versatility by mastering the jazz idiom, an accomplishment that soon led to his appointment as musical director at Paramount Pictures in Hollywood, a step made possible in 1927 by the advent of talkies.

Morros plunged into one picture after another. And with each, his reputation as a virtuoso of sound-stage orchestral direction grew increasingly. So, too, did his concern for his parents. Letters from his father indicated that of all the necessities of life in short supply in the Soviet Union, food was the least abundant.

Could Boris send them something, anything, the elder Morros pleaded?

Morros wrote to the Soviet Embassy in Washington in 1933, just after it opened following America's recognition of the USSR as a nation. The reply came back that it was all right to send food. Thus began the steady shipment of packages to his parents.

In 1935, Morros' mother became gravely ill and he decided he had to go to Russia to see her. He asked the Soviet Emassy for permission to make the trip and was given approval and a visa.

While in his homeland, Morros promised his seventy-six-year-old father that if anything happened to his mother, he would try to bring the elderly Morros to America to live with him. Boris would have wanted both parents to come to Hollywood, but his mother was invalided by her illness and couldn't travel.

On his return to the States, Morros was surprised one day by a phone call in Hollywood from a Soviet Embassy official in Washington asking the producer for "a small favor." It was a request for a letter attesting that a man named Edward Herbert was employed as a talent scout for Paramount Pictures. Morros didn't know Herbert, had never heard of him, and was puzzled by the petition—until he heard that the Russians planned to send Herbert to Germany.

Morros realized then that the mission was espionage . . .

Chapter 2

The Two Faces of Vassili Zubulin

Boris Morros was not too greatly alarmed about the request to issue phony accreditation to a man who would pose as a Paramount scout. After all, the Russians had done good deeds for him, letting him ship the food packages and allowing the visit with his parents in Russia. His mother was beginning to lose ground with her illness. She didn't have long to live. Once she passed away, he'd have to ask the Soviet Embassy to help fulfill the promise he'd made to bring his father to the United States. He sensed that he'd have to maintain good relations with the Embassy in order to get the additional request granted.

So Morros wrote the validating letter. He felt no real weight on his conscience, for the Russians ostensibly were going to spy on Germany, not the United States. What did he care about Germany? Moreover, he saw nothing illegal in accrediting someone as a talent scout so long as he had no further involvement in the activity.

Morros' mother died in 1939. It was the Soviet Embassy's turn now to do Morros a favor. He appealed to them to let his father

24

come over. A few weeks later Morros' secretary informed him that he had a visitor in his Paramount office.

He was a Soviet official from Washington.

"I am Edward Herbert, one of your talent scouts," the caller introduced himself with a benevolent smile.

Morros was somewhat startled. But he quickly gathered his wits about him and perceived that the visitor hadn't traveled three thousand miles just to make the director's acquaintance or to thank him for the letter making him a movie scout. Nor did Morros believe the Soviets would send a man all that distance from the nation's capital to discuss his application to bring his father to Hollywood.

There was more to it than that, Morros found out soon enough.

When he turned to look at Edward Herbert, he saw a man with a pleasant, square face, with just a trace of flabbiness on the jowls and some bagginess under his chin. His hair was jet black, combed back, and oily looking. It matched the mustache under a round, almost bulbous nose. He looked to be about thirty-five and like a man trying to appear younger. His suit was a powder blue double-breasted pinstripe, loose-fitting and draped on his large, slightly overweight frame the way Hollywood dandies wore their clothes in the thirties. Compared with the simple light worsted suit Morros was wearing, it would have been easy to mistake the visitor for the producer if one didn't know the movieland impresario.

Herbert sat easily in the comfortably upholstered green leather chair beside Morros' desk, his head turned slightly so he could look directly at the producer. His voice was deep, but he spoke softly because he was accustomed to people listening attentively to him when he had anything to say. The producer gave him both ears.

"Can we talk here?" the visitor asked with a hint of distrust in his voice. He turned and nodded toward the secretary's door, which was shut.

"Of course," Morros replied. "She doesn't speak Russian."

"Then allow me to introduce myself properly," the visitor said in a calculated tone—and in Russian. "My real name is Vassili M. Zubulin. I am the Second Secretary at the Soviet Embassy in Washington."

Taking two cigars from his pocket, he offered one to Morros. After lighting up, Zubulin blew a puff of smoke toward the ceiling, took a deep and audible breath, then glanced warily at the director.

"I do not know how to tell you this," he said tightly. "It is a deal that I have come here to work out with you. We are considering your request to let your father come to this country. I think we shall be able to do something. But . . ."

Zubulin paused. It was an interruption for dramatic impact, which Morros, an old hand by now in the art of hamming it up, recognized in an instant.

"You see," the man from the Embassy started to say again, "we are in need of more 'talent scout' affidavits. As you may have guessed when you prepared the last letter, it was to enable me to work freely in Germany. Confidentially . . . we are expanding our operations. Do you know what I am talking about?"

Morros nodded. Does he want to draw pictures for me, he told himself? He must think I'm a dope.

"It is espionage," he told Zubulin brusquely. ".It is dangerous business and I don't like it."

Zubulin's quick scowl was a dark flare that Morros suddenly realized could end his dream of bringing his aged father over. He decided to play it cool. He was speaking to a Communist-cloaked Rasputin.

"Well, my friend," Morros said with a forced easiness, "I have to admit that I don't have any affection for Hitler, and if my letters will serve to work against him, I'll be happy to help."

"Fine, fine," enthused the Soviet emissary. "That makes everything easy. I can assure you now that you will see your father here in Hollywood before long. I shall begin working on the arrangements as soon as I return to Washington."

As Zubulin waited, Morros summoned his secretary, asked her to dig up the copy of the affidavit he'd issued for Edward Herbert, then gave her a list of ten names supplied by Zubulin. He instructed her to type up papers for each of the persons listed on the sheet.

After Zubulin's visit, Morros began to have some misgivings about his transaction with the Russians. He wondered what might happen to him if his Paramount bosses found out he was using the studio as a cover for Soviet espionage.

By now Morros had gained a high standing in the Hollywood community. He had not only become Paramount's number-one musical director, but he had also moved into the overall production of movies. In this very period he was in full charge of his first production, *Flying Deuces*, with Laurel and Hardy. Moreover, he had contributed greatly to the advancement of innumerable Hollywood stars, not the least of whom was Bing Crosby.

But whatever second thoughts Morros had about the letters he wrote for the Russians were quickly submerged in his overriding desire to see his father in the United States.

These hopes, however, were temporarily dashed when World War II broke out. Nevertheless, the Russians did nothing to discourage the plan despite the embargo on travel imposed by the exigencies of the conflict. Zubulin promised Morros anew that his father would be brought over at the first opportunity; it couldn't be done at present because of the Soviet Union's great life-and-death struggle against the invading German armies, which were blitzkrieging their way to Moscow's outskirts at that very moment.

Zubulin never lost touch with Morros through the first three years of the war. Periodically—never less infrequently than every three months—the Russian Embassy official would phone Hollywood and keep Morros on the string with assurances that his father would be brought over as soon as passage on a ship became possible.

That day finally dawned in early January, 1943, when the elder Morros, sole passenger on a Liberty ship flying a Soviet flag, crossed the Pacific from Vladivostok. He arrived in San Francisco on January 20th.

Morros had won his one-man campaign to bring his father to the United States—but he had to pay the price. What he had done for the Russians in the past was nothing compared with what they were about to ask him to do now. The overtures came from Zubulin himself just day after Morros' father arrived.

It started with a phone call to Hollywood . . .

Chapter 3

Boris Becomes a Front for Spies

Vassili Zubulin wanted Boris Morros to meet him in New York City. The Soviet diplomat pinpointed the location—the first bench on the right on the path leading from Central Park's Columbus Circle entrance just north of 59th Street.

Morros went east by train for his encounter with Zubulin, but he was weighed down by great reluctance. He didn't want to get in any deeper. But the choice, he felt, was not his to make. He had helped procure talent scout certificates for the Soviets, and without having been told beforehand he was convinced there would be new and bolder demands as a "payoff" for the latest favor they'd done for him.

By this time, Morros had left Paramount and become an independent producer as well as the owner of a modest music business in Los Angeles, which was producing sheet music and records.

A cold, biting, late-winter wind whistled across the Manhattan landscape on the afternoon of March 14, 1943, when Morros, his coat collar turned up for warmth, walked into the park and sat on

the plain wooden bench Zubulin had designated for their rendezvous. The park was deserted and Morros felt conspicuous there by
himself.

Minutes later a sturdy, stocky man in a black fur-collared coat
and wide-brim black fedora walked briskly into the park from the
Columbus Circle entrance. Morros recognized him at once as
Zubulin.

"My dear Boris," the diplomat greeted the producer, sitting
down next to him on the bench and putting his arms around
Morros in a warm bear hug. "How is your father . . . how does
he like America . . . are you happy . . . ?"

Morros fielded the flurry of questions with answers that feigned all
the pleasantness he could summon, but his enthusiasm was not as
high as it should have been on a topic so close to his heart as his
father. Morros was all too aware that Zubulin hadn't brought him
across the continent merely to inquire about his father.

Zubulin's motives became clear minutes later when he began to
speak about the need for an "effective blind for our activities."

Morros looked askance, across the rolling grounds, their dull,
brown grass still in the clutches of winter sleep. This was it, he
told himself. A new assignment to aid Soviet espionage. But he
had no idea how extensive it was to be.

"We will require your full cooperation on a very large and
important project," Zubulin looked Morros in the eye. His voice
was subdued but the words, in Russian as they were most always
in his conversations with the producer, were precise and
meaningful.

"We are going to expand our operations in this country, and we
want you to help us. This is the plan:

"You are a motion picture producer and an expert in musical
arrangements. You also have a small music firm in California . . . We want to use that as a 'front' for our activities."

Morros looked stupefied at Zubulin.

"How do you propose to do that?" he asked in a voice that could
hardly contain his shock.

"It will not be difficult," Zubulin assured him with a char-
itable smile. "Do not worry about the mechanics. Everything has
been planned."

The Russian proceeded to outline the details of the corporate setup of the Boris Morros Company, which had been blueprinted by the Soviets. His plan appeared from the very outset to have the ominous configuration of a Kremlin effort to establish a beachhead for subversion in a totally new area.

Zubulin spoke of staffing the expanded music company with a greatly increased force of "salesmen" and "office workers" who would actually be undercover Red agents.

It would be headquarters for a Kremlin super-cell that would be cloaked in a nearly foolproof disguise.

"This will be the start," Zubulin enthused. "From this we will proceed to establish other business concerns in the United States to serve as covers for our work."

A hot-and-cold feeling swept over Morros as the impact of the proposition hit him. He experienced a peculiar, unreal, almost sickening feeling as the potential perils of the deal raced frantically through his mind. Until now he'd done nothing more than sign a few innocent documents for the Russians which, however helpful to their spy network, had ostensibly been directed against Germany, not the United States.

Now he was being asked to take part in a conspiracy against his adopted country. He wanted no part of it. He felt an obligation to the Russians for all they'd done in bringing his father to America, but he had no desire to commit himself to such a heavy price.

He wanted to refuse flatly. Yet he couldn't muster the courage to say no. He looked on himself as the architect of this incredible debacle. It was the consequence of his own foolhardiness in going to the Russians for favors. But had there been any other way?

Morros decided not to reject the deal outright. But nevertheless he'd try dashing cold water on it.

"You cannot do such a thing," he turned sharply to Zubulin. "There are too many obstacles. I can think of one immediately. It is money. My company does not have the capitalization to expand and take on the people you speak of."

The Soviet diplomat's jowls quivered with laughter. He started to say something, stopped, took out a pack of cigarets, and offered one to Morros, who politely turned it down. Zubulin lit one himself. Morros was a cigar smoker. Zubulin had quit smoking cigars and gone on cigarets. Though he had a pocketful of cigars, Morros had no inclination to smoke at this moment. He was too disturbed.

"Why are you concerning yourself with such matters as money, Boris?" Zubulin grinned at Morros. "We are going to provide all the capital you will need for the expansion."

Morros stared at him surprised.

"We have an American millionaire in our pocket," Zubulin added casually. "He has more money than your former boss, Zukor."

He was referring to Adolph Zukor, the president of Paramount Pictures, who indeed was a very wealthy man.

Morros made a casual grimace. He was still in shock, but his curiosity about the millionaire had been aroused.

"Somebody I might know?" he asked blandly.

"You might have heard of him," Zubulin said. "His name is Alfred Stern. Alfred K. Stern. He is the . . . "

"You mean he is an agent?" Morros interrupted in a startled voice. He studied the Soviet diplomat with half-hidden incredulity.

"I see you know who he is," Zubulin said, pleased.

Morros shook his head. "I can't believe it," he said, trying to reflect surprise rather than the traumatic jolt of disbelief that he actually experienced. And revulsion, too.

Morros wasn't acquainted with Stern personally, but he knew as much about him as any well-informed person who read the newspapers might be expected to know. Stern was a well-to-do midwestern businessman, who at the time was living in New York and working for the municipal government under Mayor Fiorello H. LaGuardia's administration. Stern was a member of a North Dakota banking family and a graduate of Phillips Exeter Academy who'd spent a year at Harvard. Before he was out of his twenties, Stern inherited about $300,000, moved to Chicago, went into real estate, and profited handsomely.

Then he met the pretty young daughter of the head of Sears Roebuck & Co. Her father, Julius Rosenwald, was known as "The Merchant Prince" and "Mr. Moneybags." Marion Rosenwald, who may have seen some reflections of her father's poly-dimensional qualities and multiple talents in Stern, married him in 1921. But by 1937 the attraction lost its luster, mainly because Stern saw the reflections of another glittering woman who caught his fancy—and his heart. Alfred and Marion were divorced, prompting one of the participants in the action to remark acidly:

"He did very well for himself while a member of the Rosenwald family."

By now Stern was a millionaire. With a splendid family background, a shining record of achievement in commerce—and with all that money, which is always an asset—Stern married the lovely young woman who'd caught his eye—and his heart.

She was the vivacious, charming, worldly-wise Martha Dodd, daughter of the recently-retired U.S. Ambassador to Germany, Dr. William E. Dodd. They moved into an elegant town apartment on Manhattan's Central Park West, in the same building where Frank Costello, then the nation's crime czar, made his home. They also bought a palatial country home in Lewisboro, in nearby Westchester County, where they could spend quiet weekends and long, lazy summers away from the noise and heat of the city.

Boris Morros may not have been aware of all these details about Stern, but he would soon learn them and many others that would greatly heighten the shock and disbelief that swept over him now as he was hearing for the first time from Zubulin about the capitalist's affiliation with communism.

"It surprises you, doesn't it, to hear me tell you that we have Alfred Stern in our organization?" Zubulin said in a gloating, almost pompous tone.

"Yes," Morros acknowledged, shaking his head disbelievingly. "It is hard to conceive of a man so deeply rooted in the business world, and with so much money, lending himself to . . . espionage."

Zubulin chuckled. "You will find a long line of capitalists in the service of the Kremlin," he boasted. "And the ranks are growing all the time. But our favorite capitalist is that extraordinary Hollywood genius—Boris Morros."

"You must not say that!" Morros countered in a sharp tone, as though Zubulin's audacity had to be curbed by a show of resentment. "I do not want to be classified as a member of a spy ring. When I signed those talent scout affidavits for you, I did it as a favor in exchange for the good things you were doing for me. But I do not think this should continue. Certainly not to the extent that you have demanded. I cannot lend my music company to this venture."

Zubulin sucked in a long, dramatic breath. He turned and glared at Morros with a wry, patient smile. "Is this the thanks I am to convey to the Soviet Government?" he said in a tone edged with sarcasm. "You realize that you had indicated by your actions that you would continue to serve your motherland if we brought your father over here. Now you tell us you won't . . . "

His voice trailed off and he sat in silence, sulking and staring blankly across the park. Morros felt the impact of the oral slap Zubulin had delivered. He wasn't happy with the implication that he was a double-crosser, but he couldn't bring himself to respond to it.

He felt defenseless. The Russian, after all, had delivered his father to him. There was nothing Morros had craved more than that.

Suppose he did lend his musical company to the scheme Zubulin suggested?

Look at Alfred Stern, an American-born millionaire of the highest repute. Wasn't he supporting Communist objectives?

How wrong would it really be then to employ Red agents in his music business?

How much harm could they do against the United States by operating out of his firm?

The answers were clear-cut in Morros' mind. It would be very wrong and the harm they could do to the United States could be considerable.

Over and above all other considerations was the risk of getting caught. Morros was not so much a patriot as he was a practical man. Getting caught would mean the end of his brilliant career and a probable prison sentence.

Morros tried to tell himself that he had done little for the Russians in comparison with what they had done for him. Those few talent scout affidavits he'd signed were mere peanuts compared with the Kremlin's favors to him. He owed the Russians and Zubulin something more in payment.

Still . . . no, he just couldn't do it. He'd be a traitor to the country that had given him such great opportunities.

But this was neither the time nor the place to give Zubulin a flat turndown. Try the old stall, he told himself.

"Vassili," Morros finally broke the long silence, "you must give me a little time to think about this. I have to take stock of things. I have to weigh the risks involved. You realize, of course, that you are putting me in a very dangerous position. If I am caught my career would be ruined. The dream you fulfilled for me by bringing my father here would be shattered into a thousand pieces if I were to go to jail. I need time."

Zubulin rubbed his large chin thoughtfully. "Well, I think you are entitled to think about it," he said mildly, looking Morros in the eyes. "Shall we allow ninety days for your decision?"

"Yes, yes . . . " Morros said quickly. Then, "I am indebted to you for all you have done—don't ever forget that, Vassili."

They sat quietly for a few moments, listening to the steady cacophony of city traffic streaming outside the park as the evening rush hour began.

The afternoon sun was dipping behind the imposing wall of apartment buildings lining the opposite side of the street along Central Park West. It was a few minutes past five o'clock and the numbing chill of approaching nightfall was in the air already. Morros glanced at his watch.

"Shall we say goodbye, Vassili?" he asked in a polite but firm voice.

"Not goodbye," Zubulin said with a frown and half-smile. "Let us just say au revoir. We are going to see each other . . . in ninety days, yes?"

Morros nodded. He felt an implied threat in Zubulin's tone but he let it pass without reacting.

Zubulin got up first. "Take care of yourself, Boris," he said, proffering his hand. Morros rose to his feet and shook hands.

"I shall be talking with you, Vassili," Morros said, his voice even and relieved by the ninety-day reprieve.

Morros stood stiffly erect in front of the bench, eyes riveted on the bulky, black-coated Soviet diplomat as he walked toward the nearby park exit and disappeared into the thickening swarm of office workers escaping from another day's bondage in the buildings on the periphery of Columbus Circle.

Then Morros started briskly toward the exit. As he walked out of the park, he slowed his pace and reached into his pocket for a cigar. He stopped, lit up, and glanced casually at the apartment houses on the opposite side of Central Park West.

He couldn't know then that one of those buildings housed the apartment of Alfred K. Stern and his wife Martha Dodd. Nor could he know that in the near future he'd be compelled to return from Hollywood to this New York setting to meet Alfred Stern and Martha Dodd, and that this meeting would be the beginning of a complex mixture of private enterprise and deep-laid Communist intrigue that would catapult him into the shadow world of espionage and a strange double-life.

And that it would, all of it, evolve around one central, dominating figure, whose treachery in the end would put Boris Morros' life in such great peril that it became imperative for him to flee Munich nearly fifteen years later on that dreadful night of January 19, 1957.

That pivotal, commanding figure was Martha Dodd Stern . . .

Chapter 4

Martha, the Toast of Berlin, Has a Tryst with Hitler

A group of American correspondents was sitting in the *stammtisch* in Berlin's exclusive Taverne Restaurant, whiling away the evening playing the match game and belting down their nightcaps.

It was a typical scene, repeated nightly by the passel of newsmen covering the German capital in those early Hitler days of 1934.

Suddenly, a slender, shapely, feminine figure swept into the lounge from the adjoining Italian-style dining room and slinked toward the correspondents. Even in the dim light of the saloon, she effused a rare effervescence. Her dark brunet hair was a vibrant note, and her slender, shapely figure seemed to reflect the outlines of a Roaring Twenties flapper—but with class.

Her face was pretty and would have been prettier still if it were not for her front upper teeth, which protruded buck-like. Yet it was a condition that readily could be, and was, ignored because of the stately and overpowering total pattern of lovely womanhood that she cut.

This was the amorously adventurous, indelicately articulate Martha Dodd, the bouncy twenty-four-year-old daughter of Ambassador Dodd. She had been in Berlin a little more than a year, having arrived there with her father, mother, and brother after President Franklin Delano Roosevelt had appointed the soft-spoken, absent-minded Professor Dodd from the University of Chicago to the American Embassy in the German capital.

Martha's initial glimpse of Hitler's shouting, goose-stepping Storm Troopers made her almost rapturous; she found the excitement of the people contagious, she enjoyed everything fully, and it was difficult for her to restrain a natural sympathy for the Germans. She felt like a child, ebullient and careless . . .

She was in that precise frame of mind and spirit on the early December night of 1936 when she approached the table in the *stammtisch* and sidled up to a tall, slender, blonde-haired reporter who'd noticed Martha when she first came through the door from the dining room. She put her hands on Pierre J. Huss' shoulder, sighed heavily, and looked around at the other faces staring at her, half-smiling.

"How are you boys?" she slurred a bit loudly. Her eyes were slightly aswim, which is how the optics get when several before-dinner cocktails are chased by a favorite chianti.

The correspondents, who'd turned and greeted Martha with a casual but polite hello, returned to their game. Martha tried to interest herself in it, but couldn't follow the play. She was in a restless mood.

"Having fun, Pete?" she said thickly. She patted his cheek playfully.

Of the six or seven correspondents at the table, Huss, the bureau chief of Hearst's International News Service in Berlin, knew Martha Dodd more intimately than any of the others. Martha had liked the handsome newsman ever since her father's first press conference at the Embassy in 1933.

Except for the aging and indifferent Guido Enderis of the *New York Times*, Huss was the only other bachelor at the table. This was not, of course, why Martha had taken a liking to the INS man. As we'll see, a wedding ring seldom seemed to inhibit the Ambassador's daughter when she set her sights on a man.

Martha had been dining with a "proper" Englishman in the

room next door, and had left him at the table there when she barged into the *stammtisch* so abruptly. She apparently had given him the brush-off. That became more certain when she finally leaned heavily on Huss after having stroked his cheek a while and, pressing her ample breasts against his arm, whispered a throaty invitation.

"I'm bored stiff with that Limey bastard. How about ducking out and taking me someplace else?"

A good many hours later, Martha and Pete arrived at the Embassy by the light of a full moon. Martha was feeling no pain.

In those days the American Embassy and residence were in Bendler Strasse off the fashionable Tiergarten, across from the huge block of buildings housing the War Ministry and the German High Command. A grilled black ten-foot-high iron gate gave access to the imposing three-story stone edifice, whose architecture mirrored the heavy, imposing style of Imperial Germany.

The big iron gate, of course, was locked. And all the fumbling in her handbag failed to produce the key. Pete wanted to ring the bell but Martha wouldn't let him.

Martha must have had prior experience—and practice—in the art of getting past that old locked gate. With flawless motion, she inserted her foot on the bottom crossbar of the gate and pulled herself over the top. It was skillfully executed except for one slight hitch.

Her dress and, as Huss found on closer observation in the light of the full moon, her panties got impaled on a spike. Martha's embarrassing position was somewhat heightened when she tried to free herself and tore both dress and panties, bringing on a mortifying double-exposure.

Cursing, she yelled to Huss, "Get me the hell down from here, you son of a bitch."

As Huss stood on the sidewalk trying to figure how he'd rescue her, the peculiar goings-on attracted a sentry posted at Wehrmacht Headquarters across the street, He notified the sergeant of the guard, who, in turn, whistled for the police.

When Huss spotted the *schupo* hurrying down Bendler from the top of the block, he sprung into action to avoid further complications. He climbed the gate, jumped to the ground, then reached up and virtually ripped Martha down, leaving large hunks of dress and panty emplanted on the gate and fluttering in the breeze like strange pennants of some kind.

Safe on Embassy terra firma, Martha looked disdainfully at the bewildered policeman on the outside of the gate and snarled, "Get lost!"

He must have had some familiarity with such escapades, for he pulled back, snapped his hand into a gracious salute, and strolled off.

Huss, putting the incident down as just one more hazardous episode in the pursuit of his profession, let Martha lead him up to her second-floor bedroom in the Embassy . . .

Huss, who was co-author with me of the book, *Red Spies in the U.N.*, gave me chapter and verse on his affair with Martha Dodd that night. But I do not think I should violate a confidence.

Other hazards began dogging Pierre Huss and his colleagues in the foreign correspondents' ranks in the days ahead, although they'd been abuilding for quite some time.

The significant date when the Berlin scene began to change occurred about a year after Dodd came to the German capital, and it was a change that indelibly set the stage for Martha Dodd's future conduct in the Reichland, her eventual submersion into subversion—and her ultimate involvement in the Boris Morros spy melodrama.

It was June 30, 1934, when Hitler rocked the Reich with the blood purge, liquidating Ernst Roehm, chief of the brownshirted Nazi Storm Troopers. Hundreds of others, including many distinguished military men, were cut down by the machine guns of Hermann Goering and Heinrich Himmler. Overnight the complexion of Hitler's rule of the Nazi Party changed from rowdy beerhall leadership to military mastery.

Aided and abetted by men like Propaganda Minister Joseph Goebbels, who shrewdly garbed his boss in the trappings of genius and infallibility, Hitler became "Der Fuehrer."

The era of Nazi bigwigs aping striped-pants diplomats had begun. The days when they cavorted in haufbraus and girlie dance floors were a thing of the past. Nobility of manner had taken over.

And so did creeping censorship and the cesspool of Nazi propaganda designed to camouflage the real intent to gain world domination through military might.

Before long there were only a few persons in the capital who could feed the correspondents information and data about German activity that wasn't colored or corrupted. One of these was Martha Dodd, for she was one of the favored few who had access to the high councils of the Nazi hierarchy.

Martha's entree was made possible by her intense admiration for the Nazis as individuals and collectively. She had become imbedded deeply in the social fabric of the party's high officialdom, and her petite, shapely figure cut a swath across the diplomatic frontier, dancing, dining, and drinking with the gusto and giddiness of an ambitious Hollywood starlet.

She became so infatuated with the Nazis that she found herself "heiling" as vigorously as any German. And in the great hope of closing the widening rift between Berlin and Washington, she liked to think that her conduct was dictated by the growing-up process she truly believed she had undergone since coming to Germany with her father.

Nothing in Martha Dodd's background augered this incredible love affair that she demonstrated for the Nazis—nor did her past reflect the slightest clue that she would ultimately become involved in espionage.

Martha Dodd was born October 8, 1908, in Ashland, Virginia, the second of two children in the Dodd family. The first was her brother, William Jr. Together they grew up in the staid campus atmosphere of Chicago University, where their father had advanced from Randolph-Macon College as a professor of history. He himself was a Harvard graduate with a doctorate from Leipzig University in Germany.

Martha gave her parents some anxious moments in Chicago when she married a man whose name she couldn't remember the next day. Her brother later explained from behind a wall of embarrassment that the groom was identified from court records at Crown Point, Indiana, and arrangements were hastily made for a divorce.

Had they studied her in those days, the Kremlin's supersleuths, out searching for prospective recruits for their far-flung spy network, wouldn't have regarded Martha Dodd as a likely candidate by the wildest stretch of the imagination.

They certainly would have turned away from her upon discovering that she'd served as assistant literary editor of the staid old *Chicago Tribune* for a couple of years after quitting school. Perhaps, however, they might have taken a second look if they could have discovered that Martha balanced off her rightist political leaning by becoming an avaricious reader of Nietzsche, and closely associating herself with the British left-wing Professor Robert M. Lovett, who is said to have planted in Martha the seeds of the radicalism that would lead her to commit treachery and treason against her own country.

Her father, the Ambassador, was a gentle Jeffersonian Democrat, a kindly, soft-spoken, but unimaginative Southerner who hardly exuded the qualities or talents required to handle diplomatic duties. It had always amazed a large segment of the American political family that Roosevelt should have reached out to the campus to pluck Dodd for the delicate role of representing the United States in Berlin. Except for the fact that Dodd had spent three years in Germany as a young man at Leipzig University, and devoutly believed the German people were democratic, he had no qualifications for the job.

Rumors have persisted through all the years since that the President had gotten W. E. Dodd confused with a Chicago attorney, W. F. Dodd, when he made his Ambassadorial appointment. The gossip was that Roosevelt had gotten the wrong phone number and instead of calling Walter F. Dodd, who curiously enough had been a professor, got Dr. William E. Dodd. The rumor, however, was semiofficially denied.

Ambassador Dodd, who arrived in Berlin with his wife, son, and daughter in 1933, soon showed his naiveté in the critical post he'd undertaken. His critics were quick to cite him as a bumbling old fool; they complained about his inability to get tough with the Nazis in defense of America's rights and interests, and even about the way he dealt with the veteran correspondents on the Berlin scene, who found him uncommunicative and uncooperative during the ensuing years of increasing crisis.

His tenure in the American Embassy was burdensome, often unbearable. He didn't have the armor to cope with the Big Bertha brand of shotgun diplomacy practiced by the Nazis. In truth,

Dodd was a gentleman—and in all probability he tried his best to give full service to his country, but just wasn't equal to the task against the gutter-tough Nazi officials.

He might have done far worse had it not been for Martha's willingness to project herself forcefully into the vacuum of incompetence created by her father, and the social void promulgated by her mother, who seemed to harbor an aversion to the spotlight of activity that Embassy life demands of an Ambassador's wife.

Martha Dodd was both anxious and willing to step into her mother's shoes and play hostess at Embassy functions. She was also both anxious and willing to wear her father's pants when he began to seem unable to endure the pressures of office.

It was no idle boast when she was heard to brag about her "power" at the Embassy; it became a generally accepted fact after a time that the "real" American Ambassador to Hitler's Reich in the mid-thirties was Martha Dodd.

She loved the role, too. For Martha Dodd truly began to believe she was "appointed to change the history of Europe," as she was to put it much later in a vapid, self-serving book she wrote.

That she wielded extraordinary authority is no fairy tale. Correspondents by the score could attest to having been out on dates with Martha, more often than not at her favorite spot, the dimly-lighted Taverne—where more often than not she'd be in her cups.

And at such moments it was not unusual to see Martha opening, reading, then dictating a reply to coded cablegrams Washington had sent to her father.

It takes no great mind to assess the value of having access to secret government messages. It's the zenith of attainment for any spy. It proved to be the hallmark of history's sensational "Cicero" case in Turkey. The agent called "Cicero" had found the wherewithal to photograph coded messages presumed to have been safely locked in the Ambassador's safe at the British Embassy in Ankara, and sold them to an almost unbelieving German Government.

Logically, with her position of preeminence at the Embassy being more or less common knowledge in Berlin, we can see how Martha Dodd readily could have commanded the attention and interest of the Russians, who were certainly looking for secret messages and information on intelligence matters to feed into the growing Soviet spy apparatus housed in Berlin—a proliferation seeded and given root by Boris Morros' talent scout letters to the Soviet Embassy in Washington.

As much of a drinker as Martha was, she couldn't match her brother Bill's capacity for the bottled spirits in Berlin's bars. Young Bill, who in the States seemed to be following in his father's sedate footsteps by acquiring degrees from Chicago University and Harvard, and teaching at Rutgers University and later at American University in Washington, took after his sister's ways in Berlin—in spades. He drank the bars dry and drifted into the existence of a wastrel.

Martha's weakness next to sex and drinking was dancing. At all but the most formal state functions she manifested a propensity for holding her dance floor partners tightly; more tightly under the low lights and gypsy strains of nightclub violins.

When drunk her tongue was sharpest, and she was then prone to the use of four-letter words with some frequency.

Drunk or sober, but mostly when drunk, Martha tossed her sex around with abandon, not only on Americans, but Nazis and Russians, too. This ultimately gave rise to speculation in some quarters that she was a nymphomaniac.

This opinion prevailed even in the plush interior of the American Embassy, where Martha Dodd reigned as the belle of the ball, presiding at lunches, teas, and dinners. Here correspondents and visitors, as well as Embassy staffers, fell in or out of Martha's favor at the slightest provocation.

She was subject to whims, moods, and emotions, was quick to resent those too slow or disinclined to cater to her constantly burgeoning ego. Men of all nationalities were fair game to her. She reveled in their attention at social and diplomatic events, hated it when they inadvertently ignored her.

One of the scandals of the Embassy was the way visiting Americans—industrialists, businessmen, book publishers, and even Congressmen and Senators—beat a path to Ambassador Dodd's door. Their myriad calls more often than not were viewed as pretexts to see his much-sought-after daughter rather than Dodd himself.

The first year of Martha Dodd's stay in Berlin was relatively uneventful so far as its effect on history went. She was a girl out for a good time and left no stone unturned in that pursuit. But when Hitler launched his blood purge and the clamp closed on the free dissemination of news, the changing scene quickly escalated Martha to a new plateau of preeminence.

Increasing difficulties beset correspondents in their efforts to maintain contact or association with the men waving the Swastika from the new heights of power to which Hitler had raised them. Official channels evaporated and only the Propaganda Ministry and Foreign Office were authorized to speak for the Government. Neither was acceptable as a source of news, for their releases were darkly tainted with Nazi evangelism. Newsmen had to spread afield and cultivate individual contacts and pipelines.

Because of her close rapport with the newsmen, Martha Dodd became one of the primary sources of inside information on German activity. The purge had not disturbed her connections with members of the Nazi hierarchy, with whom she continued to enjoy a close—and allegedly intimate—relationship.

The extent of Martha's closeness with Nazi bigwigs was easy to gauge, for it was evident in her association with them at their official functions. The extent of her intimacies was more difficult to determine. But Martha talked as though they not only existed, but were a vivid and vital part of her curriculum.

She seemed to derive a vicarious pleasure from spreading a tale, conceivably true, of how she had been approached to become Hitler's mistress. As Martha told the story, it was the piano-playing court jester of Hitler's early years, Putzi Hanfstaengl, who made the proposition to her. He had the crackpot idea that a pert and clever woman like Martha Dodd could change the Fuehrer for the better.

"Martha," she once quoted Putzi, "Hitler should have an American woman—a lovely woman could change the whole destiny of Europe. Martha, you are that woman."

Martha, then twenty-six years old, was not insulted by Putzi's proposition. She was eager to have him take her to a rendezvous with Hitler.

"Since I was appointed to change the history of Europe," Martha was once heard to say at a cocktail party while in her cups, "I decided to dress in my most demure and intriguing best."

But when she got to Hitler's hotel, Martha was swept with disappointment. Hitler kissed her hand politely, then sat down some distance away.

"He gave me curious, embarrassed stares," she said. But nothing more. Martha was desolate.

"I decided he was incapable of relations with a woman . . . he was a frigid celibate."

Martha thus joined the exclusive club of beautiful women of that time who were known to have tried, but failed, to become Hitler's mistress. Among these was German movie star Leni Riefenstahl and aristocratic Unity Mitford of the British beer millions.

As it turned out, Eva Braun of Munich provided Hitler with sex until 1945, when he finally married her in the underground bunker of the Berlin Chancellery just before both committed suicide.

Martha, however, was not one to pass up the opportunity to exploit this first meeting and other less dramatic ones she had with Hitler. She used them to impress other top Nazis with her importance.

Putzi steered Martha around official parties until he slipped into political oblivion in 1935 with the advent of scheming Joachim von Ribbentrop, the "champagne salesman" who wormed himself into Hitler's favor and became his Foreign Minister. But Putzi lived to see his archenemy sentenced to the gallows after the Nuremberg trials in 1946.

Even without Putzi, Martha found other Nazis willing to squire her around. Yet despite her place of priority in the Reich establishment, Martha inevitably fell under suspicion and became the target of a secret Gestapo investigation. The surveillance apparently started in late 1935 after Martha returned from a surprise tour of Moscow. Her acceptance of the Russian invitation itself stunned many highly placed Nazis who until then had believed that Martha's lessons in National Socialism had won her over to their side.

Now they began to have a more than slight suspicion that Martha Dodd was starting a love affair with an archenemy named communism.

Chapter 5

In Love with Communism Now, Martha Visits FDR . . .

Martha Dodd wasn't all ideals and convictions. She was a woman. And she possessed the prerogative to change her mind, as most women do.

As the leading party girl of Berlin's international set, Martha found the opportunity to mingle and make friends with Soviet Embassy officials—particularly after the Soviet Union was given recognition by President Roosevelt's Administration.

She was persuaded to see Russia and, on the arm of a handsome escort, the Ambassador's daughter set out for a red-carpet tour of the country. She visited the Kremlin, strolled through Red Square at twilight, boated on the Volga, bathed on summery Yalta's pebble beaches, and inspected Leningrad's factories.

When Martha returned to Berlin, she related with high glee the wonderful treatment accorded her by Soviet officials and extolled the country's virtues.

"It seemed almost like a democratic country after Nazi Germany," she trilled. "They are proving the success of socialism. I found no signs of militarism . . . no indication whatsoever of any racial discrimination . . . Churches are still open for those who want to help pay for the priest . . . "

Martha's high praise of the Soviet Union evidently didn't sit well with the Nazis, and word must have gotten to the Gestapo. The first hint of the secret probe into Martha's activities came to Pierre Huss from Karl Boemer, chief of the Foreign Department of the Propaganda Ministry, who was a Nazi with strong pro-American sentiments. Boemer, who later became an officer in the Wehrmacht with a direct link to counter-intelligence, had also dated Martha frequently in the past. The fact that he was married was a minor consideration that didn't stop him from having fun.

Speaking to Huss in complete confidence, Boemer revealed that the Gestapo not only was checking up on Martha but was also looking into those German officials seen most often with her.

"I don't dare see her again," Boemer said. "They have already interrogated me. She has been asking too many pointed questions about Nazi intentions in foreign affairs, and especially about the demilitarized Rhineland. They are wondering particularly about her trip to Moscow."

No one could blame the Nazis for wondering about Martha, after her ravings about what a wonderful country the Soviet Union was—a most peculiar phenomenon when matched against the grip of terror that Stalin's regime had going at that time. Yet long after Boemer's private advisory to Huss, other important Nazis continued to associate with Ambassador Dodd's effervescent daughter. Some of the most prominent of those who showed no hesitancy about demonstrating fellowship toward Martha were the imposing Goebbels, Goering, Hitler's adjutant Julius Schaub, Fritz Wiedeman before he was transferred to the United States as German Consul, and General Werner von Blomberg, the Wehrmacht's Chief of Staff.

Martha once confided to a group of correspondents that she had slipped off for a weekend with Goebbels on his private estate—during his wife's absence, of course. She also spoke ardently about General von Reichenau, who later commanded the German forces that swept to the Channel. Reichenau was seen toasting Martha at the round of diplomatic parties during the 1936 Olympic Games and often was heard praising her as a charming woman.

Then came a time late in 1936 when Martha concentrated her charms and attention almost exclusively upon Ernst Udet, who was then involved virtually single-handedly in building the Luftwaffe into a lethal instrument of Stukas, parachutists, and blitzkrieg daredevils. Their favorite spot for dinner was Horcher's Restaurant, where prohibitive prices always assured reservations for men like Udet, Goering, and others of their stature, and where they could feast without the slightest concern for ration cards.

The fact that Udet and other high-ranking Germans continued to see Martha openly, even after the Gestapo began its probe, raises several burning questions:

- Were the Nazis convinced as early as 1935 that Martha had started on the road into Soviet espionage?
- If they suspected that she was a Red agent, why didn't they arrest her?
- Did they play her for a double-agent—or as a come-on to keep track of what the Russians were fishing for?

In retrospect, it also becomes a curious point for consideration that while the Nazis had caught onto Martha when they did, it took her own country almost twenty years more to become fully aware of her involvement in espionage!

It's also puzzling that Martha's reputation as a playgirl and as the "real" Ambassador in Berlin never brought action from the puritanical Administration of President Roosevelt. How, one must ask, could Washington have avoided hearing about Martha Dodd's activities? And, assuming they'd heard, why did they put up with them?

When Martha Dodd started downhill into Soviet espionage, she apparently also dragged her brother along. Bill went to work for the International Peace Campaign and was handed assignments that kept him hopping back and forth between Paris and Geneva. The suspicion is that he was being used as a courier for the Comintern, or the Soviet Secret Service, or both.

And Martha also went on playing the role she believed fate had consigned to her—changing the history of Europe. But there was a difference now. Martha had lived under Hitler's dictatorship, inspected the concentration camps, witnessed the brutality, and seen the system's corrosive effect on some of her highly placed, party-loving friends.

These, all of them, were reasons for Martha to turn against the Nazis. But she didn't make the turn until she'd been to Russia.

That the Gestapo suspected her of espionage was clear. That they let her carry on with the ranking Nazis is puzzling. Unless, of course, they were playing her as a cat's-paw of German counter-intelligence by feeding her information specifically doctored for Russian consumption.

While Martha continued to go on outings with the Nazi big boys, she also was seen more and more often with the Russians. By the latter part of 1935 she had become a frequent guest of Soviet dignitaries and emissaries at diplomatic functions.

There was one particularly memorable affair in late 1935 at the drab-looking box-shaped Radziwill Palace, which housed the Soviet Embassy, and where Martha reigned goddess-like in the midst of Kremlin officialdom. It was a bash thrown in commemoration of the so-called November 7 Revolution, and the whole diplomatic world of Berlin seemed to have been invited to crowd into the red-carpeted reception room with its tremendous chandeliers and imperial adornments.

Martha arrived in her chauffeured limousine all by herself. She made a grand entrance into the lobby, which had hardly been changed since pre-Revolution days when Czar Nicholas II and his Empress stayed in the palace during their state visit to Kaiser Wilhelm. About the only noticeable alteration was in the oil painting that hung in a heavy gold frame at the head of the marble stairs. The life-size portrait of the Czar was gone. And in its place, in the same frame, was another rendering in oil—a likeness of Stalin.

First to greet Martha at this particular gala was a portly Russian whom the Berlin diplomatic set knew as a man with considerable working knowledge of Soviet affairs, one of the best informed persons in the German capital on Nazi-Kremlin relations.

He was Sergei M. Kudryavtsev, who some dozen years later would be revealed to the world as the head of Moscow's spy ring in Canada, which helped steal America's atomic secrets for the Soviet Union. Kudryavtsev was exposed in the astounding disclosures by Igor Gouzenko, the file clerk in the Soviet Embassy at

Ottawa who handled the coded messages between Moscow and its spy network this side of the Atlantic.

In 1950, Kudryavtsev showed up briefly at the United Nations General Assembly, but he didn't come to notice again until 1960 when he became the Soviet Union's first Ambassador to Fidel Castro's revolutionary government in Cuba.

Pictures and files revealed the same portly Sergei, slightly older now, waddling about in Havana. Events since support the belief that Kudryavtsev was the architect of the Kremlin's attempt to take over Cuba and arm it as a missile base for the Soviet Union. Kudryavtsev's work was done in June, 1962, after he'd helped organize and train the initial class of the "terror school," whose first graduate, Roberto Santiesteban y Casanova, led a daring band of Cubans in the abortive plot to blow up vital installations along America's East Coast.

Kudryavtsev's next assignment? No one knows for certain. But back to Moscow he went. His activities since have been blotted out by a curtain of secrecy.

Undoubtedly, Sergei Kudryavtsev already must have been an important cog in the Soviet espionage network during those pre-World War II days in Berlin. He was working out of the Tass office as a correspondent—an excellent cover for his suspected primary role in subversion. It gave him far more freedom of movement than he would have had as a Soviet Embassy attaché. That holds a remarkable parallel to the practice today which enables Red newsmen and employes of Amtorg, the Soviet trading agency, to move about the United States with far greater mobility than attachés and employes at the Soviet Embassy in Washington or the Soviet Mission to the UN in New York City.

The apparent position held by an espionage agent in his cover job means nothing compared to his real power in the intelligence community. It was true then, and it applies just as much today.

The fact that Kudryavtsev was playing a secondary role at Tass didn't preclude his importance somewhere in that baffling maze of Soviet officialdom in the German capital. He could have been a watchdog over other Russians, or he might have been serving as an active spy against the Berlin government, the United States Embassy, or both.

The innocent guise of correspondent cloaking his ulterior mission in Berlin became a bit threadbare at the Soviet Embassy reception that night of November 7, 1935. The brawn of Kudryavtsev's ranking in the Kremlin order showed through for the first time as he escorted Martha Dodd from the lobby to the main reception hall and presented her to Soviet Ambassador Nicolai Skwarzekev and his forbidding-looking wife, dressed in severest black.

Tass correspondents are not likely to handle such formalities—unless they have some other status that isn't manifest.

Martha seemed to know the couple and responded warmly as they unbent to greet her with kisses. Then Kudryavtsev took Martha to the interesting and ascetic-looking little fellow everyone knew as Vladimir Pavlov, the favorite illegitimate son of Stalin. Pavlov, who'd been circulating among the guests, urging them on to good eating and drinking, practically forgot everyone else to cater to Martha.

For the rest of the evening, Martha was in constant conversation with uniformed and bemedalled Russians, with either Pavlov or Skwarzekev at her side—but never without Sergei Kudryavtsev, who stuck close to Ambassador Dodd's daughter like a bodyguard.

This exuberant friendship with the Russians attracted not only the Gestapo but other interested onlookers. One was the First Counsellor of the British Embassy, Sir George Ogilvie-Forbes, the reliable right arm of Sir Neville Henderson, then the grumpy Ambassador from London, who seemed to have two primary goals in Berlin—to convince himself that scotch with a dash of soda was the only civilized breakfast, and to punch the nose of Hitler's stupid Foreign Minister, Joachim von Ribbentrop.

It was Sir George's task to keep Sir Neville in line and discourage him from both errands. He succeeded in preventing bloodshed with Ribbentrop but didn't do so well with his boss' mental aberrations about drinking.

Sir George was also a friend of Pierre Huss, and one day late in the winter of 1936 the correspondent was closeted with the jovial Scot in his office in the gloomy Gothic-columned British Embassy discussing a subject that seemed to stir an uneasiness in him.

"What do you make of Martha Dodd?" Sir George asked in a voice kept deliberately low so as not to be overheard by his secretary next door. "She is a strange girl, it seems to me."

Huss told Sir George that he hadn't seen Martha for some

months, but was well aware of the talk circulating in Berlin about her continued associations with high Nazis and mysterious Russians.

"Yes," commented Sir George, "it is all rather ominous. Martha is cutting quite a swath, wouldn't you say, old chap? I wonder where it will all lead to?"

Huss left the British First Counsellor that afternoon convinced that his host knew more than he let on. Sir George had been far less direct in voicing suspicion about Martha Dodd than was Karl Boemer of the German Propaganda Ministry, who the year before had revealed that the Gestapo was checking on Nazis seen with the Ambassador's daughter. Sir George seemed to have left a lot unsaid.

Even the blasé Huss was surprised one day not long after his visit to Sir George when he was approached by Martha Dodd herself during a briefing at the American Embassy.

"Will you take me to dinner?" she asked in an intoxicating tone out of earshot of the other correspondents. "I want to talk with you."

The invitation puzzled Huss, for by this time he and Martha had drifted away from their close association of past years. He had no idea what she wanted to discuss until they went the following evening to the Taverne Restaurant.

Martha drank and ate little that night, seeming to be more interested in prodding Huss with questions about International News Service, whose bureau in Berlin he headed. She asked pointed questions about INS' arrangements for selling its service to Central European newspapers and to those in other parts of the world, including the United States.

Huss told her what was fact—INS, which was owned by William Randolph Hearst, the proprietor of America's leading newspaper chain, maintained contracts with clients for news coverage in the same way as the Associated Press, United Press, Reuters, and the French agency Havas. He also emphasized to Martha that INS policy, as with all wire services, was familiar to her father—that their function was to distill the propaganda out of Nazi news before dispatching it from the German capital.

Three years later, in 1938, Hearst came to Germany and met

Hitler. The publisher's announced mission was to place an appeal before the Fuehrer to cease persecution of Jews, just as former President Herbert H. Hoover had done earlier that year.

After a time, a national magazine in the United States broke an exclusive story, with material a correspondent obtained from Martha Dodd, alleging that the owner and publisher of the Hearst Newspapers and INS had made a deal with Hitler to distribute doctored Nazi news and propaganda through his news outlets. The magazine article represented Hearst and his publishing empire as a tool of the Nazi Propaganda Ministry.

The Hearst organization sued for libel and won a considerable award in damages. But the surface vindication could never erase the smear campaign that remained alive for many years. The whisper-mongers succeeded in cutting deeply into circulation figures of Hearst newspapers across the country.

Martha's objective was quite obvious. Hearst had been waging a relentless campaign against the danger of creeping communism. He had branded Stalin a tyrant and called his regime inhuman and despotic. The crusade hurt Moscow. With Martha knowing Huss as she did, she was the logical person to send on the errand that, it was hoped, would help take the heat off the anti-Soviet attacks in the Hearst newspapers.

Her dinner date with Huss undoubtedly was plotted to provide Martha with some working knowledge about INS operations, to help build up a dossier against Hearst. The story didn't come out until three years later, but when it did it hit hard. It turned attention to Hearst's "deal" with Hitler and helped create public doubts about his anti-Communist campaign.

The Soviet Union had performed its first mission of subversion in the United States without having sent its first working spy here!

Just a few weeks after Martha saw Huss, she sailed with brother Bill for the United States on what was described as a combination vacation-shopping trip. That was in October, 1936.

In New York, Bill quickly joined the left-wing American League against War and Fascism, while Martha managed to keep her movements veiled from public scrutiny. But sometime that fall or early the following winter, Martha met the young scion of the Midwest banking family and husband of Marion Rosenwald, the debonair and wealthy Alfred K. Stern.

He was then still married to Marion, but Martha's vivaciousness and charm undoubtedly were factors accelerating Stern's conviction that the conjugal state he had begun in 1921 was not destined to endure for long.

He went back to Chicago, obtained a divorce by September, 1937, returned to New York, and took up residence at 340 East 57th Street to await Martha's return from Germany. Meanwhile, with his background as former chairman of the Illinois State Housing Board, he was appointed by New York City Mayor LaGuardia to the Mayor's Committee on Property Improvement.

Before she had rejoined her family in Berlin after her three-month sojourn in the United States, Martha flew to Washington and dropped in at the White House.

"Miss Dodd, wearing a smart peaked black hat with a veil, and a belted black caracul swagger coat," reported an Associated Press dispatch of January 8, 1937, "had no trouble seeing the President [Roosevelt], in spite of the fact that she left her letter of introduction in New York."

After her visit with FDR, who conveyed his personal greetings to her father, Martha left the White House ecstatic.

"Mr. Roosevelt is the most impressive statesman I've ever met in my life," she said rapturously.

Martha spent the rest of 1937 in Berlin in much the same way as she had before she'd gone off to the States, as the convivial, ever-ardent hostess at the American Embassy, extending friendships with increasing numbers of Soviet officials, and those Nazis she hadn't disenfranchised by her proliferating fondness for the occupants of the old Radziwill Palace.

In December of that year, Ambassador Dodd submitted his resignation to the White House. He was succeeded by Hugh R. Wilson, former Assistant Secretary of State. When Dodd brought his family back to the United States, they made a brief stopover in New York, enabling Martha to introduce Alfred Stern to her parents. Then the Dodds proceeded to the family farm home in Round Hill, near Leesburg, in Virginia.

On September 4th, Martha and Alfred stood before an improvised altar decorated with tall candles, ancient candelabra, and a profusion of potted and cut flowers that had been assembled in the living room of the Dodds' luxurious Southern-style residence, and were pronounced man and wife by the Rev. Henry B. Cole, pastor of the Purcellville (Virginia) Baptist Church.

The bride wore a gown of black velvet and lace, her brother was best man.

The marriage wasn't without irony, for it recalled what Martha had once said in earlier days, when speaking about herself and her brother:

"Our dream was one day to have an apartment together and live useful and productive lives. Neither of us wanted to marry . . . "

The apartment became a reality—the sumptuous digs on Manhattan's East 57th Street that Stern had rented before his marriage to Martha. But it wouldn't be shared with Bill.

When Martha moved in with her husband, they proceeded to live it up in a manner that was reminiscent of her halcyon days as the Ambassador's daughter in Berlin. Their parties were unrestrained, to put it mildly. Some of their neighbors who still reside in the building can recall the raucous affairs with which the Sterns' "modern" outlook carried toleration to its extreme limit.

A few months after the wedding, tragedy struck. Martha's father was driving one day near Leesburg when he hit and seriously injured a Negro child. Dodd didn't stop. Traced through the license number, he was arrested, and pleaded guilty to hit-and-run driving. The disgrace caused a partial physical breakdown and a little more than a year later in 1940, he died.

Sources close to Ambassador Dodd have said the aging scholar never suspected that his daughter and son had become tools of communism, though by the time of his death Martha was deep in the web of intrigue, along with her husband.

Within weeks of the wedding, Stern turned from his conservative, businesslike outlook and plunged into leftist causes, contributing not only his name but his money.

On the surface, however, Martha and Alfred Stern were camouflaged by a shining armor of respectability and patriotism. With the advent of World War II, Martha became an outspoken critic of Nazi Germany. She wrote one book, then another against the tyranny in that country, and took an active part in various Popular Front campaigns against Hitlerism. She also collaborated with her brother to produce *Ambassador Dodd's Diary*, published in 1941.

From time to time in the years to come, Martha also was compelled to defend her father's record as Ambassador to Berlin. Critics from various corners of the political arena raised pointed questions about Dodd's role during the rise of Hitler. Many blamed him personally for having failed to alert Washington to Germany's military buildup.

Martha flew into a rage on one particular occasion when an official of the State Department in October, 1943, stated publicly that he didn't see a single dispatch from Ambassador Dodd in the files from which the department had used 254 official documents to create a white-paper record of American foreign policy from 1931 to 1941.

Martha cried that this was an "insult" to her father and challenged the unnamed official to retract his statement that he saw nothing from Dodd that made any attempt to trace the rise of Adolph Hitler, or to warn the United States Government about the menace of German-Italian-Japanese aggression.

Martha produced armfuls of copies of reports, addressed to the highest officials of the American Government, which predicted months, and sometimes years in advance, the ruthless course of aggression pursued by the Axis powers.

Nevertheless, the State Department said it had none of the originals. The critical question then came up:

Did Dodd send those reports—or were they intercepted before they left the Embassy in Berlin?

It would seem inconceivable that Martha Dodd could have held the reports back, even though she had access to confidential files and was acknowledged as the "real" Amassador.

What could she have gained?

As an agent for the Kremlin, she should have seen that it was to the Soviet Union's advantage to send warnings to the United States about the peril of Axis aggression.

Yet the reports assertedly were missing in the State Department files—and the mystery lingers on, more than three decades later.

With America's entry into the war after Pearl Harbor,

December 7, 1941, Martha and Alfred Stern went full swing into the Communist orbit, from causes to outright espionage. Atomic espionage was their earliest assignment when they joined the conspiratorial apparatus that included Jack and Myra Soble, Jacob Albam, George Zlatovski, and Jane Foster (whom Zlatovski later married).

Then Martha became a recruiter. Her role was to sound out prospective agents and couriers, and to arrange for their introduction into actual espionage cells. Martha was adept at the job; she could play on the weakness or desire of one prospect, talk ideology with another—even use blackmail when necessary.

Her husband, too, became more than a financial angel in the conspiracy. This became very clear on that fine, brisk, windblown late afternoon of March 14, 1943, when Vassili Zubulin, the Second Secretary of the Soviet Embassy in Washington, and Boris Morros met in Central Park and discussed expanding the Hollywood producer's music company into a full-fledged front for Red espionage in America.

By now, Martha and Alfred had vacated their handsome East 57th Street apartment and moved into a still more plush, more exclusive residence on Central Park West—the Majestic Apartments—whose windows, perhaps significantly, overlooked the very bench where Zubulin held his cryptic conference with Morros about his prescribed future role in subversion for the Kremlin.

Chapter 6

Enter Jack Soble—The Plot Thickens

The blue haze of twilight hanging over New York City's streets
made Central Park look more beautiful on that Tuesday, May 13,
1943. Boris Morros held his head cocked up and quirked his mouth
in a faint smile as he allowed himself a moment's thought about
the grandeur of color that enveloped the park and the magnificent skyline to the south.

Morros couldn't help but admire the sight, and wonder about
appropriating this setting as a realistic background for a motion
picture he would film in the city. It would be a musical, he
thought. Perhaps a super-musical that would serve as a showcase
for several great stars. The idea had been on his mind since the
previous March, when he had come to New York for his meeting
with the Soviet Second Secretary, Vassili Zubulin.

Names like Walter Damrosch, Lily Pons, Rise Stevens, Fritz
Kreisler, Leopold Stokowski, Jan Pearce, and even Harry James
and Vaughan Monroe, coursed through the producer's imagination. They would all be part of the super-cast of musical artists for
this spectacular movie Morros had suddenly dreamed up. It

wasn't an entirely new thought with him, however. Bits and pieces of this idea had occurred to him earlier that year when he was producing *Tales of Manhattan* on a Hollywood sound stage.

The roly-poly producer had felt that the high cost of duplicating the city's skyscraper skyline in movie sets was extravagant—and ineffective. Despite the millions of dollars spent on background realism, stage props still came through on the screen as nothing more than—well, stage props.

It's a phony way to do a picture, Morros told himself. If I come to the location, I can produce a film more cheaply. And also everything is real here. Why bother with building replicas in studios when New York has authentic settings—and even authentic characters.

The waste! I'm going to do it. Other producers will wake up like me.

It was May 13, 1943, and at the moment this was a passing dream. Yet in time Morros' idea was to make an impression upon others, and Hollywood would never again be the incomparable citadel of film-making it once was. More and more producers would follow Morros' example and take their stars and cameras on location for authentic filmization.

The picture that Morros decided to produce in New York as he walked along the street that day was *Carnegie Hall.* In time—four years hence—his dream would come to its full realization.

But at this particular juncture in his life, making a movie in New York had to be committed to the future. There were other, more pressing matters he had to contend with, right here and right now.

He had come to New York not to negotiate for musical productions—but to discuss espionage.

The ninety-day deadline that Zubulin had invoked at their last meeting in Central Park was not yet at hand. Less than sixty days had passed. But Morros had already made up his mind. He knew what he had to do.

Morros had considered the Russian proposition that he turn over his small music-recording company in Los Angeles to the Soviet Union's spy network for a base of operations in the United States.

He had reached a decision. And now he had come to New York

from Hollywood ahead of the deadline to give his answer to the man who had demanded it.

Morros walked along the wide, curving sidewalk of Columbus Circle toward the Central Park entrance. His appointment was for 7 P.M. at the same place as the previous meeting—the first bench inside the park.

As he strode briskly toward his destination, he looked searchingly ahead and caught sight of the bench. It was unoccupied, although numerous pedestrians were promenading along the walk on this warm spring evening. Morros hardly glanced at the people as he strode past them to reach the bench. Then, with a sigh, he sat down, took out a handkerchief, and wiped away the perspiration from his forehead and nose.

Now he was able to look about him and scan the scene more closely while searching for a glimpse of the portly, severe-looking diplomat from the Soviet Embassy in Washington. Morros was not yet aware of it because he didn't have much experience with them, but Kremlin agents seldom arrive for a rendezvous ahead of their contacts. They wait discreetly in the "wings," someplace in the not-too-distant background, and scout the scene. They want to assure themselves that no one has followed the contact they're going to meet, that the FBI hasn't gotten a bead on the conspiracy.

Suddenly, Morros' eyes widened in recognition as he spotted a familiar movement. He narrowed his gaze and focused on a bulky silhouette ambling through the park entrance. It was Zubulin.

Approaching at a slow, ponderous gait, the Russian seemed to cast curious, nervous glances in the direction of the bench where Morros was waiting. Zubulin didn't indicate he could see the producer until he had almost reached the bench. Then, with all the warmth and ebullience that he had displayed in times past when the two men met, Zubulin threw his arms out in an affectionate embrace as he sat beside Morros.

"My dear Boris," Zubulin said elatedly, "how are you? This is such a happy occasion to see you again."

Morros offered his hand and a strained smile that at best were only perfunctory gestures of greeting. He didn't respond with nearly the enthusiasm of the emissary from the Kremlin's espionage network.

"I have been well, Vassili," Morros said in a subdued voice. "And you?"

"Fine, fine," Zubulin enthused. "And I will say I'm even finer if you have come to tell me that we are going to work out the business arrangement I suggested."

Morros' face, usually a healthy pink, seemed to lack color, as it had for some time now. Morros was aware of that condition and some of his close associates had been asking him whether he was feeling ill. He had been sapped of his vigor as he struggled over the past two months to come to terms with his conscience. Even now, after he'd made up his mind, he felt trapped in an onerous cloud of uncertainty.

Zubulin sat hunched beside Morros, his big hands locked on his knees, his broad dark face solemn, his eyes gazing unblinking at the director, who seemed hesitant to speak.

"Well, Boris?" Zubulin said almost impatiently.

"I am not very happy," Morros started stiffly. "I have worked very hard to become what I am . . . and now . . . well, it could all be lost in this servitude that you are forcing upon me."

He took a moment to organize his rushing thoughts and to summon a calm as he began to feel his temper rise.

"You know, Vassili, that I cannot afford to become suspect in my business. It is a dangerous position. It could be ruinous. You are asking me to sacrifice all that I have achieved because you say I owe you this for the favor of bringing over my father . . . I feel . . . "

The words drifted off all at once. In the silence that ensued Zubulin stared annoyedly at Morros, perhaps anticipating a turndown. The envoy still had no reason to believe Boris was going to accede to the request as he began talking again.

"Look at what they have done to innocent people in Hollywood," Morros continued. "James Cagney, Ramon Novarro, Lupe Velez, and Dolores Del Rio dragged into the mud because their names were found on a piece of paper . . . "

Morros shook his head despairingly.

"On a piece of paper," he repeated, his words measured.

He was referring to a 1934 episode when a slip of paper found in the apartment of Caroline Decker, Secretary of the Cannery and Agricultural Workers' Union, an alleged Communist subsidiary, had the names of those movie stars listed on it. Cagney and the others vigorously denied that they had made any contributions to Communist causes, as the information on the paper purported they had. But studio executives went into a state of panic. Getting smeared with a Red paint brush in those days was a dangerous—if not fatal—stroke. As it turned out, the matter died a quiet death.

But Cagney found himself being dragged into another Red probe in 1940 when he and seventeen other Hollywood celebrities—names like Jean Muir, Franchot Tone, Humphrey Bogart, Fredric March, Clifford Odets—were dragged into the inquiry. This time Cagney not only was accused of having contributed to Communist causes—but was even alleged to be a member of the party. Later, Cagney was given a clean bill of health by the House Un-American Activities Committee—but still the smear was there.

Meanwhile, studio chiefs had again pressed their panic buttons and careers teetered on the brink of uncertainty until the veil of accusations was lifted.

"Imagine what chance I will have," Morros said to Zubulin, "if I am investigated. They will have against me what they did not have against the others . . . evidence. How can I survive through something like that. . . ?" Boris took a deep breath.

Zubulin's face was grim. He was beginning to feel that a turndown was inevitable. But the contrast in the Soviet attaché's demeanor was startling when Morros picked up the sentence he had interrupted.

" . . . but I know it is not right not to show you my appreciation for what you have done for me. Therefore . . . I will do what you want."

The smile on Zubulin's face would have torn the skin of a man with less resilient epidermis. It was ear-to-ear.

"Wonderful!" he almost shouted, thrusting his hand at the producer. "Let us shake on that." Their conversation still was all in Russian.

For several minutes afterward Zubulin bathed Morros in mountainous waves of praise for his "patriotism to the motherland" and inundated him with glittering promises. "The great rewards that you can expect from Stalin will far exceed anything you have attained here. Just wait and see."

Then Zubulin got down to the core of the hard business that lay ahead.

"I was so certain that your answer would be affirmative," Zubulin began, "that I asked Martha and Alfred Stern to expect some visitors this evening. They are very anxious to meet you and to begin the big project that we have been speaking about."

Taking Morros' arm while the movie-maker was still seated, the Red agent tugged gingerly to lift him off the bench. "Let us go."

Zubulin took Morros out of the park and, still clutching his arm, escorted him across heavily-trafficked Columbus Circle. Even though it was wartime and there was gasoline rationing, the two hurrying pedestrians had to dodge a heavy evening flow of cars and taxis headed for the Times Square theater district a few short blocks south.

Although the former belle of Berlin and her millionaire husband resided on Central Park West, Zubulin didn't head in the direction of the Sterns' apartment house.

Instead he took Morros to the west side of the Circle and ushered him through a pair of narrow swinging glass doors, and up a flight of stairs into a Chinese restaurant sandwiched between a men's clothing store and a barber shop. The small foyer, reeking with the odors of Cantonese cooking, led into a dim, unpretentious dining room. Tables cluttered the center of the floor and booths hugged the walls. White tablecloths gave the place an antiseptic look which also tended to brighten the drabness of age afflicting the decor.

It was now past the peak of the supper hour and a mere half-dozen patrons were seated at the tables. As they went into the dining room, Zubulin released his grip on Morros' arm and stood for a moment glancing about at the occupants. An instant later he recognized someone and tugged at the tail of Morros' jacket.

"Come, our host is waiting," he said eagerly. He led the director across the floor like an agile halfback, swivel-hipping past chairs and tables to a booth on the far side near the back.

A man was seated alone at the table. His solemn dark eyes betrayed instant recognition of the approaching diplomat as he looked up from a spread of serving bowls bearing an assortment of Chinese foods. The feast served as a barometer of his ravenous appetite.

He was bald and sat tall, erect in his chair. The skin beneath his eyes was dark and wrinkled but his face seemed smooth and young. His eyebrows were almost jet black and bushy, lending a conspiratorial quality to his appearance. Morros sized him up as a man in his fifties.

As Zubulin approached the table, the movie producer at his side, the man rose to his feet and put out a hand in greeting to the Soviet attaché.

"So good to see you, Vassili," he said, the words garbled as he swallowed a mouthful of food.

Zubulin, turning to Morros, made the introductions.

"I want you to meet Jack Soble," he said in a modulated voice.

"How do you do," Morros smiled pleasantly.

The two men shook hands. Soble invited them to join him.

Zubulin slid into the booth and Morros edged alongside him so that they were both seated opposite Soble. Morros sensed a penetrating, investigative stare, for Soble seemed to be sizing him up.

"Are you going to eat, gentlemen?" Soble asked, stuffing the rapidly disappearing food into his mouth. This was no man to interrupt his meal, no matter how important the business at hand.

Morros and Zubulin declined the menus proffered by the waiter who was hovering over them.

"We are not having anything," Zubulin told the waiter, who left.

Still chewing, Soble struggled to speak. "Did Boris agree to our plan?" he asked, looking at Zubulin.

"Positively," the diplomat replied quickly. His attitude toward Soble seemed extremely respectful, almost humble. "Boris is willing to participate fully." Then turning to Morros in a prodding tone, "Isn't that right?"

Soble leaned forward, swallowing the last morsel of his food, watching the movie producer with a slight, intent frown, seeming eager to hear an affirmative word from him.

Morros stared squarely at Soble. In a reply that was almost a grunt he said, "Yes, I am willing."

"Good," Soble snapped. "Now we can move ahead. Martha and Alfred are waiting." He lifted the napkin from his lap, wiped his thick lips, which were moist from a last gulp of hot tea, then summoned the waiter. Paying the check, he got up.

"Let us go, gentlemen," he said in a voice that was obviously backed by some authority.

It was apparent to Morros even as they went out to the street that Jack Soble was not just a rank-and-file member of the Soviet espionage network, but somebody in the higher echelons. How high, he wondered? A notch below Zubulin? On the same level? Or was he above him?

These questions traveled through his mind as they walked across Columbus Circle toward Central Park West. After they had crossed the street, Morros felt a familiar hand on his arm. It was Zubulin, who now also brought his head close to Morros' ear and whispered.

"I must tell you before we go upstairs that I am not going to be involved too much more in the operation that we are establishing. I have my duties in Washington and I have been instructed to turn over direction of this project to Jack."

Then tightening his grip on the movie-producer's arm once again, Zubulin added, in a tone that suddenly sounded ominous, "He is the boss . . . he will give the orders. Listen to him and do exactly as he says."

Morros didn't like it. All his dealings had been with Zubulin, whom he knew as a man of substance who commanded public respect as a bona fide diplomat—even though he was really a spy. Even consenting to become partners with Martha and Alfred Stern didn't repel Morros, for they also were respected members of the community—even though they, too, were spies.

But who was Jack Soble? And why must he, Boris, take orders from him?

Morros had no solution to these and other burning questions that now vexed him. But he was certain of one thing—Jack Soble was a key man in the Soviet espionage machine that was based on these shores, waiting to be fueled with recruits who would put it into high gear.

In time, Morros would learn more about this stranger, a slim, neatly built man despite his obvious gluttony, who had just been foisted upon him as a superior. But for the time being, Jack Soble would remain a man of mystery to Boris Morros.

Chapter 7

Benedict Arnold with a Russian Accent

There was something about Jack Soble's accent that told Boris Morros it wasn't quite Russian. He thought it sounded more like the way people speak his native tongue in the Baltic countries.

He was absolutely right, for Jack Soble was Lithuanian. He was born Abroma Sobolevicius in the village of Vilkaviskis, on May 15, 1903. He was one of four children of a prominent manufacturer of bristle and animal-hair brushes which were sold in Lithuania as well as other European countries and North Africa. The father also had sidelines in timber and breweries.

There were two other sons, Boris and Robert, and a daughter, Ania.

As a teenager, Jack was taken to live in Russia for a few years immediately following the Revolution. It was there that he attended high school and met a pretty Russian schoolgirl named Myra Perskaja. They fell in love but before they could marry as they had hoped, the Sobolevicius family moved back to Lithuania.

Vowing that they would wed someday, Jack said a poignant farewell to Myra and left for his new home, in Kaunas. A short time later his parents sent Jack off to Leipzig University, and after graduation as an economics major he pursued further study at the Sorbonne in Paris.

When he had completed his education, Jack returned to Kaunas, where his father began grooming him to head the brush business and the other family enterprises. This son had a flare for the business and interested himself deeply in its operations, learning it thoroughly.

All the while, he had been corresponding with Myra, whom he still wanted to marry. Finally, in 1927, Myra obtained a visa, came to Lithuania, and became Mrs. Jack Sobolevicius.

The next dozen years passed with a heavy veil around Sobolevicius, whose activities aroused the curiosity of some people at home who wanted to know just what he was doing. He made frequent and unexplained trips out of Lithuania, sometimes to Western Europe, sometimes eastward into Russia. For the tongue-waggers in his city, those trips were something to clack about; in their idle moments some even suggested there was something clandestine in Sobolevicius' travels.

But even the wildest stretch of the imagination couldn't have conceived of what was actually happening, and of how the quiet, studious, altruistic young member of the respected Sobolevicius family was in fact being groomed by the Kremlin for espionage.

Why he was recruited for a key role in international intrigue is still a secret locked deep in the vaults of the Kremlin, yet it is an incredible truth that when Jack Sobolevicius did finally enter the shadow world of intrigue, he was directed and guided personally by the greatest Red spy of all, the infamous and dreaded Lavrenti P. Beria, chief of the Soviet Secret Police.

Why Beria picked Sobolevicius for this special role has never been made clear. But this much is known: Beria initiated Sobolevicius into the Kremlin's intelligence service by assigning him to spy on Western European groups aligned with Leon Trotsky, the exiled Russian revolutionist. Later he also engaged in collecting, evaluating, analyzing, selecting, and interpreting any and all available information he could gather in Germany, France, Czechoslovakia, and other countries. Some information was military, some was industrial, and some was commercial.

All of it was designed to aid the Soviet Union in planning for the day it was sure was coming—when a Hitler double-cross would send the Nazis' vaunted Panzer units storming across Russia's frontiers in what would prove to be the Reich's greatest single mistake of World War II.

During Sobolevicius' cloudy years in Lithuania he was extremely aloof and apparently committed to a barren social life with few intimates. Only one person could be called a close friend, Jacob Albam, a man born and raised in the same town, and whose own pursuits seemed as vague and surreptitious as Sobolevicius' doings.

The year 1939 saw the birth of Jack and Myra Sobolevicius' first child, a son whom they named Lawrence. Two years later, just before the Nazi legions burst across the border, Jack suddenly took his wife and son into Russia where, the FBI believes, he was given his most important espionage assignment—he was ordered to spy on the United States.

By now Martha Dodd and Alfred Stern had been recruited into the Kremlin's spy network and given their assignments in America.

By now Vassili Zubulin had recruited Boris Morros to perform his modest, yet significant little chores of providing talent scout accreditations to Soviet undercover agents.

The groundwork had been laid to launch a major espionage operation in the United States. Just a few strings had to be tied together to make the network all-encompassing and operational inside Uncle Sam's frontiers.

After receiving his orders, Sobolevicius returned to Lithuania to find an austere reception from an unfriendly community which had begun to suspect the worst of him because of his Russian trip. He was arrested and condemned for Red activities; but his influential father arranged to have his son exchanged for a Lithuanian prisoner incarcerated in Russia.

Brief months later, when Russia invaded Lithuania, Sobolevicius returned to his native land; he told his relatives he was disillusioned with communism and urged a number of them to join him in leaving the country.

The record shows the family left Lithuania, traveled across the vast reaches of Soviet Union into Siberia, then crossed the Manchurian border into China, and finally reached Japan. With a visa issued by the U.S. Embassy, they sailed from Kobe for the

United States, landing in San Francisco in the latter part of 1941. Time had been on Sobolevicius' side. Just a few short weeks later, the Japanese dropped their bombs on Pearl Harbor and the American Embassy in Tokyo was closed. Had Sobolevicius delayed his departure from Lithuania for just that brief span of time, he might not have obtained a visa so readily—if at all.

From the city by the Golden Gate, they went north and east, to Canada. Finally they reached Montreal, where Boris and Ania settled down with their parents. Jack, Myra, and young Lawrence, along with brother Robert, made their way back to the United States.

Robert headed for New York City and eventually acquired a position at Rockland State Hospital, a mental institution not far from Manhattan, as a psychiatrist, a specialization for which he had been prepared in European medical schools. He also shortened his name to *Soblen.*

Jack took his family to Boston, stayed there for a year, and then he, too, moved to New York. Along the way, Jack also shortened his name, going his brother one letter less and making it *Soble.*

Jack, Myra, and Lawrence settled into a pleasant six-room fourth-floor apartment at 321 West 78th Street, a fashionable neighborhood between West End Avenue and Riverside Drive, within sight of the broad Hudson River and the rising Palisades on the New Jersey shore.

The year was 1942. Half of Europe and a vast sector of the Pacific already were aflame with war. For Jack Soble, an immigrant who answered the draft call to serve in the armed forces of his newly adopted land, there was no military service; he was rejected for physical reasons.

With the vigor characteristic of so many of America's immigrants who came from abroad to achieve success in the free-enterprise system of a democracy, Jack Soble plunged into business. He started a small brush and bristle exporting firm, a trade he knew well but also one whose operations were greatly restricted by the war. Nevertheless, Soble was able to enjoy modest success in exporting his wares to Canada and Mexico, as well as some South American countries.

The business also gave Soble the perfect front that he needed to conduct his primary pursuit—espionage for the Soviet Union.

The authorities are not quite certain at what precise point he began his nefarious duties for the Kremlin on these shores. The author was unable to uncover a shred of evidence to show what subversive activity Soble engaged in from the time he entered this country to that eventful Tuesday, May 13, 1943, when Boris Morros was introduced to him by the First Secretary, Vassili Zubulin, in the Far East Chinese Restaurant overlooking Columbus Circle.

That he had been busy as a spy during the period preceding his first recorded espionage activity ought not to be doubted. For how else could he have commanded the rank and position to act as Zubulin's replacement in the plot to spy on the United States, for which Boris Morros had just been recruited as a full partner?

Although Morros was uneasy with the prospect of dealing with a total stranger, he didn't betray his feelings that Tuesday as he was escorted by Zubulin and Soble in the elevator up to the apartment of Martha Dodd and her wealthy husband Alfred Stern.

Morros found the Sterns' apartment precisely what he expected it would be—elaborate, luxurious, and breathtaking. Stern obviously had spared no cost in furnishing the quarters with the most expensive furniture and appointments imaginable.

And Morros found the Sterns themselves just about what he expected, too—dignified, decorous, and debonair. But, he also decided after a bit, they were somewhat dull.

At the beginning, conversation centered almost entirely on Morros' Hollywood achievements. He was praised lavishly and excessively for his accomplishments by Martha and Alfred. Although he pretended to enjoy these effusive compliments, Morros knew for damned sure he hadn't been brought there for that.

Why don't they stop this patronizing horseshit and get down to business? Morros asked himself bluntly. He knew the score and the chatter wasn't necessary to prepare him for the main event—his assignment in subversion.

Some thirty minutes and several cocktails later, Martha and Alfred finally got down to brass tacks. Martha provided the opening with a gratuitous declaration that she was delighted to have "a man of your caliber join our cause."

She extended her hand across the couch to Morros, her fingers dangling loosely like those of a reigning empress. The movie director forced himself to take his cue and hold Martha's hand for a moment.

"What plans are you giving to me?" he asked quickly in a voice edged with impatience.

"My dear Boris," Martha sighed. It was a very regal sigh as though Martha were sitting on a throne and Boris, one of her subjects, had been brought before her for an audience.

"We have an ambitious program that is going to require everyone's maximum cooperation," Martha said slowly, enunciating her English clearly so that Boris, the "foreigner," might more readily absorb what she was saying. "We are gathered here this evening to make certain that we all understand our assignments."

Boris told himself the dialogue sounded like something out of a Grade-B movie plot. He hated amenities but more than anything else he hated cornball prefaces, though many times he was compelled to grind lots of corn in his movies.

Martha looked at Morros for a silent moment, her eyes grave and impassive but deeply penetrating. She drew in a long careful breath.

Now she thinks she is Bette Davis, Morros amused himself.

"Your task will be to allow us a maximum of free movement inside your music company," Martha said, beginning to get to the nuts and bolts of the conspiratorial structure. The words dropped from Martha's dry, thin-lipped mouth as though they'd been rehearsed many times over.

For the next hour, it was Martha Dodd's show, as she spelled out explicit plans of how the Boris Morros Music Company would expand its staff with Red agents who'd conduct their espionage assignments under the guise of music salesmen.

Then Soble took over center stage, amplifying, expanding, altering, or confirming the Master Plan for the Red takeover of Morros' recording firm which Martha had detailed.

Zubulin said very little and Morros himself next to nothing. The only times the director spoke were in response to specific questions about the size of the firm, its income, and its potential to tolerate a sudden expansion with the infusion of new money and an enlarged staff (of spies) without attracting too much attention, but more importantly—without arousing any suspicion.

"If it happens," Morros explained at one point about the sudden enlargement of his company, "we will not attract any suspicion because people will think I found an angel to invest in the business. It is done all the time in Hollywood."

Martha seemed pleased with that explanation.

Her husband said even less than Morros, and to Boris it was spotlight clear that this millionaire was a puppet dangling at the end of a string manipulated by his wife.

The most significant statement Stern made all that long evening came just before the gathering broke up. He looked up from a small notepad he was fondling and declared, "Well, I'm going to put up $100,000 on this venture . . . That should certainly get us started rather auspiciously."

During the meeting Morros had sought to find out what intelligence the Communist ring that was to operate out of his company would be seeking. But he learned little and Soble cautioned him to be patient. His instructions would come at the appropriate time.

"It is much too soon to go into that now," Soble said. "First we must work on expanding the company."

Morros was told by Soble to reorganize the music firm so that it could absorb a greatly expanded staff of Red agents, as well as support the more extensive business operation that was necessary to justify hiring so many additional employees.

"We will advance the money as soon as you have completed this plan," Soble advised him.

The meeting ended on a note of optimism with a toast by Martha Dodd, who by now seemed to be feeling no pain after having downed at least a half-dozen cocktails.

"Let us work together for success," she slurred. "And let us proceed with caution and good sense."

That was how it began for Boris Morros, a nearly fifteen-year career as a full-time, trusted, devoted, faithful agent for the Kremlin who was to take part in one incredible plot of espionage after another.

For all of those nearly fifteen dangerous years he was to be one of the main cogs in a ring that furnished the Soviet Union with information ranging from biographical material on the 1944 Republican Presidential and Vice-Presidential candidates, Thomas E. Dewey and John W. Bricker, and on Dewey's running mate in 1948, Earl Warren, who later became Chief Justice of the United States Supreme Court—to the names, locations, photographs, and personal habits of American military intelligence agents abroad.

Morros even supplied documents, writings, photographs, negatives, notes, and other data connected with the national defense of the United States.

In those fifteen years Morros was to travel hundreds of thousands of miles for the Kremlin's spy machine, holding clandestine meetings in restaurants, cafes, hotels, movie studios, filming locations, theaters, and even street corners and back alleys in what would one day come to be regarded as the twentieth century's most fantastic double-life.

Because all the time Morros played at being a spy he continued exercising his genius in the musical and theatrical worlds, producing one film after another to enhance his reputation as one of the best-known and most respected musical directors in all of movieland.

He seemed to have an inordinate facility for handling both jobs, making it seem that his cloak was a tan camel's hair coat straight out of Hollywood; his dagger a sharp wit; and his supreme self-confidence, a family-bred trait that taught him never to doubt himself whether conducting the Imperial Symphony Orchestra for the Czars in Russia before the Revolution, or leading Hollywood's musicians in performing lilting rhapsodies and sonatas for the screen.

In time, Morros would be faced with still another role, which would weigh him down even more strenuously with the responsibility of living not two, but three lives: spy, Hollywood impresario, and—we'll get to that third role presently.

For now, let us continue to study Boris Morros and the espionage system that was being established to give the Kremlin spy apparatus the wherewithal to launch the greatest cloak-and-dagger operation in history, an operation that would bring some of America's most guarded secrets cascading into the insatiable gullet of the Red Monster of subversion.

And through it all loomed the bulky figure of Boris Morros, who at that meeting with Martha Dodd, Alfred Stern, Vassili Zubulin, and his new *boss*, Jack Soble, had finally thrown the cloak on his shoulders to play his part as the twentieth century's Benedict Arnold—with a Russian accent.

Boris Morros had hitched his droshky to Mother Russia and he was going to spy for her in a great big way . . .

Chapter 8

Honor among Spies—Cross and Double-Cross

When Boris Morros returned to Hollywood after his brief adventure in the council of the Red conspiracy at the Majestic Apartments in New York, he knuckled down to the familiar business of grinding out movies. He wasn't yet ready for anything so lavish as *Carnegie Hall*, but there were plenty of Grade-B movie scripts around that he could produce on a low budget. For the next few months such film-making chores kept his nose to the celluloid grindstone with few thoughts of his commitment to communism.

Nobody was pushing him—yet.

Then came mid-December, 1943, and Morros received an urgent phone call from Washington in his office. Vassili Zubulin was at the Soviet Embassy and he had a question to ask.

"Have you prepared the reorganization plan?" the chief Kremlin spymaster in America asked. His tone was impatient.

"Yes," Morros replied quickly. "It is all ready. But there is a slight problem . . . "

The producer proceeded to tell Zubulin that reorganizing the Boris Morros Music Company on a scale comparable to the one envisioned as a cover for a nationwide espionage ring would require more than the initial and very generous $100,000 that Alfred Stern had volunteered to invest in the enterprise.

"How much will it take?" Zubulin asked annoyedly.

"Oh, somewhere in the neighborhood of $150,000," Morros replied grandly.

Zubulin said he didn't think that was too much of an obstacle and ordered Morros to head east once again.

"Be in New York on the twenty-third," he directed. "I will meet you at the main information booth in Grand Central at two o'clock in the afternoon. We must see Martha and Alfred. The time has come to put our plan into action."

Morros tied up the loose ends of his Hollywood business quickly and left for New York. He met Zubulin at the station just as it had been arranged and was led to the street to a waiting limousine with a chauffeur behind the wheel. He was employed by the Sterns.

But instead of heading uptown to the Majestic Apartments, the driver bore east to the Franklin D. Roosevelt Drive, then turned north. A powdery snow was beginning to fall, augering a white Christmas.

It wasn't until the car had crossed the Triborough Bridge's Harlem River span and was tooling along Eastern Boulevard (now Bruckner Boulevard) in the Bronx that Morros suddenly awakened fully to his strange surroundings.

"Where are we going?" he asked as he looked around at the passing parade of warehouses and factories.

"To the Sterns' country home," Zubulin said brightly. "You are going to see a capitalistic paradise. It takes only money to live the way they do. That is why I told you it would not be much trouble to get the $150,000. They have the money."

The Sterns' patrician country estate in Lewisboro, just across the Connecticut state-line from Ridgefield, was an eye-opener even to one as blasé as Morros, whose years in Hollywood had taken him past the thresholds of the most resplendent and ostentatious mansions in the movie colony. But the Sterns' villa was wholly different. It had a distinctive, aristocratic flavor that set it apart from any palatial West Coast home Morros had known.

Zubulin and the movie producer were greeted warmly by Martha and Alfred Stern, who escorted them into the living room.

A fresh pile of blazing logs in the fireplace was crackling furiously, giving the room the perfect touch of needed warmth and coziness on this snowy winter afternoon.

Warm and cozy, too, was the slender, dark-haired figure slouched in one of the living room chairs near the fire and working on a quart of the Sterns' imported vodka. He turned his head slowly toward the approaching party. When he caught sight of Morros, he gulped from his glass with quickness, struggled awkwardly to his feet, and came forward unsteadily with hand out in greeting.

"Glad to see you, Comrade Boris," he said with a gentle coarseness that Morros remembered with repugnance from his last encounter with Jack Soble. "Come, have a drink, my friend."

After several minutes of chit-chat, Zubulin brought the meeting to order with an announcement to Stern.

"Alfred," he said meaningfully, "Boris tells me $150,000 will be needed for the expansion of his company. What do you think?"

A frown of desolation all at once seemed to carve itself on Stern's thin, wrinkled face. Up to the time his path crossed Martha and Marxism, he'd been strictly a man of fat cigars, old brandies, and mahogany-paneled board-of-directors' rooms in which questions of high finance never flustered him so long as the investment promised a healthy return on every dollar. And there was always a profit in any deal Stern made.

After the minister tied the knot at Martha's ancestral abode in Round Hills, Virginia, and his wife's tender brainwashing had latched him to communism, Stern acquiesced to certain departures from his old capitalistic way of life. While it shocked the stiffnecked doormen at the Majestic, Stern took it as part of his new mode of life when he got to greet the coterie of odd-ball friends calling on his wife—world-savers, America-haters, tipplers, bearded cats who weren't called beatniks in those days but radicals, high-falutin' bums disinherited by their families, and discredited debutantes turned sexpots. He began to feel more at home with this lot of Kremlin aficionados than with a chairman of the board.

And, spurred on by Martha, he joined every Communist front—and wrote generous checks every time the Red collection basket was passed around. But no money tray ever had a $150,000 contribution tag on it. Maybe he was in love with the Kremlin, but not to such an absorbing degree that would make him pour a fortune into a pig in a poke.

"What guarantee can you give me?" Stern turned to Morros somberly. "I want to help all I can to set up your company expansion for our cause, but I've got to have assurance that it is also going to be a sound business investment."

Alfred Stern's ideology may have been Communistic but his heart was still very capitalistic.

"I know all the great artists of Hollywood," Morros said with a sweep of his hand. "They all will make records for me."

Stern had no reason to doubt the director's credentials as a big man in the movie capital. But he was disinclined to agree that many of the film city's musical greats would flock to Morros' music company.

"You've got RCA Victor, Columbia, Decca, and so many other recording firms to buck," Stern said soberly. "I'm not as optimistic as you are."

Soble interrupted almost angrily to point out to Mr. Moneybags that the primary goal of the investment was to create a huge spy front for Russia, and that profit should only be a secondary motive. Stern couldn't agree more—but he still wouldn't part with $150,000.

After hours of dickering, he consented to a compromise— $130,000.

But for that kind of loot, he said, he'd want a hand in the business. He let the gathering know that he was going to open a branch office on the East Coast to keep an eye on things as vice-president, a title he bestowed on himself after a sip from his glass of brandy. The thought of a vice-presidency seemed to warm Stern more than that swallow of burning booze.

By making that decision, Stern in effect had also become a sort of spymaster for the Soviet Union on the Eastern Seaboard.

In a matter of days, Stern had rented an office suite on a high floor at 30 Rockefeller Plaza in New York City. He spared no expense on elegant furnishings. Morros was duly impressed by the branch office and when he went west to the home office, he promptly closed it down. And had it redone with furnishings and decor even plushyer than Stern's. When it came to extravagance, nobody could outdo Boris Morros. Just ask Paramount.

Stern put up the money in two installments in early 1944. In January, he handed over a check for $50,000 to the corporation and in March he surrendered the remainder of his commitment, $80,000. In return Morros issued two promissory notes in the same amounts, bearing four per cent interest in dollars—not rubles.

See what a businessman Stern was? A chip off the old capitalistic block, that's what he was.

Just as operations began going into high gear, the espionage entente received a jarring that rocked it right down to its corporate bootstraps. Vassili Zubulin, the distinguished Second Secretary of the Soviet Embassy in Washington, was caught redhanded by the FBI trying to obtain secret U.S. Army manuals.

The State Department declared him persona non grata and requested the Kremlin to recall him. The incident barely received notice in the newspapers. It was wartime, the Soviet Union was America's ally, and publicity about an act of treason on Moscow's part at a time like that wouldn't work in the best interests of either country.

So it was a quiet departure for Comrade Zubulin. But a historic one, nevertheless, for he was the very first of what would be an endless procession of Soviet diplomats who were to get the boot in years to come for espionage activity while stationed here in the guise of ministers or envoys.

Zubulin's ouster elevated Jack Soble to chief Soviet spymaster in America. No sooner had Soble taken over than he was beset by a grave internal problem. It sprung up in April, 1944, when Stern looked over the company books in his skyscraper office in Rockefeller Center and discovered that most of his $130,000 had been spent.

Ripping mad, he tore out to Hollywood. A look at the lavish front Morros called his office made it clear to Stern why he was seeing red. A glance at the books made it doubly clear to him. Only a sprinkling of capital had gone into cutting records. And what records had been pressed, Stern disliked violently.

"Who told you to make such trash?" he demanded sternly of Morros. "This is all trash, this stuff you call 'Rum and Coca Cola' and 'Chattanooga Choo-Choo.' Why don't you record 'Nutcracker Suite' or some beautiful Russian ballads? Anything is better than this junk."

Stern glared at Morros' desk, spotted an ash tray, and picked it up.

"This ash tray," he roared. "Why did you pay $100 for it? You're wasteful. You're throwing money away."

Morros studied him, pinch-faced and sober. His tight expression finally eased. He burst into a sudden, explosive laugh.

"You are talking about saving money, are you?" Morros growled, the blood rushing to his face. "What do you call this—$5,000 for entertainment. Entertainment for what?"

Morros had an expense statement in his hand and was waving it in Stern's face.

Stern blushed. He'd forgotten to explain that little item. It seems that the comrades working out of the East Coast office had wanted to do a little something as a remembrance for Vassili Zubulin before he left for the salt mines.

"I gave him a farewell party and bought Mrs. Zubulin a going-away present," Stern said thinly. "You know, Vassili can do our firm a lot of good back in Moscow."

"Ha," Morros sneered. "And you are talking about saving money. Go back where you came from and stay there. You let me run this business. I am the musical genius. I will pick the songs we record."

Stern was boiling mad. "I'm asking my attorneys to dissolve the company and sue you for return of my investment," the millionaire shouted and stalked out of Morros' office.

"You sue, you'll see what you get," the producer bellowed at the departing Stern.

Morros immediately phoned Soble, the new spy chief, to report the trouble. "Don't worry, Boris," Soble comforted him, "I'll take care of everything."

Several days later, when Stern had reached New York on the train, Soble called on him and Martha at the Majestic. He was in a gloomy mood.

"Let us not have any trouble now that we have started everything moving," he said severely. "I am just getting our agents their jobs with the music company. We cannot afford difficulties now."

Martha cut him short. She was deeply disturbed.

"Jack," she said slowly as she stood by the living room window staring out at the budding spring foliage in Central Park. "I don't trust that Morros. That son of a bitch is no more of a Communist than J. Edgar Hoover. In fact, I'll bet that $130,000 that he's an FBI stooge. That's why Alfred and I are so worried about the money."

Soble disagreed violently. "He has been checked out thoroughly," the Number-One Kremlin spy chief in this country assured the Sterns. "I have the complete record on him. He has cooperated fully since the 1930s with the Soviet Embassy in Washington. Even Beria likes him. I have a note from Lavrenti that he wants someday to meet Boris. So please don't talk about him like that. If you want your money back, I will try to get it. But give me time. Don't spoil the organization we have started."

Martha and her husband were adamant. They demanded their investment be returned immediately. They assured Soble they'd sink the cash into another front, any kind of front just so long as it didn't involve Morros.

"I will run it personally," Stern offered.

Soble said he'd try to get the money back. But that was easier said than done. Morros balked.

"I am doing smashing business with 'Chattanooga Choo-Choo' and 'Rum and Coca Cola,'" he told Soble on the long-distance phone. "I refuse to return the money. I have other songs ready for the Hit Parade."

The situation was serious. Soble regarded the Sterns and Morros as valuable agents, even if they had clashing personalities. The company had to be sacrificed—and Morros had to accept that decision. But Soble didn't feel he was equipped to be Boris' persuader. He notified Beria.

Moscow dispatched an agent who was qualified both by background and training to talk sense into Morros. He was Stephen N. Choudenko, alias the Professor, an outstanding authority on murder whose kit of work tools had the guarantee of making every fatality appear—even to the world's finest police—as nothing more than certain suicide.

Choudenko was assigned to Washington as a Second Secretary at the Soviet Embassy. Then he joined the Red conspirators in New York late in the spring of 1944. He spoke to Martha and Alfred Stern and satisfied himself that there was no way to settle their differences with Morros. Choudenko went to see the producer in Hollywood.

A man of a few words, the Professor had only to speak one, in Russian, to convince Boris of his future course.

"*Likvidirovay!*" the visitor from the Kremlin said with utter finality.

"Very good, very good," Morros said tremblingly. "If you want me to liquidate, I will liquidate."

It was either liquidate the business or have himself liquidated, Boris quickly gathered. That's why *liquidate*, standing as the Professor's only spoken word, carried so much meaning and impact for him.

Boris closed shop immediately. But Stern didn't get back his full investment, only $100,000. Yet he was satisfied. Just to be rid of Boris Morros was worth that $30,000 loss.

The effect of the whole episode was that Morros, despite Martha's charge that he was an FBI counterspy, became a bigger man in the Kremlin. Martha had repeated her suspicions to Choudenko, but his reply was a stiff reprimand.

"Director Beria has his own opinion about Boris," the Professor said huffily. "Our chief says anybody who returns $100,000 the way Boris did is a worthy person who can be trusted. Actually, he is angry with *you* because you forced the company out of business. Now we have no place to headquarter our spies."

Stern quickly volunteered to open another business as a front for the espionage operations.

What kind of business, Choudenko wanted to know.

Stern wasn't sure.

But Soble, who also was at the get-together in the Sterns' Lewisboro home, had a thought that he'd been toying with for some time. The Kremlin had drafted a bold new espionage plot. It was to be a major spy offensive in Washington, D.C., with the White House, the Pentagon, and the various Government departments as targets.

Nerve center of the spy network would be a fashionable Washington haberdashery that just happened to be up for sale.

"We want to buy this shop but we cannot put up the cash if it will be traced to Moscow," Soble explained. "Therefore, Alfred, this is the opportunity you asked for."

Stern was nonplused when he learned it would take $300,000 to buy out the business.

"No haberdashery is worth that much, not even the one where

Harry Truman [then a U.S. Senator] used to work," Stern said prissily. "I can think of a hundred other businesses that can be bought for far less and could serve the purpose just as well."

Soble turned to Choudenko for guidance. "Not my business," the Professor shrugged. "Talk with Gromov."

Anatol B. Gromov, another Soviet Embassy Secretary, had taken over the spy machinery in the nation's capital after Zubulin's departure. Arrangements were made to bring Martha and Alfred Stern down to Washington to see Gromov, nicknamed Alex.

The meeting was held in front of the Lincoln Memorial at ten o'clock in the morning of the first Sunday in June, 1944, a time when weekend tourists were beginning to flock to the monument. The Great Emancipator would have squirmed in his marble chair if he'd been able to hear the voices of the plotters. But they'd retired to a convenient restaurant to get away from eavesdroppers.

Gromov agreed that $300,000 was too much to sink into a haberdashery, and he didn't think the Squire of Lewisboro should be peddling $1.98 ties. This wasn't a business with class, and if Stern went into it he might attract some FBI agents as some of his first customers.

The Soviet diplomat had another idea. Alfred and Martha, he said, could serve the Soviet Union in two other vital areas—providing a meeting place and message drop for Soviet agents and recruiting new ones among their large circles of acquaintances. He went on to tell them that later on he'd have an even more important assignment. He would want them to establish a base of operations in Mexico City, where the Soviet espionage and sabotage services for Cuba and all Latin American countries were to be established eventually.

"We must have someone like you to pass information between Mexico and the United States," Gromov said.

The Soviet espionage apparatus needed Americans of the Sterns' stature who, because of their habits as frequent international travelers, could cross the border with impunity as *Fellow Travelers*.

Chapter 9

"Easy as a Callhouse"

With the encouragement and new direction given them by Alex Gromov, Martha and Alfred Stern went back to New York and began living up to their first two commitments. They made their apartment in the Majestic available for the meetings Gromov suggested and began to receive the Communist Party faithful.

Among the more notable comrades who attended cell meetings there in the months that followed were Hans Eisler, Moscow's top political wire-puller in the United States, and Bill Browder, brother of Earl, head of the Communist Party, U.S.A.

In the recruiting end, the Sterns did a brisk business, too. One of their best catches of Red tenderfoots was an old chum of Martha's, a shapely, amply endowed blond named Jane Foster, about thirty, and a native of California. Jane had a fascinating face to go with her figure and possessed Martha's zest for booze and boys.

The fact that she was married to tall, blond, good-looking George Zlatovski of Duluth, Minnesota, didn't stop Jane from having fun. Jane managed to make a lot of men happy in the sack because around that time—December, 1945—husband George, who came to America from Russia when he was eight years old, was serving with the U.S. Occupation Forces in Vienna.

And of all things, he was attached as a lieutenant to the Army's Counter-Intelligence Corps!

When she ran into Jane in New York City on that cold December afternoon, the warmth of Martha's greeting could have melted an iceberg. And when she heard about Jane's husband being in the Counter-Intelligence Corps, the heat of Martha's passion could have thawed the whole Arctic.

As for what Jane had been doing all these years that Martha hadn't seen her, there was a simple explanation: she'd been on the Dutch island of Sumatra in the Dutch East Indies, with the hush-hush Office of Strategic Services, America's wartime intelligence organization.

The excitement over this news was almost too much for Martha to bear. Jane simply had to come up to Martha's apartment on Central Park West to talk over a very important proposition—espionage.

Jane was all ears. And she was certain husband George would be just as elated about working for the Kremlin. Jane declared herself ready to start at once.

Martha sent for Soble and, knowing the boss subscribed to sexual interludes with his female underlings, she prepared the guest bedroom with a spray of perfume that gave the place a fragrance one might expect to find in an Egyptian cathouse.

When Soble arrived, Martha made things clear at the outset. She ripped off Jane's blouse and shoved her into the spy boss' arms.

"This is Jane," Martha said breathlessly. "Take her, Jack. She's yours. You'll find she's a wonderful girl."

The bald, stiffly erect Soble had no qualms about retiring with Jane to the spare boudoir after he gave her prodigious charms the once-over. Years later, when he repented his role in the Kremlin's servitude, Jack Soble would recall this incident with some frankness.

"It was," he said, "as easy as in a callhouse."

He not only accepted Jane, but also a fifty-page report she

wrote at his request—a report on everything she had seen, heard, and learned while stationed in Sumatra with the OSS.

Just two months later, in February, 1946, Soviet Delegate Andre Vishinsky stood up in the temporary quarters of the infant United Nations at Lake Success on Long Island and rattled the hall with a harangue against Dutch rule in the East Indies. His key arguments were passages taken verbatim from Jane Foster Zlatovski's fifty-page thesis.

Her contribution pleased Beria so much that he broached to Soble the idea of promoting Jane to Vienna where she could join her husband. Two can be more effective than one in playing the espionage game, and in postwar Vienna, a divided city occupied by the Soviets and the Western Allies, espionage was the biggest game of all.

The onset of the Cold War had put diplomats at each others' jugulars and the secret services of East and West were staging their own duels—in blood. Hardly a day passed that the blue Danube didn't turn red with the unidentified corpses of rival agents who'd been stabbed, shot, or dismembered.

Those events in that far-off snakepit of murderous intrigues cast their shadows all the way into the Majestic Apartments in New York on May 2, 1947, which was memorable also for an event in the film world that was of some moment—the world première of *Carnegie Hall*. After years of planning and plotting, Boris Morros finally produced the super-musical and now it had finally opened at two New York theaters—the Winter Garden and the Park.

By eleven o'clock that night, the *New York Times*, *Daily News*, *Herald-Tribune*, and *Mirror* were on the street with their reviews. What the critics had to say about the film was something Morros was better off not reading.

But the night wasn't a total loss for Morros. Other critics were giving the producer rave reviews—right in Martha and Alfred Stern's apartment. Everyone present, however, was under an admonition to keep his voice low, so as not to wake up the baby.

It should be noted right here, right now, that Martha and Alfred Stern, infected by the yearning for parenthood in the midst of all their spy activities, had adopted an infant son and named him Robert.

Mindful of the sleeping baby, Jack Soble spoke in a modulated tone as he unfolded the news to Martha and Alfred that Lavrenti Beria had decided to shift Morros to Vienna as a key figure in the expanding international network.

"You must try to overcome your hostile feelings toward him," Soble said sternly. "The Director decided that you will serve as his New York contact. I personally appeal to you to make an effort to get along with Boris, for the sake of the Communist cause. And, besides, he is not a bad fellow."

"He stinks!" cried Martha, trying gamely not to let her voice rise too loudly in anger lest it wake little Robert. "Don't mention Morros and communism in one breath. I always thought and still think he's a phony. He's working for the FBI."

Stern, who was sitting inoffensively in a corner drinking from a goblet filled with red wine, struggled clumsily from his chair and turned with a sheepish smile to his wife.

"Now, Martha, my dear, you're too hard on him," he said in a tremulous voice. "If he were double-crossing us, we would have had the FBI on our necks long ago. I'll try to work with him if I have to."

Martha stalked across the room, retrieved her drink from the serving table, and wheeled around with a glower for her husband.

"All right, damn you, if you want to be a sucker, be one," she said wearily. "I'm not going to fight you, but you wait and see. You're going to kiss my ass in Macy's window if you're ever wrong about him."

Soble shook with laughter. He turned to Martha and said softly, "If Alfred is wrong he will not do his kissing in Macy's window—it will be in Leavenworth Penitentiary."

Martha shook her head in despair, muttering, "That's what I'm afraid of."

Martha Dodd Stern never was more in error than she was that night—and all the days and nights of the past four years that she'd known Boris Morros. The man she suspected was a counter-spy for the FBI had never so much as spoken to an agent of the Bureau or even ventured past the door of an FBI field office in all the time he'd toiled as a Red spy.

But this much should be said about Martha. Time was to prove her a woman of remarkable intuition, possessed of an extraordinary clairvoyance.

For precisely ten weeks later, on July 14, 1947, the FBI office in Los Angeles was fated to receive a phone call . . .

Chapter 10

Boris Really Goes to the FBI!

"I am Boris Morros, the film producer," the caller introduced himself on the phone. "I would like to see somebody from the FBI about something very important . . . "

Agents met Morros and unburdened him of his strange, bewildering story of how, for some dozen years, he'd yielded to Soviet pressures that had started in the 1930s when he wanted to send food packages to his parents. He told every detail he could remember about the scores of meetings with Zubulin and Soble and Martha and Alfred Stern, about the recording company, about whatever else he could recall.

Morros was astounded several times when the FBI agents corrected him on minor points about which his memory was hazy.

"How did you know that?" he'd cry out, flustered.

A better question would have been: What don't you know?

The truth of it was that the FBI had been on Morros' heels for years—as it had been on the tails of the Sobles, the Sterns, and more recently the Zlatovskis.

What to do with Morros was resolved in Washington by none

other than J. Edgar Hoover himself, who recommended that the movie director stay with the spy network as if nothing had happened—and operate as an FBI counterspy. If he was willing.

Morros swore he'd do anything to atone for his past guilt, and if being a double-agent was what the FBI wanted him to be, he'd accept the assignment.

Now Martha Dodd Stern's obsessive fears about Boris Morros at last had a foundation in fact.

Morros took his assignment to work for the Reds in Vienna with uncharacteristic eagerness. Being an FBI counterspy seemed to give Boris new bounce.

Following instructions from Moscow, Morros went into movie production in Austria's capital and also began importing Soviet films to the United States. This dual business enterprise provided Morros with the cover he had to have to perform effectively for both the Soviet Union and the employer he was now moonlighting for, Uncle Sam. He could meet actors, writers, financiers, as well as Red agents—or FBI men. He could also make journeys for either side behind a wall of legitimate business reasons. He had virtually unlimited freedom of movement, which was required in his precarious dual existence.

His value as an FBI counterspy soon became apparent when he began delivering into the hands of American security authorities secrets of Soviet espionage in Vienna—such as the doings of Jane and George Zlatovski—that U.S. agents could not keep track of.

Using her body and face as a lure, Jane enticed officials of international anti-Soviet organizations into compromising positions, wheedling information on the routes of underground pipelines into Iron Curtain countries and the names of prominent refugees and informants against the Kremlin.

Zlatovski, still a lieutenant with the OSS, became a man to be watched even more closely by agents of his own Counter-Intelligence Corps as he pilfered Army documents from American headquarters, or cuddled up in his spare moments with the Austrian secretaries of U.S. agencies in Vienna to let them whisper in his ear some of the secrets they'd picked up in their day's work.

But most of the documents he stole, most of the information uttered under the breath to him in Viennese nightclubs was so much worthless data, for it all had been carefully planted by U.S. authorities alerted to his activities by Boris Morros.

Morros himself soon became known in Vienna as a big-talking good-time Charlie. With top hat, silk suit, flashy diamond stickpin, and a sleek convertible, the producer's roly-poly figure cut a nightly swath through the city's nightclubs, dancing waltzes, sipping bubbling champagne, and fondling the tender flesh of doe-eyed Viennese starlets. It was the way a film impresario was supposed to behave, and Morros was playing the role to the hilt.

Travel became one of his most important duties. The Kremlin wanted Morros to serve above all else as a courier because of his unquestioned right to flit about from country to country in his role as a movie producer and film exporter-importer.

His first trip back to the United States came in late November, 1947, when he was ordered to meet Alfred Stern and Jack Soble in New York City to deliver instructions directly from Beria to them, and to accept a packet of documents pertaining to the defense of the United States that were bound for the Kremlin. Buried among the theatrical papers in his briefcase, no Immigration agent would know to search for the hidden documents. And especially would no agent search for them after the Immigration people had been given orders to lay off Morros, to give him unhindered clearance.

Morros met Stern and Soble at the Essex House, not far from the Majestic Apartments. The site was Stern's idea. He didn't think Boris should come up to Central Park West because Martha still had no tolerance for him. She never stopped believing Morros was a double-crosser. More than ever now, in fact, she was convinced of it and she was secretly trying to do something about it.

A short time after Morros returned to Vienna in January, 1948, he received orders to head for Paris and rendezvous with Jane and George Zlatovski. By now George had finished his tour in the Army and was mustered out at his own request. He returned to the States just briefly, then went back to take a Kremlin assignment, one of the most important of the day—to assist in a plot to assassinate Yugoslavia's Marshal Tito!

The plan was to murder Tito on a train taking him back to his summer residence. It was to be executed in such a way that the killing could be pinned on "American hired killers." But for reasons unknown to this day, the assassination was called off only hours before it was to have happened. That's when George and Jane were ordered to meet Morros in Paris.

Meantime, in New York, Martha and Alfred Stern read the

orders that Beria had sent with Morros. They had finally been given that plum in Mexico City which had been mentioned earlier by Alex Gromov, the Soviet Embassy Secretary in Washington.

Stern was instructed to go into the money-lending and house-development business in the Mexican capital—at last a cover worthy of his social and financial status.

With his immense wealth, Stern established his base of operations below the border very quickly. Then he and Martha began commuting between New York and Mexico City, as vital links in the conspiracy to spread the tentacles of communism into Cuba and Latin America, as well as to expand operations to an even greater extent in the United States.

The Paris meeting between Morros and the Zlatovskis was also engineered by Beria. They had been instructed to lay the groundwork for Jack Soble, who would arrive soon to open another spy front in the French capital—a brush factory. He had been given $100,000 of Soviet money to expand his New York business with a branch abroad.

Everything went well for the spy team in Paris for the first few weeks, according to Morros' reports to the FBI. But then something unexpected occurred. Something embarrassing. Jane apparently had gone on a date with a certain Frenchman; of course George had never let jealousy interfere with his wife's romances, so long as they served the interests of Moscow. Whether George noticed that Jane was carrying on somewhat beyond the call of duty is hard to say. But this much is known:

George slapped Jane around in their hotel room. Jane, in turn, ripped George's shirt and clawed bloody grooves into his back. Then George got angry. He tore off Jane's dressing gown, walloped her, then dragged her—stark naked—out into the Paris traffic.

"Luckily," Jane wrote Martha sometime later, "it was a warm day."

Martha penned her condolences back to Jane. She told her to be forgiving with George—but to watch out for that "dirty, double-crossing FBI rat, Morros." Martha said other things about the man she despised and implored Jane to do her own little investigation of the producer to see if she couldn't come up with something on him.

Jane found the occasion one evening when she dropped in on

Morros in his Raphael Hotel suite with a visitor, a woman from the Foreign Ministry of France who was recruiting agents for the Soviet espionage network in her country. Morros took them to a French nightclub, a gilded trap called the Monseigneur.

The French woman finally left but Jane sipped champagne with Morros for hours, while she pumped him for information that might lay bare the slightest clue to support Martha's suspicions. Jane wearied of this pursuit after draining nearly a dozen glasses of the bubbly stuff, and finally she reached a state of drunkenness that brought on collapse. Before she passed out, she brayed to Morros:

"Boris, somehow I don't believe you're a loyal Communist . . . I think you're a . . . "

Some days later, Jane whipped off a note to Martha to report her failure to find any clue that "our Hollywood friend" is an FBI counterspy. But in passing she mentioned that Morros was heading for Moscow—summoned there personally by Lavrenti Beria . . .

Chapter 11

Boris Is Marked for Death!

The trip to the Kremlin had been arranged some weeks earlier, in mid-1949, after Boris Morros had been brought to Geneva to meet Alexandre Mikhailovich Korotkov, head of the GPU's foreign branch, which was called the INO. Korotkov was on his way to join the diplomatic staff of the Soviet Embassy in Washington.

Korotkov told Morros that Beria was anxious to meet him personally, but the movie producer couldn't give the Soviet spy chief an immediate reply. He had to consult the FBI first to see if they didn't think a trip to Moscow might be too risky. Morros stalled for time, giving as an excuse that he had urgent movie business to attend to back in Vienna.

Korotkov directed Morros to meet him in Lausanne a month hence—with his answer.

Ordinarily, an agent in the Kremlin's service would never refuse a summons to Moscow. But Morros had always conducted himself aloofly, playing the prima donna. He had been advised to keep up that act by the FBI. It would continue to earn him the respect of the Kremlin hierarchy if he didn't step out of character.

Morros was given the green light to go to the Kremlin. The FBI knew that Martha Stern distrusted Morros, but shared the producer's confidence that her suspicions probably hadn't rubbed off on anyone else. All the conspirators in the spy ring seemed to accept the movie mogul as a loyal Communist. But make an exception of Jane Zlatovski, who seemed now to have come under Martha's influence.

After reading Jane's note telling of Morros' forthcoming trip to Moscow, Martha sprung into action. She dashed off her own personal note to the chief of the dreaded Secret Police, denouncing Morros as a traitor. It was the first direct communication Martha had with Beria.

Incredible as it may seem, the note was delivered to Beria at the very moment Morros was sitting in Lavrenti's Moscow office. Beria read the message, then gazed quizzically at Morros.

"Boris," the Kremlin spymaster said evenly, "why does Martha Stern dislike you so much . . . why does she always accuse you of being a traitor to communism?"

Morros felt a chill course through his body. A cold sweat started to cling to his flesh. His answer had to be fourteen-karat because only a few steps out of Beria's office were the stairs leading down to the infamous blood-splattered cellar where Kremlin agents stood in readiness to apply the third-degree.

Morros forced himself to burst out in raucous, hilarious laughter that almost shook the spy boss' office.

"That Martha," Morros managed to sputter, trying desperately to make his tone sardonic. "She is such a dedicated woman, but such a hateful person. She never forgives . . . "

He gave Beria a purposeful wink.

"I don't understand," the Chief said impatiently. Frowning, he leaned over his desk to grasp at what the movie producer was trying to say. That Beria, very slow on the uptake.

"Well, Lavrenti," Morros said, deliberately lowering his voice as if he didn't want the others in the room to overhear, "I don't know if you have gotten reports about Martha's extracurricular sexual peregrinations, but I must tell you she is quite the thing . . . "

Morros proceeded to paint Martha as a woman who hadn't changed since those early days in Berlin when she was "sleeping with every Nazi, and even tried to get into Hitler's bed." He said that even marriage to Stern hadn't cured Martha's sexual urges

94

for other men, that she still went after anybody who wore pants. And she was always demanding to receive every man's attention.

"My trouble with her," Morros told Beria, "was that I would not go for her advances. I gave her nothing back, not even a look. That is why she has been trying to get me."

The explanation apparently satisfied Beria, who undoubtedly had heard the reports about Martha's promiscuousness, which had prompted further reports that she was a nymphomaniac. So far as Beria was concerned, Morros was clean. So it was back to work for the movie producer—with bigger and more important assignments in international espionage.

Although the conspiracy had many worldwide ramifications, the primary target above all others always remained the United States and its numerous operations in foreign lands, which the Kremlin sought to infiltrate and subvert.

In the broadest general terms, as the Justice Department would tell this author before he began to write this book, the conspirators had three principal goals in their sights.

- To penetrate U.S. intelligence agencies, the U.S. Department of State, the Department of Defense, and even Congress, as well as technical organizations and anti-Communist groups.
- To gather information about military research and development, strategic geographic areas, defense plans, nuclear and missile research and development, industrial research, methods, and production, and political-economic changes.
- To spread Communist propaganda through speeches, press releases, printed material, radio and television, and personal contacts.

In short, the assignments were geared to greatly extend the beachhead of communism that already had been established on America's shores and in those lands that depended upon the United States for military and economic aid and assistance.

To enumerate the step-by-step operations of this far-flung spy ring would require massive tomes thicker than the twenty-three-volume *Encyclopaedia Britannica* (plus its Index and Atlas). The object of this book is merely to show that the web of intrigue and espionage indeed existed, that to a large extent it had an effective existence, and to narrate the story of how it all started. The story behind the story, so to speak.

But now let's continue with the story we have been relating.

While the FBI was alert to the treasonable alliance and had agents assigned to watch the various known members of the conspiracy, while much of the information that many of the known Kremlin operatives received had been "doctored," and while Boris Morros kept the FBI informed of the ring's doings—still in all, it was impossible to keep tabs on all the far-reaching tentacles of the Soviet spy machine. Even if every G-man in the Bureau had been assigned to the case, the whole plot would never have been uncovered. It was too deep, too widespread. For example:

There were links and ties with the notorious Julius and Ethel Rosenberg, who were ultimately executed for their part in the theft of America's atomic secrets; there were connections with David Greenglass, Harry Gold, Klaus Fuchs, and the many others who had a hand in that same case; there were still other bonds with Morton Sobell and the Soviet super-spy Colonel Rudolph Ivanovich Abel (who years later was jailed, then swapped for American U-2 spy-plane pilot Gary Francis Powers).

The links and ties, the connections, the bonds go on and on—endlessly.

And so does the roster of Communist agents . . .

For example, there was Jack Soble's boyhood friend, Jacob Albam, who remained behind in Lithuania when the Sobolevicius family emigrated to Canada and the United States. Albam followed his pal over in 1947, took an apartment in Manhattan, and joined the spy ring.

Myra Soble, Jack's wife, also had a considerable role working as a courier who transmitted stolen U.S. defense documents.

Then there was Mark Zborowski, a former Soviet Secret Police agent who made his way to the United States in the early 1940s. An anthropologist, he became a research assistant at the George White Health Unit of the Harvard School of Public Health, an independent unit of Harvard University. Zborowski, whose home was at 18 Alton Place in Brookline, Massachusetts, was observed by the FBI for a period of years in the mid- and late-1940s meeting clandestinely with Soble and other members of the spy team.

And lastly—but far from least—there was Robert Soblen, Jack's brother. He went on to make his mark in medicine as a respected psychiatrist at Rockland State Hospital—a perfect cover for his role in the web of Soviet espionage that was spun so thickly over the United States and beyond.

The day of reckonin' for the conspirators began dawning very gradually after that meeting between Beria and Morros in 1949. After Morros was given his clean bill of health by the spy chief, he went back into the shadow world of intrigue and continued to pose convincingly as a Soviet spy.

As he did so, every step was kept under the watchful eyes of FBI or OSS agents, who never were more than feet away, whether Morros' assignments took him to Paris, East Berlin, Vienna, Munich, New York, Washington, Hollywood, or any other port of call that his work required him to visit.

Morros crossed the Atlantic no less than sixty-eight times, traveled several hundred-thousand miles, maintained contacts and relationships with more than two-score Red agents over the next seven years that the conspiracy flourished.

Then came that day of January 19, 1957, when Morros received that one-word cabled warning—"CINERAMA"—in his hotel room in Munich, precipitating his flight back to the United States and the sudden lowering of the curtain on the long-playing, danger-packed international drama of intrigue and espionage.

The message had been sent to Morros by the FBI.

Why had the Bureau all at once decided to end a spy sham that had endured for ten long years?

Simply because Martha Dodd Stern at last had succeeded in convincing the Kremlin that Boris Morros was "an FBI stooge."

Martha had never ceased firing off poisoned darts at Morros, but so long as Beria was the head man in Moscow her suspicions always fell on deaf ears. But in July, 1953, a momentous event rocked the entire Soviet espionage apparatus. Lavrenti Beria, who in all the years past had done the liquidating, was himself liquidated by Premier Nikita Khrushchev.

In the next three years, Beria's six deputy directors, some seventy subdirectors, several thousand local Secret Police chiefs, and up to fifteen thousand small-fry "thumbscrew and confession experts" were scragged. The new order was formed, and atop the piles of corpses stood a thin-lipped sadist named General Ivan Serov, the only veteran purger who'd escaped being purged himself.

In late 1956, when Serov had settled down after the tremors of the shakeup had faded away, Martha ripped off a note to the new spy boss. And to make certain he got it she sent the message directly to the Soviet Embassy in Washington with instructions that it had to go to Serov unopened.

Its flap was wax-sealed with the imprimatur of the United States State Department (a seal she apparently appropriated from the U.S. Embassy in Berlin when her father was the Ambassador). Soble himself delivered the envelope to the Soviet Embassy in the capital. Although he hadn't seen its contents, he suspected strongly that it had to do with Martha's vendetta against Morros.

How effective Martha's last rap at Morros was can be gleaned from the swift-moving events that followed. On January 10, 1957, Morros was passing through East Berlin on a mission for the Kremlin. He ran into an old crony, Vladimir Posner, who had been a cameraman for Morros in his early Hollywood days. Posner was now head of East Germany's movie industry. They arranged to have dinner. Later, however, Morros received a cryptic message that Posner wouldn't have dinner with him.

To Morros that was a tip-off that something was wrong. But he didn't sense any peril until the next day when his travel itinerary was abruptly canceled and he was ordered to return to Vienna to meet a Soviet agent he'd never heard of.

Morros promptly notified the FBI agents who were shadowing him. The G-men, with information quickly provided by U.S. Central Intelligence Agency operatives in Vienna, learned that the agent Morros was to meet was a bloodhound sent from Moscow by General Ivan Serov.

He was the same Stephen N. Choudenko, the Professor, who had ordered Morros to liquidate his music company back in Hollywood. He'd come to Vienna under an alias to await Morros. This time, no doubt, his job was to liquidate Boris.

Boris Morros had suddenly become a marked man—marked for death!

Word was flashed back to FBI Director Hoover in Washington. A hurried consultation was held with Justice Department lawyers, then with State Department officials. A decision was reached: bring Morros home.

Thus the cablegram to the movie mogul in his hotel room in Munich, where he'd gone to await word from the FBI on whether it was advisable to proceed to Vienna for his appointment with the mysterious agent dispatched by General Serov.

That one word "CINERAMA" told Morros he couldn't go back to Vienna, that he must leave immediately for the only safe haven left to him—the United States.

Chapter 12

Boris the "Bum"

It was January 25, 1957, when newspapers from New York to California clarioned the news with big black screaming headlines:

SEIZE 3 AS SPIES, CHARGE THEY STOLE U.S. SECRETS FOR KREMLIN

The stories described how "three foreign-born New Yorkers were arrested by the FBI as members of a highly-organized Soviet spy ring and charged with delivering U.S. defense secrets to Russian agents."

The accused were identified as Jack Soble, aged fifty-three; his wife Myra, fifty-two; and Jacob Albam, sixty-four.

No mention was made of Martha and Alfred Stern. There was no word about Jane and George Zlatovski. Nothing about Mark Zborowski. The only reference to Dr. Robert Soblen was to identify him as Jack Soble's brother.

And there wasn't a whisper about Boris Morros.

At least not that first day, nor for many, many days to come. The Government seemed satisfied to shock the nation for the time being with the news that a Soviet spy ring had been broken up and to toss only the Sobles and Albam on the coals of justice for a long overdue roasting.

But U.S. Attorney Paul Williams, head of the Justice Department's operations in the Southern District of New York, who appeared in behalf of the Government at the accused trio's arraignment in the Federal Courthouse on Foley Square, told U.S. Commissioner Earl N. Bishopp:

"The upper members of this espionage group are not at the present time identifiable . . . the case has been under FBI inquiry for more than ten years."

The stocky, bleached honey-blonde Myra Soble, standing beside her husband before Commissioner Bishopp, was smiling and sarcastic as Williams addressed the court. She put a copy of the complaint up to her face when photographers tried to take her picture. By contrast, Soble made no effort to avoid the cameras. Twice he turned smiling to his wife and stroked her hair gently, as though trying to comfort her.

But she lost her smile and composure quickly when Williams proceeded to characterize Soble as the chief Soviet spy agent in the United States since 1944, when he replaced the ousted Second Secretary Vassili Zubulin. The statement prompted Myra to cry out, "Wha-a-a-t?"

There was another outburst from Myra when Williams asked for high bail on the grounds that the Soviet Union was "allegedly implicated as a principal conspirator," and it was "conceivable that it would be in the interests of that power to make funds available for the defendants in order that they might flee the jurisdiction of this court."

Myra tightened her lips in anger and snapped, "Fantastic!"

She had more to say after the prosecutor told the court that a special grand jury would be impaneled the following Monday to hear evidence in the case, which moved Commissioner Bishopp to hold the three suspects in $100,000 bail each.

At the mention of the $100,000 bond, Myra bellowed, "We never saw so much money. How can we raise it?"

The prisoners, of course, pleaded not guilty. And as they were led away to detention, Myra turned to the spectators in the courtroom, shrugged her shoulders, and muttered resignedly, "There is no choice."

Back at their sixth-floor apartment at 321 West 78th Street, where some hours earlier the Sobles had been seized by FBI agents and taken to the Bureau's headquarters at Foley Square for questioning, the arrest of his parents left Lawrence Soble, the accused spies' only child, now seventeen years old, in a state of dazed disbelief. The well-mannered blond youngster, a student at a coeducational private school in Manhattan, admitted reporters to the apartment and spoke freely, although evidently under great emotional stress.

Lawrence defended his father as an honorable man and cited a dozen reasons he couldn't have been a Soviet spy.

"I know him well," he murmured, almost as much to himself as to reporters. "He wouldn't be so idiotic as to spy. He'd know that he would be caught. He would think of me and of my education . . . If he were spying he'd get paid for it. Believe me, he had to work to make a living. And this thing ain't going to help him any. I am 101 per cent sure of my father's innocence."

The Sobles' neighbors were also astonished at the news of the arrests. They spoke of Jack and Myra as ideal tenants and neighbors who minded their own business.

Over on Riverside Drive, Albam's neighbors were just as shocked at his arrest. They praised him highly, as did the employes of the Hudson Tea and Spice Company in Brooklyn, where he'd worked as a production foreman.

On Monday, January 29th, after two days of careful screening, nine women and fourteen men were impaneled by Federal Judge Sidney Sugarman and promptly began hearing evidence against the three accused Russian spies. Before sending them off to begin, the judge warned the panel:

"During your investigation it may be necessary to expose to you highly confidential information of great importance to the security of the nation. All such information must be kept secret. Disclosure is forbidden unless permitted by the court."

U.S. Attorney Williams indicated that the Government hoped to obtain an indictment by the end of the week. He told the grand jurors:

"The bulk of the work will be presented to you today and tomorrow."

Among the members of the panel was Arthur Gershwin, who had startled the court momentarily when he said that his brother had recently returned from Russia. He explained that his brother, Ira Gershwin, had toured the Soviet Union with an American *Porgy and Bess* troupe.

Later, when Williams reviewed the prospective jurors' occupations, he said to Gershwin, "I see you're a composer."

"The unknown one," Arthur Gershwin answered succinctly.

The prosecutor's forecast of an indictment by the end of the week was accurate—the grand jury handed up its findings on February 4th. It was a six-count indictment, which accused Soble, his wife, and Albam of twenty-three overt acts of conspiring with Soviet intelligence agents to transmit information about the national defense of the United States. The first count was a bombshell. It charged the defendants with violating the peacetime provisions of the 1954 Espionage Statute—which carried a death-sentence provision. The statute had never before been used.

Under that law, if a defendant was found guilty, the judge had the option of sentencing him to death. But the court in its discretion could also impose life imprisonment, or a lesser term.

The indictment also pointed accusingly to a number of co-conspirators. Some were identified, others were not. Those not named obviously were either safely out of reach of the long arm of the law, or couldn't be implicated formally at that time for lack of sufficient evidence.

Of the first group, as events in time would support, the grand jury certainly must have been thinking about George and Jane Zlatovski and Alfred and Martha Stern. The Zlatovskis were sitting tight in Paris and the Sterns were safely ensconced in Mexico City.

And the panel may or may not have been aware at this time of the second group, persons like Dr. Robert Soblen, who was still practicing psychiatry on the patients at Rockland State Hospital (and shaking his head mournfully for his poor brother, swearing that neither Jack nor his wife was capable of being a spy), and Mark Zborowski, the Harvard anthropologist (who was saying nothing).

They were, all of them, fated to step upon the scales of justice. But now was not yet the time.

As for the others accused by name by the grand jury as co-conspirators but not defendants, they made a formidable roster. They were the thirteen Kremlin diplomats and aides who'd served in the Soviet Embassy in Washington at one time or another in the course of the fourteen-year-long conspiracy. All were charged with having a part in the plot to transmit "documents, writings, photographs, and other information relating to the national defense, particularly to intelligence activities of the United States and the United States armed forces."

Like the Zlatovskis and Sterns, all thirteen members of the Kremlin diplomatic corps were no longer within the territory of the United States. They were back in the Soviet Union, and the last to go had been Vassili Mikhailovich Molev, who was declared persona non grata by the State Department only the day after the Sobles and Albam were arrested.

Why was Molev allowed to leave despite the Government's awareness of his part in the spy plot? Molev had been actively engaged in espionage in the United States; he had installed the Sterns as spymasters in Mexico City.

Molev and the other Soviet emissaries could not be prosecuted. They enjoyed diplomatic immunity—the safest cover for a spy in the United States.

The other Soviet diplomats named in the indictment along with Molev were:

Petr Vassilievich Fedotov, Alexander Mikhailovich Korotkov (head of the GPU's foreign branch, the INO, and the man who told Morros that Beria wanted to see him), Vassili M. Zubulin (who had played the biggest role of all in the espionage case), his wife, Elizabeth; Mikhail Chaliapian, Stephen N. Choudenko (the Professor, who persuaded Morros to return Stern's investment and later was assigned to "liquidate" Boris in Vienna), Anatole B. Gromov, Leonid Dimitrievich Petrov, Vitaly Genadievich Tcherniawski, Afanasi Ivanovitch Yefimov, Christopher Georgievich Petrosian, Igor Vassilievitch Sokolov, and Vladimir Alexandrovich.

As they had done at their hearing before Commissioner Bishopp following their arrest, Jack and Myra Soble and Jacob Albam again entered innocent pleas at their arraignment on the grand jury indictment before Federal Judge Gregory F. Noonan. Soble was the most vocal when asked how he pleaded.

"Not guilty!" he shouted.

One element of mystery remained after this phase of the case had ended. The indictment mentioned an unidentified "individual" as having met in New York, Paris, Zurich, Vienna, and other cities with Soble and the various members of the espionage ring. The name remained a secret until New York attorney George Wolf, counsel to the Sobles, asked for a list of all Government witnesses to be produced before trial.

The hearing on the motion was held in Judge Noonan's chambers and Assistant U.S. Attorney Thomas B. Gilchrist Jr. said he had no objection to giving up a list of witnesses. But he noted:

"As of this moment, our only witness is—Boris Morros."

At last Morros' name came out. But there were no trumpet blasts, no drum rolls to hail him as an FBI hero or a patriotic American. He was made to look like a bum, or more precisely a spy. Here's the way the *New York Daily News* reported the story:

> A prominent Hollywood film figure with a disarming Russian low-comedy accent and a background as a child musical prodigy was dramatically accused by the Government yesterday of being a sort of underground mailman in the asserted Soble-Albam Soviet spy ring.
>
> For almost nine years, the Government charged, Boris Morros, director and producer and longtime musical bigwig with Paramount Pictures, had traveled between New York, Paris, Vienna, and Zurich, meeting with both the defendants and Russian secret agents, receiving and passing on various "writings" which were not further described.

Other newspapers reported the story in the same vein. The treatment greatly disturbed Morros, who now wanted his role as an FBI counterspy made public. His annoyance grew into exasperation, then into anger. He pleaded with the U.S. Attorney's office to release the story of his life as a double-agent. Or, better still, allow him to tell his story to the public to show he was a loyal American who'd risked life and fortune in helping to expose Soviet espionage.

But the answer was no. At least, it was no for the time being.

In the ensuing weeks, lawyers representing the Sobles and Albam assaulted the courts with petitions to dismiss various counts of the indictment, including the charge that carried the possible death penalty. Even as the appeals were taken under advisement, Judge Richard H. Levet unexpectedly convened court on April 10th, after being informed the Sobles wanted to enter new motions.

Attorney Wolf went before the bench and told the court that his clients, who had wrestled for more than a week with the thought, had decided to change their original pleas of not guilty—to guilty.

It was a startling turnabout. When the Sobles stepped up to face Judge Levet, they pleaded guilty only to the second count of the indictment—conspiracy to obtain documents, writings, photographs, and other data connected with the national defense for transmission to Russia. The maximum punishment they could receive if convicted of the charge was ten years in prison and $10,000 fine.

There was no mention of the remaining five charges, including the one carrying the death penalty. It was apparent that a deal had been cooked up with the Justice Department. Jack and Myra would cooperate with the grand jury investigation of espionage. If they talked, and talked plenty, the other charges would, in time, be dropped. But for now there was no move to dismiss them; they would hang over Jack and Myra like the sword of Damocles to make certain they "sang" the right tune before the jury.

After the hearing, attorney Wolf spoke to reporters in the courthouse corridor and told them the couple's story was "an amazing tale which borders on the fantastic—more fantastic than 'War and Peace.'" Wolfe intimated that the Sobles had been unwilling tools unable to escape "the long arm of Russia." He suggested that they had to do what they did to protect relatives living in Russia.

"They had a burden they wanted to get rid of," Wolf explained. "They told me they wanted to recapture their souls for the first time since they came to this country. They were two anguished individuals, suffering intensely from experiences they had gone through before they emigrated to this country and since."

Meanwhile, Harold O. N. Frankel, court-appointed attorney for Jacob Albam, said he'd discussed the Sobles' plans to change their pleas with his client, and would talk with him again now in view of their surprise confessions of guilt.

Surprising or shocking or whatever their turnabout may have meant to the many persons closely connected with the case, the admissions fell like a ton of bricks upon young Lawrence Soble, who, until that desolate day, believed with all the loyal strength a seventeen-year-old can summon that his parents were innocent of the terrible charges.

But late that morning of April 10th, when his mother and father had their day in court, Lawrence was taken out of class at Rhodes Preparatory School on West 54th Street and brought downtown to Foley Square to hear the news from his parents' own lips. It was a crushing blow, yet Lawrence's faith was unshaken.

"I respect them and love them more than ever before," he told reporters bravely. "Not many people in their position would have admitted their guilt." He spent three hours talking with his parents in a court anteroom. It was a meeting that started with tears and kisses and ended with cold-water shock for young Lawrence.

"They didn't do this [spy] because they wanted to," the youth sobbed, "but because they had to. It's an old story—to get out of Russia, they had to do what they did. If they didn't, they [the Russians] threatened to 'take care' of my parents' relatives who were left there.

"Mama told me, 'After this is all over, we'll tell you everything from the beginning.' My father said they pleaded guilty to clear their consciences and because he regrets they didn't do this when they first came to this country."

Just a little more than a fortnight later, on April 26th, Jacob Albam followed the Sobles' lead and pleaded guilty in Federal Court to conspiring with Soviet nationals to obtain national defense data, just as Jack and Myra had admitted.

Then Jacob joined his boyhood pal and the latter's wife before the grand jury that indicted them, with the announced purpose of baring the inner secrets of the spy ring. How much this trio told the jury has never been disclosed. But it must be assumed that they spilled details about the conspiracy that would never have been made known to an ambivalent and peripatetic counterspy like Boris Morros.

Whatever the testimony, the Federal grand jury which listened to the Sobles and Albam—and to Morros, as well—must have found enough evidence to justify indictments against George and Jane Zlatovski. They were named in five counts as active members of the Kremlin-directed spy ring and charged with thirty-five overt acts of espionage.

But George and Jane, watching from three thousand miles

away in a dingy Left Bank flat in Paris where they had been living for the past two years, couldn't be touched. Although France and the United States had an extradition treaty, Assistant U.S. Attorney William F. Thompkins, in charge of Internal Security, shook his head ruefully and lamented that there was no way to get the couple back. The Franco-American pact didn't include extradition for political crimes, such as espionage. Thompkins expressed hope that because many of the subversive acts had taken place in Paris, the French Government might be inclined to take some action. But it never did.

George and Jane Zlatovski were permitted soon afterward to leave the country under their own power. They headed for a permanent new home behind the ancient walls of Prague, the capital of Red Czechoslovakia, which was soon to become the dumping ground for a dozen-odd Americans who were in a fix somewhat like that of the former OSS man and his wife, Americans who had outlived their usefulness as spies in the United States and couldn't go elsewhere.

It would be only a matter of a few short months before Jane and George were joined by the most honored Red spies of all, Martha and Alfred Stern, the capitalist celebrities who for nearly twenty years had committed treason against the country of their birth.

Their hegira to Prague was to be precipitated by the same grand jury that spelled downfall for Jack and Myra Soble and Jacob Albam, and doomed George and Jane Zlatovski to exile. And when that day came on September 9, 1957, and the grand jury returned its three-count indictment against the rosy-shaped Ambassador's daughter and her gullible millionaire husband, the revelation that Martha Dodd and Alfred Stern were spies came merely as an anticlimax.

Chapter 13

Morros Was Motivated by Fear, Not Patriotism

For fully a month before Martha Dodd Stern and her husband were legally accused of espionage, the whole country, indeed the world, had known about their complicity in the vast Soviet espionage activity in the United States.

It started subtly at first after Boris Morros, given his chance at last to tell his story, went to his public and related how he'd started down the road to espionage in the early 1930s, how he'd gotten involved deeper and deeper in the Red conspiracy, how he'd served as a double-agent for the FBI.

Of course, it must be made clear that Boris Morros never let on, in his first all-out account that day of August 12, 1957, when he held a press conference in the office of Assistant U.S. Attorney Gilchrist in the U.S. Courthouse in New York, that any crimson showing on him wasn't his patriotic red-blooded Americanism.

Exhibiting a deliberate disregard of conflicts in dates, Morros told the public a story that was meant to make it appear that all his years as a spy were paralleled by his heroic service as an FBI counterspy. He neglected to mention anything about his four years of total servitude to the Kremlin, from 1943 to 1947, before he ever offered himself to the other side.

As a case in point, in his own prepared statement issued to reporters in Foley Square on that August 12, 1957, Morros said:

> While my work for the FBI actually commenced in *1947*, coincidentally with my services as a "Russian agent," my contacts with the Soviets go back to 1935 when I went to Russia to see my very ill mother. I told my aged father at the time that if anything happened to my mother I would try to bring him to America to live with me . . .
>
> After my mother's death, I got in touch with Soviet diplomatic representatives here and started my one-man campaign to bring my father to this country. It was finally arranged and he came . . .
>
> From the time of my father's arrival, overtures from the Russians started and developed to such a phase that in *1945* they asked me outright to become an active agent for them.
>
> I went straight to the FBI and reported what had happened. I was told to agree to the Russian proposals and make my contacts, which I did . . .

But we know what the truth was—that Boris Morros did not go to the FBI until July 14, 1947. And he went to them not because of his sudden engulfment by patriotism but, as this writer has learned, because he was convinced that the FBI had the goods on him and that he'd be grabbed as a spy sooner or later.

Although he didn't identify her by name when he uttered his first public statement about his dangerous dual role in espionage, Morros left little doubt as to whom he was talking about when he said:

"A prominent American woman, whose name will startle everybody when it is revealed, not only said she didn't believe I was a Communist, but she reported her suspicions to the Second Secretary of the Russian Embassy in Washington. I had a number of close shaves but none closer than when this woman's 'report' on me was received in Moscow while I was there 'conferring' with the heads of the Russian Secret Police."

Although Morros didn't name the woman, the Fourth Estate took care of that soon enough. Some bright newsmen put two and two together. They dug up a clip of a story that had been buried in the inside columns of the *New York Times* back on May 2nd. It told how a wealthy American couple living in Mexico was fined $50,000 the previous day by Federal Judge Levet in New York for contempt of court; they had failed to answer a subpoena before the grand jury investigating the Soble-Albam-Zlatovski espionage case.

Then, to boot, the story identified the couple as Alfred K. Stern and his wife, Martha—"daughter of the late William E. Dodd, a former United States Ambassador to Germany."

The reporters put the story in perspective and tied Martha and Alfred to the Soble-Albam-Zlatovski spy axis.

The facts relating to that contempt citation against the Sterns were these:

Papers had been served on the Sterns in their Mexico City penthouse and the couple promised to appear before the grand jury in New York. But then Stern wrote the U.S. Attorney:

"I insist on payment of witness fees and travel expenses by the U.S. Government, a right granted all witnesses under the law."

Uncle Sam dutifully sent them a check for $978.34—but the Sterns never showed up, compelling the court to levy the fine. The $50,000 represented assets Stern had in the United States, which the Government seized.

However, when the Sterns had left New York for Mexico City they took with them at least $350,000 in cash, while another $1,000,000 in holdings was quietly transferred to Swiss banks.

Thus it was reasonable to conclude that Martha and Alfred Stern would never return to America. They left nothing behind—well, almost *nothing*, if you don't count that $50,000.

On August 17, 1957, just five days after he trumpeted the hair-raising but somewhat inaccurate details of his role as a double-agent, Morros went before staff agents of the House Committee on Un-American Activities and bluntly named Martha Stern as the "prominent American woman" he'd mentioned earlier.

After the grand jury returned indictments against the Sterns the following month, the State Department requested the Mexican Government to extradite the Red-loving U.S. renegades. But there was no more hope of getting the Sterns back than there was of bringing home the Zlatovskis. The U.S.-Mexican extradition treaty only provides for the return of fugitives charged with crimes of violence. Yet even if spies had been covered by the pact, the Sterns couldn't have been brought back anyway.

They'd already flown the coop.

With forged Nicaraguan passports and tickets to Zurich, they left July 2, 1957, on a KLM Royal Dutch Airlines plane which took them, via Montreal, to their destination. From Switzerland they went on to Moscow and no doubt to a red-carpet reception at the Kremlin, then to their new home port—Prague.

By now Myra Soble and Jacob Albam had been meted their punishments. This had come to pass on August 9th in Judge Levet's courtroom.

Myra, weeping softly as she stood before the bench, and Albam, his eyes shifting nervously, heard themselves sentenced to prison terms of five and one-half years each. Jack Soble was not at his wife's sentencing, but she was at his side when it came turn for his day in court on October 8th.

When Judge Levet asked, as a matter of form, if Soble had anything to say, to the surprise of all he pulled himself slowly to his feet, ran his hand drearily over his eyes, bowed his head, and said in a tearful voice:

"Your honor, I can say only one thing. I deeply regret my past and my crimes which I committed against the country. And I hope that by my full cooperation I will partially do good to the country.

"I cannot forgive myself. In the past I had plenty of opportunities to straighten out my life when I came to this country, but I did not. I beg you to believe I am telling the full truth now. It is very hard for me, but I know what I did to this country which gave us refuge, and which could have made us happy and respectable citizens. Thank you."

Myra, who was seated at the counsel table, sobbed as her husband was sentenced to seven and one-half years.

Justice moved slowly but surely for the remaining conspirators in the Soviet espionage ring.

Harvard anthropologist Mark Zborowski was subsequently indicted for perjury, not espionage, because he'd told the spy grand jury he didn't know and had never met Jack Soble. Zborowski was convicted and sentenced to five years on December 8, 1958; the conviction was then upset on a fluke in the higher courts. The Government said it would try Zborowski again.

Earlier that year, in February, despondent, repentant, and torn by conscience, Jack Soble swallowed a pound and a half of rivets, nuts, and bolts in a suicide attempt at the Federal Penitentiary in Lewisburg, Pennsylvania. The effects of this assorted hardware in his stomach didn't begin to tell until thirty-six hours later when he'd been brought to New York City to testify before the grand jury, which was still investigating espionage.

Soble was rushed to Bellevue Hospital, an operation was performed to remove the indigestible metal, and he pulled through.

Why was Soble so despondent, repentant, torn by conscience as to try suicide?

Because the testimony he was giving to the grand jury had to do with Zborowski—and still another as yet unidentified individual.

It wasn't so much his testimony against Zborowski that bothered Soble, but that against the unnamed individual, who was finally named.

Who was he?

Jack Soble's brother, Dr. Robert Soblen, the psychiatrist.

Just as he'd been required to be the key Government witness at Zborowski's trial, so again was Soble summoned to take the stand at his brother's trial.

It was brother against brother in one of the most dramatic situations that had ever occurred in a court proceedings. Twenty-five feet separated the brothers as they took their places at the conspiracy trial, Soblen at the counsel table, Soble in the witness chair. The contrast was startling, like a negative and positive of the same man.

Soble, who'd been convicted and was serving time for his treasonable acts, appeared to have prospered by his confession. His brother, who had steadfastly maintained his innocence, was gray with inscrutability.

The witness was vivid, dressed in bright tweed jacket, dark tie with bold white stripes slanting across it, dark blue trousers. He was tanned, swarthy complexioned, and his heavy black beetle brows looked more like awnings than ever. His black eyes glittered. And his silvery hair looked vibrant and alive.

The defendant wore a pale blue suit and a dull blue tie on a white shirt. There was nothing special in his sartorial make-up. His face was sallow and fallen, his sparse hair far more gray than his brother's. There was a sense of pain and tightness around his mouth and creased forehead. His face had the appearance of a death mask. Soblen, according to his attorney, was dying of lymphatic leukemia. The court had been warned that he had less than a year to live.

During the trial, Soble often clawed at his brother's lawyer in oral combat. He became irritated by the frequency with which attorney Joseph Brill hurled questions at him. At one point during the trial, Soble lost his temper, leaped to his feet from the witness stand, and denounced the counsel's tactics. A great hubbub followed as everyone began talking at once.

Through it all Soble shouted, "You see, I can be very calm. But I can fight back, too, because for me it is a personal tragedy to sit [in court] with a brother. And for me it is not just a case and publicity. This is what I want to make clear—for four-and-a-half years I have been begging him to tell . . . "

Judge William B. Herlands commanded Soble to restrain himself, admonishing him not to "get into any personal arguments with anyone."

Brill asked for a mistrial. It was denied.

Soble went on to tell the court the bald facts of life that traitors must face when they engage in espionage work for the Soviet Union. The pay, he said, is lousy.

"We [Soble and his brother] had funds and we were such stupid fools that we told the Russians about it. The Russians—they gave us peanuts," the witness stated bluntly.

"I was living on my father's money. I do not owe one penny to the Russians. They owe me my life and the life of my wife and my brother. That is what they owe me. We spent our own funds on this spying."

In the end, Dr. Robert Soblen was convicted and sentenced to life in Federal prison. But a year later, on June 25, 1962, while out on bail and just after the United States Supreme Court had refused to consider an appeal against his conviction, Dr. Soblen managed to book passage aboard an El Al Airlines plane at New York's International Airport with forged passports and an alias, and made it to Israel, only to be arrested there two days later, then ordered deported.

On the flight back, although in custody of a United States marshal, Soblen managed to get a steak knife, then stabbed himself in the stomach and slashed his wrists in a vain suicide attempt. He was taken off the plane in London and rushed to Hillingdon Hospital in suburban Uxbridge. He ultimately recovered, but by then legal moves in London as well as Jerusalem, by lawyers who felt Israel's peremptory expulsion of Soblen was shabby treatment even for a convicted spy, fought to keep him from returning to the United States.

The fugitive American spy appealed to Prime Minister Harold Macmillan to let him stay in England at least until the legal moves in Israel were adjudicated. A stay was finally granted by the British courts, but by late August Soblen's battle seemed to lose ground. His return to the United States now was inevitable.

But the doctor pulled one more trick out of his hat in order to thwart his extradition—he swallowed an overdose of drugs.

Soblen went into convulsions, then into a coma. His wife flew to London to be at his bedside in Hillingdon Hospital. Five days later, on September 11, 1962, without regaining consciousness, Dr. Robert Soblen was dead.

Just hours later in Washington, the Justice Department announced that his brother, Jack Soble, had been released for good behavior from the Federal Correctional Institution at Danbury, Connecticut. Soble had been freed on August 31st but the disclosure was held up for nearly two weeks because of the flak that was flying over his brother's extradition wrangle.

Soble's wife, Myra, and Jacob Albam had both been given mandatory releases earlier in the year after doing four of the five and one-half years of their sentences.

Even after he gained his freedom, Jack Soble was again in the espionage spotlight for a brief time when he returned to the witness stand of New York's Federal Court and testified once more against Mark Zborowski, who was being retried for perjury after the Court of Appeals had reversed his earlier conviction on a technicality—that Judge John M. Cashin, who presided at the first trial, had refused to hand over to the defense Soble's grand jury testimony relating to the defendant.

This time the material was produced in Judge Levet's court, but it made no difference in the end for the defendant. The jury found the owlish-faced Zborowski guilty and he was again sentenced to five years.

Today, more than a dozen years after they finished paying

society for their crimes as spies, Jack and Myra Soble are living quiet, unobtrusive lives "somewhere in the United States," perhaps even under assumed names so that no one will know who they are, not their old friends and neighbors—and especially not their old comrades.

The same is true of Jacob Albam.

Chapter 14

Dare They Come Home?

What has happened to the rest of the cast in this intriguing real-life spy drama?

Jane and George Zlatovski and Martha and Alfred Stern are still holed up in Prague, one of the few cities in the world that will have them. Of the two exiled spy couples, the Sterns are living by far the more elegant life. They have a ten-room penthouse with a misty view of the Vltava River and many of its thirteen bridges and thousand-year-old palaces. Ten rooms make for a lot of living space in a country where you can't own a cow or occupy more than one room per person, but the Sterns have it all.

And at the opera, or wherever Communist big shots gather, Martha is still the belle of the ball—just like in those good old Berlin days. But she is an aged belle now and the atmosphere is quite a bit different from the carefree gaiety of her life in the Nazi German capital. Martha's parents are now both dead, and brother Bill, who finally broke away from leftish causes in the 1940s, tried unsuccessfully to run for political office in Virginia, then went west to California to work for a publisher, is also gone. He died in 1955 of cancer.

There are only her husband Alfred and son Robert now—and of course their circle of fellow Communist spies. Not long ago, Stern told a Czech reporter:

"We feel sincerely sorry for the oppressed American people."

As long as he feels that way, perhaps Alfred Stern can see it in his little old Red heart to send Uncle Sam that $978.34 witness and travel fee which he and Martha pocketed.

Or perhaps they could bring it back in person, if they dare.

But dare they? Can they afford to chance that priceless luxury—homesickness?

Part II

*From Little Red Books to Sexy Red Hookers
and Passport Crooks*

Chapter 15

There's More to Ceylon than Those Tiny Tea Leaves

The wind swirled angrily along the banks of New York City's East River and tiny flakes of snow whipped down like showers of confetti onto the heads and shoulders of pedestrians hurrying to their destinations on that cold evening of March 5, 1957. Winter's end was approaching, but the Old Man still had enough punch to drop the thermometer to twenty-six degrees and threaten a blizzard.

Downtown in Foley Square the weather was no better, but it was warm and pleasant upstairs in the offices of the Federal Bureau of Investigation at the Federal Courthouse. Businesslike agents in shirtsleeves somewhat hurriedly coursed in and out of the offices.

They had an assignment.

Once again their target was Soviet espionage, and they had barely finished tying up the loose ends of their investigation into the many-faceted and complex Boris Morros Case.

In their sights now was a Soviet espionage agent of dubious background who had been sent here from Moscow to represent his country as First Secretary of the Soviet Delegation to the United Nations. But that was a diversion.

For Vladimir Arsenevich Grusha, the diplomatic assignment to the UN was merely a cover that enabled him to carry out his primary mission in the United States—espionage.

The FBI had been wise to Grusha's movements for months. But even from the outset, when it became aware of his real assignment, the Bureau was not startled or even surprised. Over the years since the United Nations had been established in this country, J. Edgar Hoover and his operatives had become accustomed to expect that the Soviet Union would not hesitate to misuse and abuse diplomatic privileges granted to members of missions accredited to the UN.

The world body based in New York City had become a diplomatically immune island for Soviet espionage. Agents from the Kremlin had been engaged in subversive activities from as long ago as 1948 when Valentin Gubitchev teamed up with American government-girl Judith Coplon and stole valuable data from the Justice Department.

This activity was separate and apart from the espionage network operated by Vassili Zubulin and his successors in Washington. But the goals were the same—to gather secret data, no matter what its nature, for the Kremlim spy machine.

The Soviet's goal was wide-ranging. It covered the gamut of politics, industry, business, commerce, agriculture, labor, transportation, and—by far most importantly—the military. The FBI has had to be alert to the plots and tactics of Moscow's trained agents who, for the most part, are sent to New York under the guise of diplomats representing their nation at the UN, or in their Embassy in Washington.

In effect, the Soviet Union has put not only the entire United States under a Red spyglass—but the whole Western Hemisphere and indeed much of the world.

But New York is unique for this illicit activity. As in no other city in the world, there is a grouping in Gotham of diplomats from all nations on the face of the globe. Their emissaries to the UN live, eat, and sleep in the nation's biggest city or its immediate suburbs. And they have offices in Manhattan—offices that house the voluminous records pertaining to the business their countries are conducting at the UN.

Much of the business is political and much of it is publicized in the world press. But there are many matters that are by their very nature restricted from public scrutiny. In particular, a nation's own documents are matters of intensely private substance.

One example of this could be a country's confidential code.

We selected that criterion because that was precisely what was at stake and occupying the focus of the FBI on that wintry evening of March 5th. The agents scurrying about at the Bureau's offices in downtown Manhattan were preparing to go out into the night on what they expected would be the payoff on the case that had held their attention for more than three months.

It all began unobtrusively, as most espionage cases do. A mere suspicion was all it took to command the FBI's interest. That was a week before Christmas, 1956, when an FBI agent spotted First Secretary Vladimir Arsenevich Grusha in company with another foe whose name poses a formidable challenge to orthographers, Dhanpalo Samarasekara, a Ceylonese national employed at the UN in a third-level Secretariat post.

It should be explained here quickly that the FBI doesn't watch every Soviet diplomat at the UN every hour of the day and night. Such thoroughness would cost the United States an astronomical portion of the taxpayers' dollars. But G-men are ever on the alert—and they do watch for early signs portending unusual activity.

The signal for the FBI to watch Grusha was his meeting with Samarasekara in an East 45th Street restaurant about a block west of the UN Building.

D.S., as we'll call Dhanpalo Samarasekara for obvious reasons, was a swarthy, dark-haired, thin reed of a man with glistening ebony eyes and a Valentino head of straight black hair, slicked back against his skull. All he needed was a whip and a burnoose to play in a 1957 version of *The Sheik*.

That was the opening gun of a social relationship between the Ceylonese and the Russian that made little or no sense to the FBI. All it took was a little poking here and there, in the places Grusha and D.S. went to on their rounds, to tell the G-men that the man from Moscow was playing the part of Santa Claus in his relationship with the man from Ceylon.

Sure it was Christmas week, but this Red Santa Claus undoubtedly wasn't being benevolent because he was gripped by the spirit of Yule. At least the FBI didn't think so. Grusha, concluded the agents watching the action, was out for something.

But what?

Looking at it realistically, the FBI couldn't conceive too readily what the Russians might be after. After all, what in the world did Ceylon have that another nation coveted. Tea?

But the FBI was aware of one indisputable fact:

Russia, by its monolithic nature, touches every base. Her aim, as we have been told so repeatedly over the years, is ultimate supremacy over the world. Stalin, Khrushchev, and even Brezhnev, in pursuit of the Kremlin's design to dominate other nations, have employed espionage in ways that no other nation in all of recorded history had ever attempted. Through subterfuge, deceit, and deliberate circumvention of regulations, the Soviet Union has managed to infiltrate and undermine nation upon nation and to draw them into the Soviet orbit.

The Kremlin's chief weapon in the fulfillment of this objective is subversion. For once Red spies obtain the secrets of a nation, they have the upper hand. They know the industrial and military strength as well as the potential of that nation. And they can map their takeover accordingly.

Even as the FBI was beginning its inquiry into the Grusha-Samarasekara alliance, the feeling had surfaced that Moscow was out to get something from Ceylon. Something that Red agents in Colombo could not get, obviously.

At this very moment in Ceylon, the Communists had scored heavily in the national election of 1956 and the People's United Front, a coalition of Trotskyites, Buddhists, and the very Communist-oriented Sri Lanka Freedom Party, had defeated the United National Party, which had been in power for twenty-five years and stood as a bulwark of moderate republicanism and anti-Communism. So Moscow had gotten what it wanted in Ceylon. But . . .

What could Grusha be after in New York?

And why had he targeted on Samarasekara?

The FBI wasn't aware of how the Soviet diplomat had shopped around for a decent Ceylonese traitor—if that was what D.S. was. Yet it went without saying that Ceylonese traitors were in short supply because, let's face it, who needs a Ceylonese spy? There simply wasn't much of a demand for them.

Nevertheless, there was D.S. being squired around town by Vladimir Grusha, who was lavishly wining and dining the Ceylonese on the Russian's expense account and even picking up D.S.'s personal restaurant tabs as well as his suddenly multiplying bills at some of the East Side's swank cocktail lounges.

The FBI hasn't made a public pronouncement on how it came to know something about D.S. that even Grusha didn't know—that D.S. had an affliction known as acute lip-flapping, plus a propensity for smearing his newly acquired pin money in the wrong places.

But the G-men happened to be watching Grusha, and through him they apparently decided to do a backgrounder on D.S., who otherwise might never have come into the FBI's sights.

And that was when the FBI arched its collective eyebrow and focused in on the squandering Ceylonese. The G-men's trained vision told them that D.S. had all the earmarks of a man who had been bought.

The FBI's tail was pinned on D.S. that week before Christmas and by mid-March it was on him so tightly that G-men were doing everything but sharing D.S.'s morning shower with him. But even at that, they were practically outside his bathroom door.

Ditto, it can be said, for Grusha.

It came to pass, on that evening of March 5th, that the Russians, unaware of the fact that D.S. and Grusha were traveling in a crowd, had given D.S. an assignment to carry out. This became quite obvious to the two FBI agents trailing D.S. and the other two G-men who were following Grusha.

There had been a two o'clock meeting that afternoon between D.S. and Grusha on First Avenue and 59th Street under the Queensborough Bridge. Their talk was urgent. The FBI observers sensed that the time had come for action—it was D.S.'s turn to repay Grusha for his many favors.

One of the agents on the tail immediately phoned the FBI office to report the rendezvous. That called for a blanket of G-men to cover the case, for no one now could foretell where the trail would lead or how diffuse it might be. Other conspirators conceivably could be waiting in the wings to take an active hand in the plot.

Harvey Foster, the Agent-in-Charge, gathered ten of those shirt-sleeved G-men in his office and reeled off their assignments. They were specific. Two men were posted to watch the Soviet UN Delegation Building at 136 East 67th Street. Two others were assigned to stake out the Ceylon Delegation, which was housed in a building at 417 East 57th Street, off York Avenue. The others, in two three-man teams, were assigned to radio-equipped cars to cruise in the vicinity and be prepared to shadow any of the participants in the spy drama.

Four other agents were already on the street—the two watching Grusha and the pair on D.S.'s trail.

It was shortly after 6 P.M. when Foster sent his men out into the field. That was just seconds after the call came in reporting that D.S. had left his apartment on the East Side, hopped into his tiny red Volkswagen, and begun cruising in what seemed like an aimless course over East Side streets until . . .

He wheeled to a stop in front of the East 57th Street building housing the Ceylonese Delegation to the UN.

The G-men shadowing D.S. had an idea at once that their quarry was up to no good. At that time of day the Delegation's offices were locked tight. D.S.'s presence there at such a late hour was like a drumbeat warning that something unusual was about to happen.

At 6:56 P.M., an FBI car bounced to a gentle stop directly across the street. The three agents in the car spotted the two G-men who had been following D.S. They were in their car up the block. A signal from the man behind the wheel of the latter car told the newly arrived agents where D.S. was—about fifty feet west of the Ceylonese Delegation Building.

An instant later, the agents in both cars were talking to each other on the radio. The story was that D.S. had been walking up and down the block for nearly a half-hour in what was an obvious attempt to "case" the headquarters of his nation's mission to the UN. Evidently he was trying to make certain that the last of the mission employees had gone home. Quitting time was 6 P.M. but late work sometimes kept them over.

That wasn't the case on the night of March 5, 1957. The Mission, which used rented quarters on the fourth floor of the building, was already closed.

Despite his being accustomed to the warm climes of Ceylon, D.S. didn't seem to mind the bitingly cold wind and the icy snowflakes being whipped in his face as he trudged back and forth on the sidewalk.

The G-men weren't close enough to observe D.S.'s face but there certainly must have been an expression of relief when he finally deserted the freezing outdoors and made his way into the heated building at No. 417.

Within seconds after D.S. went in, two agents followed. They would not readily attract his suspicion even if he saw them because other tenants rented space on various floors of the building.

When the G-men entered the lobby they immediately caught sight of D.S.'s back disappearing into the elevator. An instant later the doors closed and D.S. was on his way up. The FBI agents watched the dial for a clue to his destination—as if they really needed one.

It was no surprise. The elevator stopped on the fourth floor, just where it was expected to.

The agents decided that their best way up was via the stairs. Enroute they had one problem to contend with. They knew that their tail could not extend beyond the limits of United States territory. That may sound silly but it was a technically significant point.

For all intents and purposes, the Ceylonese Delegation's offices are "foreign soil." They are diplomatically immune islands and not subject to our laws—or to the invasion of our law enforcement officials. Not even if we are working in their interest—unless the Ceylonese have given us permission to enter their preserve.

So the FBI men who followed D.S. upstairs were bound to adhere to the law. They could walk through the fourth-floor corridor but they could not go beyond the door leading to the mission.

To say that this restriction posed a handicap to their investigation and their efforts to learn what D.S. was up to would be a gross understatement. And to have sought permission of the Ceylonese Chief Delegate or Ambassador would have been premature. For the agents still had no evidence that D.S. was involved in espionage.

But the two agents following D.S. were in for a big surprise.

When they reached the fourth floor they found the hall deserted. The elevator door was closed. That raised the question at once: Had D.S. fooled them? Had he stopped the elevator at the fourth floor only to throw anyone who might be following off his trail?

But where else but the fourth floor could D.S. be bound for?

The answer became apparent to the G-men once they entered the corridor and saw the open door—the one to the Ceylon Mission's offices. They had only to tiptoe down the hall to establish without any question that D.S. possessed a very cumbersome characteristic for a spy. He was clumsy and incredibly amateurish.

There he was busily rifling a filing cabinet and examining its contents without the least concern for the door he had conveniently left open for the G-men. And he had no idea that he was performing for an audience.

D.S. spent about ten minutes combing the cabinet before he evidently found what he wanted—a red book that he glanced through quickly, then jammed into an airline-type handbag. As he started out, he turned off the lights and then shut the door and locked it with his key.

Meanwhile, the FBI agents had ducked back into the hall to avoid being seen by D.S. When they observed him heading for the elevator, they dashed down the stairs and got out of the building before he had descended to the ground floor.

The agents signaled to the car across the street as they reached the sidewalk, then hurried to their own cruiser parked near D.S.'s Volkswagen.

Seconds later D.S. walked out of the building at a brisk pace, carrying the bag. He got into his car and started off in the direction his auto had been parked—westbound. The car with the G-men who had just tailed him fell in behind the Volks.

At the same time, the agents in the car across the street made a U-turn and fell in behind the first team of G-men.

Traffic at that hour of the evening—it was 7:40 P.M. by then—had thinned after the homebound crush and his FBI pursuers had no trouble keeping track of D.S. as he made a turn at the end of the block and headed north on First Avenue. Moreover,

D.S. didn't seem to be in much of a hurry. His pace was leisurely, almost a crawl.

The first FBI car was right behind D.S. as he plied along on First Avenue for a block and turned east again into 58th Street. Then D.S. did the unexpected. He stopped suddenly in the middle of the block.

So suddenly that the FBI car—a black 1957 Oldsmobile sedan—had to stop on a dime to avoid plowing into the rear of the tiny compact. D.S. had failed to signal that he was going to stop. Even worse, his red brake lights weren't working.

The screech of brakes apparently startled D.S. The silhouette of his head, picked up in the headlights of the FBI car, turned and tilted as if he were peering into his rear-view mirror to see what had happened behind him. Evidently sensing that he had almost caused an accident by stopping short, D.S. turned and politely waved his hand at the FBI agent behind the wheel of the Olds. It was an apology.

D.S. then started out again. This time the second FBI car fell in behind D.S. The first one picked up the rear. There was good reason for this tactic. D.S. might have suspected he was being followed if the first car had continued to stay on his tail.

D.S. went to the end of the block and turned south on York Avenue before stopping at a red light—at the corner of 57th Street. This was where the around-the-block caravan had started and it was beginning to have overtones of a Keystone Cops chase.

It was now 7:50 P.M. and suddenly whatever comic aspects had seemed to encroach upon the drama faded away. All at once the deadly seriousness of the cat-and-mouse game was apparent. Standing on the corner of that intersection at that precise moment was Vladimir Arsenevich Grusha, the Soviet First Secretary.

The G-men in the two cars following D.S. were expecting he'd be there because they had been receiving advisories over the radio of Grusha's position from the agents who were shadowing him. They had followed the Russian from the Soviet Mission Building. Two teams of G-men were trailing him—two on foot and two in a car, the latter being protection in case he suddenly jumped into a taxi or bus.

D.S. and Grusha didn't meet physically despite the fact that

129

they came within a dozen feet of each other. Yet it was obvious to the FBI men that a contact was in the making between the Ceylonese and the Russian.

D.S. simply drove on after the light turned green. But the G-men were certain that D.S. had seen Grusha—and that Grusha had seen D.S.

D.S. went driving through the streets of the East Side for the next hour—always within sight of the FBI. His maneuvers were weird, if not ludicrous. He went over and over the same streets, occasionally stopping in front of the Ceylonese Delegation as if to check on the place to make certain that no one had discovered his unauthorized visit there earlier and his unauthorized removal of the little red book.

By now, of course, the FBI was fully aware of the contents of the stolen document. The Ceylonese Mission's Chief Delegate, who was made aware of the goings-on at his offices just minutes earlier, was sped to the building on 57th Street by FBI men. He checked the cabinet that D.S. had pilfered and found that the only document missing was a small red book—a description that fitted precisely with the book the G-men saw D.S. lift from the files.

The book contained Ceylon's confidential code!

A veritable treasure trove for the Soviet Union.

It was now 8:30 P.M. and Samarasekara (we promise to go back to D.S. after this) again was taking his car along 57th Street. But this time his course changed. He made a turn south on Second Avenue, went to 51st Street, west to Third Avenue, north to 52nd Street, east to First Avenue, and on up to 58th where he turned east.

About three-quarters of the way into this block he stopped his car in double-park position. Suddenly, from between two parked cars, stepped the unmistakable tall and erect figure of Vladimir Arsenevich Grusha. Without a moment's delay, he opened the door, got in beside the driver, and was whisked away.

Still on his trail, the FBI followed the red Volkswagen down York Avenue to 57th Street. At the corner, the car stopped and Grusha got out. D.S. drove on.

As they passed Grusha the G-men spotted a manila envelope, about eight by ten inches, in his right hand. The first FBI car continued to follow D.S. but the second vehicle stopped and let out two agents who took up Grusha's trail by foot at a discreet distance.

Grusha headed for his own car, which he had driven from the Soviet Mission earlier and parked on 56th Street off Second Avenue. The agents, who had walkie-talkies secreted under their overcoats, flashed an advisory to the G-men in the cars. The second car quickly headed into 56th Street and fell in back of Grusha's Chevrolet sedan as he pulled out. He went just where the FBI men expected he would go—to the Soviet Mission on 67th Street.

Meanwhile, D.S. drove back to the Ceylon Delegation's building and, as he had done earlier, he took the elevator to the fourth floor. And as they had done earlier, the FBI agents followed him up the stairs.

Still as careless as ever, D.S. left the door open so that his shadows could observe him opening the same file cabinet that he had worked on earlier. This time, instead of taking, he was putting the red book back.

He had completed his mission in espionage and it must have seemed like such a nice, neat job to him. He had no idea that the FBI had covered his every move every step of the way.

Nor for that matter did Grusha know. He had betrayed no sign of awareness that he was being watched or followed. He didn't spot the FBI operatives who had tailed him uptown for nine blocks from the UN Mission to 56th Street, watched him park his car, then walk to 57th Street and York Avenue.

It had been dark at 7:50 P.M. But there was enough illumination from the street light at the corner to enable the G-men to spot the cloak-and-dagger maneuver that was engineered. It all happened in a flash.

D.S. stopped for the red light. Grusha was standing on the corner. D.S. reached across to the right side of his small car and rolled down the window. Then he tossed an object out. That object was the handbag—containing the Ceylonese code book. Then D.S. drove on.

Grusha quickly stepped off the curb, bent down, picked up the handbag, and scurried across the street and around the corner of York Avenue and 56th Street to where he had left his car. He got behind the wheel and drove back to the Soviet UN Mission. As he went into the building, the G-men saw him holding the handbag that D.S. had tossed out of his car.

In exactly twenty-two minutes—at precisely 8:24 P.M.—Grusha emerged from the Soviet's UN headquarters and returned to his car. He drove back to the very spot he had parked in before—the space was still available because it was a fire hydrant and diplomatic immunity gives a motorist that kind of gall.

Grusha parked and walked two blocks uptown on First Avenue to 58th Street, then east along 58th toward the end of the block where D.S. was waiting in his Volks. Grusha got in, obviously to return the code book to D.S.

The FBI was quite certain that Grusha also crossed D.S.'s palm with some balm for his troubles.

In the days that followed the FBI kept both D.S. and Grusha under strict surveillance. However, the agents noted no further meetings between the two men and as the days passed into a week and then two, it began to look as though D.S. and Grusha might never meet again.

D.S., it was conceded, apparently had done the dirty work that the Soviets demanded—getting the code book to them. It was deemed unlikely that Grusha and his cohorts were interested in any other secret Ceylonese documents.

After all, how many secret documents could Ceylon possess?

What, you might ask, could the Soviet Union do with the document Grusha brought to the Mission for that twenty-two-minute stopover?

In those twenty-two minutes, the FBI concluded, the expert Red agents posted in the military section were able to make photostatic copies of every page of the Ceylonese code book.

Its value?

That's hard to say. It was hardly likely, however, that the Soviet espionage masterminds, desperate for some way to earn their oats on an otherwise dull day, had decided to secure the confidential code of Ceylon just on the off-chance that it might prove worthwhile. More than likely, the truth lies in the theory the FBI leaned to:

The Soviet Union felt it could use the Ceylonese code to crack secret messages passed between that island nation in the Indian Ocean and other governments, especially those of nations in the

British Commonwealth; that is, India. It certainly couldn't do any harm to know the code.

In light of later world developments—the border disputes involving Red China and India and the conflicts between India and Pakistan—it would now appear that the Soviet Union was preparing itself back in 1956 for a crisis eight years before it occurred!

Now that D.S. had done the dirty work the Soviets had subverted him for—the theft of the code book—and since there was no further contact between him and Grusha or any other member of the Soviet delegation, the FBI decided this espionage plot had run its full course.

So it was time to pull Samarasekara in and put him on the grill. The handsome Ceylonese was taking a shower when the G-men rapped on his door.

Dripping wet and with only a towel around his middle, D.S. opened the door with a look of bewilderment clouding his face.

"Yes, what can I do?" he asked gently, managing a benign smile.

"Sorry to bother you at a time like this," one of the three agents in the hall apologized. "There's a small matter of utmost importance that we want to discuss with you. It's a Government matter . . . may we come in. We are from the Federal Bureau of Investigation."

The affable D.S. seemed almost impressed by the announcement. Evidently he never suspected that the FBI had taken an interest in a case of espionage involving two foreign nations—his and Russia—and was under the impression that the business they wanted to talk over was something completely different.

"Come in, gentlemen," he said. "Please sit down. I will dress and be with you right away."

For the next several minutes silence dominated the scene in D.S.'s modest three-room apartment. It was the silence of waiting, when three men certain they are holding a royal flush in their hands, are up against a man who doesn't even have a pair.

D.S. finally came out of the bedroom, neatly attired in gray slacks, a maroon silk sport shirt, open at the collar, and black moccasins. He reeked heavily of an exotic perfume that one of the G-men later described as "Canal Far East."

"What sort of Government business do you wish to discuss?" he asked with inordinate curiosity. Evidently D.S. had given some

133

thought to his visitors while dressing. He seemed at this moment a bit uneasy even though his unexpected guests had not indicated precisely why they were there.

"We want to ask you about your relationship with a certain member of the Russian Delegation," one of the G-men finally said.

"Yes, yes," the Ceylonese national replied, his voice pitched high and on the verge of cracking at any moment, perhaps out of panic.

"Do you know Vladimir Grusha?" the agent asked flatly.

D.S. seemed to search his mind for the answer. Then all at once as though he had suddenly placed the name, he blurted:

"Oh, yes, I know him."

Then the questions came faster. And D.S.'s answers became progressively more hesitant, less clear, and were uttered in a voice that seemed to acquire new fear and apprehension with each subsequent query.

In essence, the FBI agents refreshed D.S.'s memory of his visit to the Ceylonese Delegation offices on the night of March 5th, his circuitous ride around the East Side, his stop at 57th Street and York Avenue, his meeting with Grusha, and finally his return to the Ceylonese Delegation with the stolen document.

D.S. admitted he'd been to the building. He admitted he had driven around. He even admitted he had met Grusha—as he had met him a number of times before.

"But," he pleaded, "I did not steal the code book . . . I didn't even touch it."

Yet he had no logical explanation either for his unauthorized stopover at the Delegation offices or for his furtive driving around town, which led to his furtive "drop" of the handbag that Grusha retrieved and later to the meeting with the Soviet emissary in the car.

There was no way the FBI agents could draw out any more information from D.S. He insisted he was telling the truth. But D.S. made a determined stab at trying to contribute some logic to his get-together with Grusha.

"He is a very good friend," D.S. stammered. "We both work in the Secretariat."

The FBI men finally left D.S. and reported the results of this interview to their superior, Harvey Foster. A full report on the case was then prepared by Foster and forwarded to the Bureau in Washington. In turn, the facts were brought to the attention of the State Department.

On March 25th, Vladimir Grusha was declared persona non grata and the Soviet Union was asked to expedite his departure to Moscow or wherever else, but for certain out of this country.

The head of the Soviet Mission in New York filed the usual protest that followed all such requests when Soviet spies were caught red-handed, denying that its diplomatically immune emissary had engaged in any form of espionage. But on April 10th Grusha and his wife left New York for the Kremlin.

Meanwhile, the State Department instructed the U.S. Mission to the UN to request Secretary General Dag Hammarskjold to dismiss Dhanpalo Samarasekara from the UN Secretariat on the grounds that he had engaged in espionage activity on American soil.

On July 5th, D.S. was suspended with pay and a committee was appointed by Hammarskjold to investigate the allegations against the Ceylonese.

On December 16th, the Secretary General informed the U.S. Mission that he had terminated the employment of Dhanpalo, who was being summoned back to Ceylon.

Although this case did not involve an attempt to steal American secrets, it clearly showed that the United States is not the only target of espionage by the Soviets on our own soil.

This was the first—and so far the only—instance in which the FBI broke up a spy plot involving two foreign countries in the United States.

In cracking the case the G-men proved that the Kremlin will go to any lengths in stealing another nation's secrets, no matter how small—and even if it has to do so on a neutral nation's soil.

There is serious doubt that Grusha was received with welcoming arms in Moscow. In the more than fifteen years since his return there, not a word about him has been heard here.

And what of good old D.S. or, if we may be allowed for one last time to mention him by his full name—Dhanpalo Samarasekara? What was his fate?

No one knows either. But D.S. may be much better off in Ceylon

135

than Grusha in Siberia. There are no salt mines in his island homeland.

At worst, it may be speculated, D.S. may have been relegated to a future of counting those tiny tea leaves.

Chapter 16

The Spy Who Sought Only Our Secrets
of Mass Destruction

It may have been spring on that night of April 18, 1956, but the snarl of Old Man Winter still lingered in Washington and the city's celebrated Japanese cherry trees were cringing dormantly on the banks of the Potomac.

No one could fault Hugo Tiomkin for keeping his windows rolled up and running his heater full blast as he sat in his car parked on 5th Street near the corner of Van Buren Street in the northwest section of the capital. A thirty-mile wind with gusts reaching fifty plummeted the thermometer into the chilling thirties.

But the frosty weather didn't seem to annoy the tall, husky man bundled in a black woolen coat whose huge collar was turned up almost to the brim of his gray fedora. He had emerged from the darkness of a doorway on 5th Street and was walking at a gingerly gait toward the parked car in which Tiomkin was seated.

If the cold had no apparent effect on the pedestrian, it was perhaps because he was accustomed to much colder climes. For the man was Ivan Aleksandrovich Bubchikov, who was born and raised in one of the many ice boxes of the Soviet Union—a city called Smolensk.

As we will learn from the FBI on a day long after that night of April 18th, Bubchikov was born on June 9, 1918, with black hair and gray eyes. He grew into sizable manhood, achieving a height of five feet ten inches and a weight of one hundred and seventy pounds.

Bubchikov joined the Red Army as a private in 1940, the FBI told us, and worked his way up the ranks to a commission. During World War II, he distinguished himself as a tank commander and ultimately he was made an instructor in tank warfare at the famed Frunze Military Academy in Moscow.

By 1950 he had attained promotion to colonel. Four years later, Bubchikov was advised that he was being sent to Washington to serve as Assistant Military Attaché at the Soviet Embassy. By now Bubchikov was married and had a small son.

But it was not because of the settled family life to which Bubchikov had become accustomed in the Soviet capital that he objected to his new assignment.

"He declaimed that he was too honest and too straightforward to become involved in diplomatic machinations," our source in the FBI said. "He didn't like the idea of shaking hands or sipping cocktails at Embassy functions."

But Bubchikov's protests were dramatically silenced after he was summoned to a meeting with Lavrenti Beria. The spy boss made it crystal clear to the colonel that his services were required in Washington. And Bubchikov quickly agreed that it was wrong of him not to have leaped at the assignment in the first place.

His leap brought him to the capital with his wife and son, and his assignment to the Embassy's military staff drew the instant attention of the FBI. Not that he had become enmeshed in subversive activity so soon, but the Bureau has standing orders to keep tabs on all Soviet diplomats—especially those assigned to the military staff. They are the prime architects of Soviet espionage in the United States.

In the first year of Bubchikov's Washington tour the FBI found no basis to suspect that he was involved in illicit activity.

But on July 24, 1955, two agents assigned to keep an eye on the Soviet Embassy picked up Bubchikov as he left the building on what seemed like an urgent and unusual errand. It was 10:15 P.M.—much too late for a diplomatic call.

The G-men followed Bubchikov in their car to a private residence about a fifteen-minute drive from the Embassy. They watched their quarry enter the house, waited, and saw him come out shortly after 11:30. He drove back to the Embassy.

When they returned later to the FBI Building, the agents filed a report on their observations. The next day, other agents made discreet inquiries and learned that the person Bubchikov had visited was Hugo Tiomkin, a fifty-five-year-old engineer employed by a major petroleum firm in the Washington area.

A further check revealed that Tiomkin had emigrated from Russia to the United States in 1920 and that he had become a naturalized citizen. By day's end, discreet inquiries at his place of employment revealed that he had been working there for some dozen years and was regarded highly.

There was nothing in his dossier to show that Tiomkin had any serious ties with his native land. But further investigation showed that during World War II Tiomkin had apparently fraternized with some members of the Soviet Embassy in Washington.

The FBI report on that activity read:

> Tiomkin appears to be something of a promoter and an operator. He seems to be a big talker and the Russians appeared to have an extraordinary interest in him. But he has not done anything to indicate a furthering of the friendships that developed during World War II days. Many of the members of the Embassy have since been transferred out of Washington and Tiomkin seems to have cut off any ties that he had.

Yet on that July night in 1955, the two FBI agents were not mistaken. They had seen Colonel Ivan Aleksandrovich Bubchikov drive up to Hugo Tiomkin's door and pay him a visit of approximately an hour.

What was that all about, the FBI was asking?

Before their own investigation into the incident could be launched, the FBI received a phone call. Tiomkin wanted to see someone from the Bureau.

"I have something very important to tell you," he said in a voice that trembled. "Please send someone to my house."

The next evening, two FBI agents dropped in on Tiomkin. They listened as he told them about Bubchikov's surprising visit.

"I did not know him," Tiomkin informed his visitors from the Bureau. "He merely called me up the night before and told me that he was coming over to discuss a very important matter."

When Bubchikov dropped by that July 24th, Tiomkin related, no words were wasted.

"He came right to the point. He wanted to know if I still felt as friendly toward the Soviet Union as I did ten or fifteen years ago. My answer to him was, 'Once a friend, always a friend.'"

Bubchikov seemed pleased with that response. He told Tiomkin, "That is very encouraging to hear. We need friends and we need help."

What kind of help, Tiomkin wanted to know?

"We know about your work as a consulting engineer in petroleum and its by-products," Bubchikov said. "We are very interested in learning about developments in your industry. Most of all we want to know details about aviation fuel."

Tiomkin told the FBI men he was horrified to find that the Russians had singled him out for subversion.

"In my mind the proposition was the most repulsive thing I ever heard," Tiomkin said in a tone reflecting his unquestioned outrage. "How did they come to pick me out for espionage?"

"Undoubtedly that friendship you cultivated with them during the war years had something to do with it," one of the G-men told Tiomkin. "You know that the Soviet Union considers anyone born in Russia to be a loyal son of the motherland regardless of where he may be living. Your citizenship here means nothing to them. They expect you to feel the same way. That's why they make these approaches. You're not the first one who has been put in such a position and you won't be the last."

Then the agent assured Tiomkin that he had no reason to be concerned about his loyalty to his adopted country.

"You did the right thing in calling the FBI," Tiomkin was told.

"But what shall I do?" he asked, puzzled.

"Play along with them," said the agent. "We'll guide you. And we'll also protect you and your family. You have nothing to worry about."

Tiomkin was asked on what note he had concluded his discussion with Bubchikov.

"I told him I would think the matter over," Tiomkin said. "It was the only answer I could give him. I wanted time so I could notify the FBI."

Before the agents left, they briefed Tiomkin on the strategy he was to employ on Bubchikov or any other Soviet agent in the future.

"Don't call them," Tiomkin was told. "They will get in touch with you. If you show anxiety to work with them, they will become suspicious. You've got to pretend that you are hard to get—and afraid of what will happen to you if you are caught."

Tiomkin was also advised that the most important element in his dealings with the Soviets was to make it clear to them from the outset that he was "hungry for the almighty dollar."

"You've got to make them think that you are reluctant to take any chances unless the price is right to make it worth the risks you will be taking," the agent who had been doing most of the talking said. "We will tell you how much payment you can demand after they approach you for specific information. Every secret has a different price tag."

Although the agents kept in almost daily touch with Tiomkin after their initial visit, there was no contact with the Soviets over the next few weeks. The FBI, however, felt confident that Bubchikov or someone else at the Embassy would eventually get in touch with the engineer and set forth the terms of the conspiracy in more detail. That is the pattern of Soviet espionage—the process entails long periods of waiting during which their agents make careful studies and further evaluations of the person they have selected for a role in their subversive schemes. If in that time they should happen to find that a candidate they have picked poses a threat to the successful completion of the conspiracy, they will avoid him like the plague. They don't want boneheads, fools, or patriots lousing up their spy network.

Evidently Hugo Tiomkin passed the Soviets' scrutiny, for early on the evening of August 22, 1955—exactly a month after the first approach—the long-awaited summoning finally came. The phone rang just as Tiomkin had sat down with his family for dinner.

"Hugo," the voice on the other end said, "I want to meet you tomorrow night. I have a very good proposition for you . . . "

The caller was Bubchikov. He asked Tiomkin to meet him outside a restaurant in a nearby Maryland suburb.

"I will meet you at the park bench at the side of the restaurant," Bubchikov told Tiomkin. "Be there at eight o'clock."

Tiomkin promptly notified his contact at the FBI about the meeting. He was advised to keep the appointment—and to "show a willingness to cooperate in any request that's made to you."

The next night, Tiomkin went to his rendezvous with the Soviet colonel. Tiomkin arrived about three minutes late, found the park bench, but saw no sign of Bubchikov. He sat on the bench to wait for him.

No more than a minute went by. Tiomkin heard a rustling in the bushes behind the bench. He turned and was startled to see Bubchikov emerging from the yews and junipers.

"Good evening, my friend," the man from the Embassy greeted with a toothy smile. "It is good to see that you could make it."

Bubchikov sat heavily on the bench beside Tiomkin and plunged immediately into business.

"Have you given much thought to the matter I discussed with you?" he asked.

"Yes," Tiomkin said.

"And what is your answer?" Bubchikov inquired almost eagerly.

"Well," Tiomkin hesitated, "I am not completely certain what you want from me . . . I will be glad to help, but I must know what you are after . . . "

Bubchikov was apparently buoyed by the response, as far as it went. For he interrupted to say, "That is exactly what I want to talk to you about. I am primarily interested in obtaining information dealing with weapons of mass destruction."

Tiomkin was stunned.

"But . . . but . . . I have nothing to do with such things," he stammered. "You know what my field is. I only have knowledge about petroleum, rubber, and aviation fuel . . . "

Bubchikov began to laugh.

"I know that," he said with a casual air. "But I also know that you have the means to look into these other matters and to put your hands on such information."

What sort of information, Tiomkin wanted to know.

"Well," Bubchikov came back, "I am anxious to receive specific details about developments in biological and chemical warfare. Then I also wish to obtain data on guided missiles and on the new types of atomic and hydrogen weapons that the United States is developing."

Although Tiomkin knew full well that there was no method at his disposal to gather even the most fragmentary information on such top-secret weaponry, he pretended that he was in a position to put his hands on that data—if the price was right.

He was being guided now by what the FBI had told him:

"No matter what you're asked to get, say okay, that you'll try. And always ask whether they're going to pay well."

"By all means, comrade," Bubchikov said grandly when Tiomkin brought up the question of money. "You will be well compensated. Of course, you understand, it will all depend on the quality of the material you deliver."

The meeting on the bench lasted an hour and forty-five minutes. The time was exact, for it was clocked by two FBI agents in a parked sedan near the restaurant. The G-men had the intimate little gathering under surveillance from beginning to end—and they also shot about two hundred feet of movie film of Bubchikov and Tiomkin in their discussion, which at times was extremely animated. The agents were puzzled over Bubchikov's frequent movement of his hands, which often resembled a player's motions in a game of charades.

As they were to learn later, Bubchikov's virtuoso performance with his hands was a necessary adjunct of a carefully outlined procedure that he laid down for the engineer to follow in future dealings with the Soviet spy.

"He is a very ingenious man," Tiomkin told his FBI contacts late that night after returning home from his rendezvous with Bubchikov. "He designated two locations where we are to meet in the future. He told me exactly where I am to park my car and precisely what I am to do when I am to meet him or deliver material."

One of the locations was at 19th Street and Kalorama Road. This was to be used only in the event Tiomkin wanted to meet Bubchikov at a time other than the one agreed upon.

"He gave me this package of putty," Tiomkin told the agents. "He said I was to form an X with a piece of the putty and affix it to the top of a metal pillar at that location. He said he would see it and get in touch with me."

Bubchikov also designated a wooden post next to a tennis court

143

complex near Garfield Street and 34th Place Northwest for the times when he would want to meet Tiomkin in an emergency. Again an X shaped by the putty would signal an urgent need for an encounter when one was not scheduled.

But the arrangements for deliveries of stolen secrets were something else again. Strictly cloak-and-dagger stuff.

"He told me that when I brought material that I was to pass on to him to carry it in a suitcase. He asked me what kind of suitcases I owned. I told him and he decided I was to use a brown one that has a Mexican eagle stamped on it. He wants me to carry it in my left hand."

Bubchikov also assigned a role to Tiomkin's other hand.

"He said I was to stuff my right hand into my shirt—like Napoleon."

That gesture would indicate all was well, that Tiomkin did not suspect he was being followed or watched.

Bubchikov also took pains to arrange a code for such contingencies as when he himself might not be able to meet Tiomkin and a substitute spy had to make the pickup.

"The man whom Bubchikov will send is to ask me, 'How far is it to the park?' And I am to reply, 'It is quite near from here.' In that way we will each know that we are dealing with the right party."

As specific and detailed as Bubchikov was in arranging meetings and deliveries, he was just the contrary when Tiomkin tried to pin him down on the matter of how many rubles he would receive for his efforts.

"He told me not to worry about money," Tiomkin informed the agents. "He said I will be well paid. And he assured me that it was going to be all tax-free money because the Soviet Union wouldn't report the payments to Uncle Sam."

Tiomkin also told the G-men that Bubchikov had promised to prepare an "itemized list of mass destruction weaponry" that the Soviets were interested in and would deliver it to him on September 30th at 5th and Van Buren Streets.

At 8:30 P.M. on the 30th, Tiomkin met Bubchikov at that Washington locale and received the list. As he glanced over it, he raised his eyebrows at such items as "jet fuels," "radio-detecting devices," "bacteriological warfare," and "atomic reactors."

"You know that information about such things will not be easy to obtain," Tiomkin said. "I will need time."

"Yes, yes," Bubchikov agreed. "I am not in a hurry."

Then Bubchikov proceeded to outline a careful new plan for delivering the material. The suitcase with the Mexican eagle was still to be used to carry the stolen documents, but the meeting arrangement worked out for passing the suitcase to Bubchikov was off.

The colonel designated a site at the Collingwood picnic area along the Potomac, and he told Tiomkin the precise spot where the suitcase was to be left—in a clump of bushes near the river.

"When you go there," Bubchikov said, "carry a fishing rod to throw off any suspicion . . . "

The procedure he had now designated is known as the "drop" method. It provides a much greater latitude of safety for the participants in subversion. A Soviet agent who is to receive delivery of secrets can avoid physical contact with the conspirator by the "drop" method. He can lie back in hiding and stake out the area where the material is deposited. He can observe whether others—such as FBI agents—are shadowing or watching the conspirator making the delivery. If the coast is clear after the "drop," the Red agent knows it's safe to retrieve the material left for him. He has taken no chance at being caught receiving the evidence.

With material assembled by the FBI, which used Bubchikov's list for guidance, Tiomkin proceeded to make periodic deliveries of "secret" information on bacteriological warfare, atomic reactors, radio-detecting devices, and other military matériel that had been requested. All of it, of course, had been carefully doctored beforehand so as to make the data totally useless or unworkable when the scientists and military men in the Kremlin tried to make a practical application of it.

On November 10, 1955, Tiomkin met Bubchikov at Garfield Street and 34th Place Northwest, where they had agreed to rendezvous after the engineer, acting on instructions from the FBI, had left a puttied X on the pillar at 19th Street and Kalorama Road, indicating a need for an emergency get-together.

"What is the matter?" Bubchikov asked when he met Tiomkin.

"So far you have not given me any money," Tiomkin complained, following a well-rehearsed speech that had been prepared by the FBI. "I am tired of working for nothing. You promised me big money."

"I am very sorry," Bubchikov apologized. "I should have paid you sooner."

He put his hand into his pocket, extracted his wallet, and handed Tiomkin a wad of bills. "There is $150 here," he said. "Does that please you."

"No," Tiomkin said angrily. "I am not working for hundreds of dollars. I am only interested in thousands."

And with that, he told Bubchikov to keep his money.

"But you have not delivered any of the key information that I asked you to get," Bubchikov complained. "So far you have only given me scraps. When will you begin to produce the important information?"

"When you pay for it," Tiomkin said sarcastically.

Bubchikov swallowed his pride and tried to mollify his recruit in espionage.

"I promise you, Hugo, that I will talk to the boys back at the Embassy and make them realize that they must pay you better," he said. Then all at once he had another request.

"Do you think you can get information on the F-1 Safari plane?" Bubchikov wanted to know.

"Perhaps I can," Tiomkin replied coyly. "But not if you don't pay well for it."

"Agreed," Bubchikov smiled, shaking Tiomkin's hand.

Three weeks later, Tiomkin lugged his suitcase to the picnic grounds along the Potomac and deposited it in the shrubbery. An hour later, an FBI agent watching through field glasses spotted Bubchikov picking up the valise, which contained more worthless data on rockets and atomic reactors—but no information on the Safari, which was manufactured by the Frye Corporation in Fort Worth, Texas.

According to the prearranged plan, Tiomkin returned to the Collingwood site the next day and retrieved the suitcase, which had been left in the bushes after it was emptied of its contents.

When Tiomkin brought the suitcase home and opened it, he found a terse note:

"What happened to the Safari?"

In place of a signature were these significant markings: "$$$$"

Over the next three months, Tiomkin delivered two more suit-cases of doctored secrets for which he received about $400. But whenever he was asked for information on the plane, Tiomkin gave Bubchikov a stall.

Finally, on the night of April 5, 1956, Bubchikov phoned Tiomkin at home and told him he was coming over. An hour later, the colonel stormed into the house, grabbed Tiomkin by the lapels of his jacket, and began berating him.

"Hugo, you have let me down," he scolded. "You have been stall-ing me. You promise to deliver but you give me meaningless infor-mation. You have not lived up to expectations."

Bubchikov accused Tiomkin of not being able to control his con-tacts—the people supplying the engineer with the data the Soviets were seeking.

"Look," the colonel thundered. "Introduce me to those people. I will develop them properly. And when I do I will turn them back to you for all the future dealings. Let me assure you I am not try-ing to take your bread and butter, but I must make sure they im-prove their productivity so that this operation is a success."

Tiomkin turned Bubchikov down flatly.

"I will not let you meet my contacts," he said. "You will deal only with me."

"Then produce," Bubchikov shot back, "or I shall have to go to someone else for the information."

Tiomkin reported what Bubchikov said to the FBI.

"Get in touch with him and let him know that you have finally gotten the Safari data," Tiomkin was advised.

Thus the stage was set for Hugo Tiomkin's response to Bubchikov's ultimatum—it was that cold April 18th night when the engineer drove out to 5th Street near Van Buren.

When Bubchikov stepped from the shadows of the doorway on 5th Street and headed toward the car, he motioned Tiomkin to join him on the sidewalk. But the engineer pretended not to see him. Bubchikov was compelled to open the car door and sit beside Tiomkin.

"Here," Tiomkin said, handing a large manila envelope to the Soviet Military Attaché. "This is what you wanted."

Bubchikov tucked the envelope under his arm, got out of the

car, and before slamming the door shut he said, "I will contact you very soon."

The two men did not meet again until May 21st. Bubchikov arranged the get-together for 9:15 P.M. at 17th and Kearney Streets Northeast. They were both on foot and Bubchikov greeted Tiomkin with unusual courtesy.

"My dear friend, Hugo," he smiled, taking Tiomkin by the arm. "We were very pleased with the Safari data. And I have brought you a down payment for your troubles."

He handed the engineer a wad of twenty-dollar bills.

"There is $200 there," Bubchikov said. "But there will be much more. We have sent the information you delivered to Moscow and as soon as they notify us that they are satisfied, I will be in a position to pay you perhaps as much as $1,000 more."

When Tiomkin reported the results of his encounter with the Soviet spy to the FBI, he was told:

"Don't count on that thousand, Hugo, When the Kremlin goes over that information they will know they've been taken. They couldn't build a plane to stage a dogfight with the Wright Brothers at Kitty Hawk from the stuff you gave them."

Then came the news that Tiomkin had been waiting to hear for nine long and arduous months.

"It's all over, Hugo," one of the agents told Tiomkin. "We're sending the colonel home very soon."

On June 14, 1956, the State Department advised the Soviet Embassy that Colonel Ivan Aleksandrovich Bubchikov had been declared persona non grata for engaging "in espionage activities incompatible with his continued presence in this country."

Ten days later, on June 24th, Bubchikov and his wife and son flew from Washington to New York's International Airport where they boarded an airliner for London. They were on their way back to Moscow.

Ivan Bubchikov hadn't wanted the assignment to begin with, but Lavrenti Beria had convinced him to take it.

Beria had shown some poor judgment with Bubchikov, as he had with other spies he sent to this country. In fact, in light of his dealings with Boris Morros, one could say Beria was a boob.

At any rate, Bubchikov did not have to answer to Beria because by now Nikita Khrushchev had already exterminated the spy boss.

The question that lingers to this day is not so much who said what to Bubchikov—but what happened to him? For, just as nothing is known about the subsequent activities and final end of Vladimir Arsenevich Grusha and other Kremlin spies who failed in their missions in the United States, the fate of Ivan Aleksandrovich Bubchikov remains a dark mystery.

Chapter 17

Play for Pay Girls—A Danger to Our Security?

Even to this day all of Great Britain blushes like a nervous bride on her wedding night at the mention of John Profumo, Christine Keeler, Mandy Rice Davies, Dr. Stephen Ward, and their strange, Boccaccio-like tale of revelry that for a time both shocked and titillated the island kingdom of John Bull, and indeed the entire world.

From the grave and ancient paneled halls of Old Bailey flowed a stream of revelations as bizarre and nakedly lustful as anything those ten Florentines ever spun out in the pages of the *Decameron*.

Profumo, Christine, Mandy, Ward, and a scarlet company of others held a hypnotized world in absolute thrall throughout the most sensational sex scandal a civilized government had ever known, and before the tumult had ended the nation was aboil with crises and Her Majesty's Prime Minister, Harold Macmillan, realized it had cost him his political life.

Yet in the great worldwide notoriety of wooden canes, black net stockings, plunging décolletage, whips, orgies, and men of high station pervertedly cavorting in black masks and nothing else, little was said and even less understood about the sinister web that bound Old Bailey to Moscow, to Prague, to Budapest, to Washington—and finally to the richly carpeted salons and reception halls and quietly elegant cocktail lounges of the United Nations.

Neither was there any deep appreciation of the role played in the improbable ignominy of the Profumo scandal by an astonishingly beautiful, sloe-eyed blonde of international origin named Mariella Dibbins, or—as she was carried on the vice records of the New York City Police Department—Maria Novotny.

And buried even deeper in the surrealistic complexity of the tale unfolded from the dock before the Lord Chief Justice, was the shadowy figure of Maria Novotny's mentor, a man whose full scope and range in international espionage is still not quite clearly in focus, a man called Harry Allan Towers, a former executive of the British Broadcasting Corporation.

Of all the fact and fiction known about Harry Towers, one thing stands out as a matter of record. For approximately eleven years, perhaps longer, Towers employed one of the most effective weapons known to the ancient art of espionage—the female body. And he is suspected of having brought it to its most virtuoso capabilities with his stable of call girls at the United Nations.

Maria Novotny, the police records show, was one of them.

She was also well-known in that substratum of London society in which Christine Keeler, Dr. Stephen Ward, and their friends traveled, and it was in fact at a cocktail party in Maria's suburban London home that Christine and John Profumo first met.

The national crisis in Britain developed, of course, from the fact that Christine was having an affair with John Profumo at the same time she was sleeping with the Soviet Naval Attaché, Captain Yevgeny "Eugene" Ivanov.

British officials feared that Christine, perhaps only inadvertently, was transmitting her nation's top-secret information to the handsome Soviet. The implication was that during his relationship with Christine, Profumo may have let spill a secret or two or more about Her Majesty's Government.

The roles played by Maria Novotny and Harry Allan Towers in the Profumo scandal are imprecisely known, largely because

Maria Novotny was never a defendant and never fully questioned, and because Towers by then had vanished behind the Iron Curtain.

Better documented were their activities on this side of the ocean, where for years New York City police were cognizant of a call-girl ring operating within the very structure of the United Nations itself, yet were unable to penetrate the diplomatic barrier and flush them out.

Aware of the call girls, too, were the heads and high consular officials of most member nations, who warned their people of the prostitution ring's suspected true purpose—espionage.

Although no concrete evidence has ever developed that Towers indulged in espionage, his flight to Czechoslovakia and later Moscow, at the cost of $10,000 bail, strongly indicated that his procuring operation could have been directed ultimately from the Kremlin.

Neither is there any way of producing evidence of the number of times that members of the various national diplomatic corps have fallen victims to traps purportedly set by the Kremlin via the sex and pleasure route.

Yet through all the many years of the UN's existence, rumors have abounded about sex traps that are skillfully operated and expertly camouflaged by the Soviet Mission to the UN. We doubt that even the crack agents of the FBI—if indeed it were their job to do so—could ever ferret out hard evidence to nail down the suspicions that have existed.

The nearest approach to the probable truth stems from the revelations involving Harry Towers, a man who had once been known widely, in television circles from Broadway to Fleet Street, as suave, handsome, and glib as any man could be.

In London, for instance, where Towers often made his home between trips to New York, one of his closest friends was the late Dr. Stephen Ward, who took his own life in the aftermath of the shame that involved him in Britain's Profumo scandal. And Towers, like Ward, had been accepted in the highest ranks of British society. His story should begin with a brief description of how he initiated and developed his UN call-girl ring.

With so many nations represented at the UN, and so many of them ostensibly marked by Communists for espionage, call-girls and call-girl combines were always suspected through the years of preying on diplomats and aides of the various missions assigned to global headquarters.

The FBI and the police of New York City knew of their existence, but were powerless to act because they have no jurisdiction in the UN itself. And when it came to the activities of the call-girls on the outside, the authorities entertained the greatest reluctance to move in because of the possible embarrassment the action would create for the diplomats.

Harry Towers' prostitution ring appears to have been one of the largest in operation at the UN, and in many ways was typical of them all. It was expertly managed and so adroitly did it transact its illicit business that it took the better part of a dozen years before it was detected.

Towers himself had the perfect "in" at the UN for his operation.

To begin with, Towers was accepted in the highest echelons of American and British enterprise, through his franchise in Great Britain for the TelePrompter Corporation. TelePrompter, a giant industry, has not only installed communications facilities in more than a hundred military bases both in the United States and abroad, but also has been responsible in a large measure for the training of military officers and enlisted personnel in the use of TelePrompter equipment.

Cape Kennedy, the Pentagon, the White House, and the U.S. Navy's European Command Headquarters in London are just a few of the locales where TelePrompter communication systems are supplied and serviced under Government contracts.

TelePrompter also supplies speech-prompting devices, but these are only a small part of the firm's overall business. TelePrompter chiefly develops and rents complex communication facilities.

Yet it was primarily the speech-prompting devices that gave Towers his "in" at the United Nations. This operation was, in fact, a front for Towers, it was the opening or entree to the UN and its diplomats, according to a secret report prepared by the Central Intelligence Agency after an investigation of Towers and his ring of high-priced prostitutes who cavorted between the two continents.

Towers' modus operandi was almost a perfect approach. In his

New York City office Towers employed a coterie of "secretaries" and "typists" who were actually doubling as ladies of the night. His business in New York was technically of a dubious nature, for Towers did not have the franchise in this country to supply the speech-prompting equipment provided by TelePrompter.

According to Irving B. Kahn, who was then the president of TelePrompter, Towers had an agreement with the firm for distribution of its units only throughout England, through the Towers Company of London. Yet Towers managed to extend his dealings into New York by becoming a sort of illicit subcontractor.

Though the terms of his own franchise specified that he could not violate the exclusive territorial rights of franchised distributors in this country by shipping back speech-prompting equipment consigned for England, Towers got around this barrier by obtaining the equipment from a New York supplier. Then, in turn, through his own office set up privately in the city, he was able to solicit United Nations delegates for his services.

Here is a typical sample of the way that Towers ran his business:

A delegate would call Towers' office and ask for a prompting device needed for making a speech either at the General Assembly or at a banquet or some other function. The unit itself is a small, portable, screenlike device which illuminates and at the same time enlarges the words of a script prepared for delivery.

Towers would send one of his girls—the CIA said he had fifteen to twenty girls working for him—to the UN, where she would not only deliver the unit in its carrying case but frequently sit with the delegate and help him in the preparation and typing of his speech. She could also serve as audience of one, giving a delegate her reaction to the speech.

Incidentally, the CIA report showed, the reaction almost always was complimentary.

From this meeting, the CIA went on, there could blossom—and indeed did blossom on innumerable occasions—an after-business-hours friendship that often led to cocktail, dinner, the theater, and finally a night in bed for the "secretary" and the delegate.

Very often Towers himself would go to the UN to deliver a piece of equipment. Those at the UN who remember Towers, and not many have forgotten him, recall that his visits were always engineered to focus prime attention on his arrival and departure, for Towers almost always was accompanied by one or two delectably eye-catching girls.

He was, of course, parading them for surreptitious inspection by the men who craved to wine and dine them in the city's bright nightspots or dimly lit supper clubs, and then, for a usually handsome fee, spend the night with them.

There's little doubt that Towers enriched himself immensely by personally pocketing his cut, probably as much as fifty per cent of the play-for-pay girls' evening fees. But in the light of subsequent evidence there were strong indications that Towers' primary objective may not have been the accumulation of a private fortune, but rather the systematic gathering of secret and vital information for transmission to the Soviet Union's intelligence headquarters in Moscow.

Basic in the case against Towers was the certain knowledge by Western intelligence that the Kremlin never wastes time on a dilettante or a money-hungry procurer. And since Towers was later given refuge behind the Iron Curtain, where he remains to this day, the only allowable conclusion is that Towers was in fact a bona fide agent of the Soviet spy network operating in the United States.

On the basis of his entire record going back to 1950, the CIA concluded that Towers was receiving his instructions directly from the Soviet Mission to the UN. The Russians, according to the CIA, imported many of the call girls from abroad, outfitted them with counterfeit identities, backed by fraudulent documents, frequently quartered them in fashionable apartments paid for by a camouflaged third party, planted juicy gossip among the non-Communist UN diplomats designed to whet their appetites for the lovely ladies, and in dozens of other ways did whatever they could to keep Towers' V-ring functioning at its fullest efficiency.

This, again, is not the author's conclusion but the CIA's.

The CIA further concluded, ruefully that a great many of the UN diplomats became easy marks for the call-girls, with results that will probably never be entirely known. Except that the top-secret files of victimized governments conceivably could tell some sorry tales of trusted servants gone bad under the influence of the kind of sex sold by Harry Towers.

Ironically enough, the development that turned the world spotlight on Soviet sex weaponry in the UN, and for a while raised such a clamorous scandal that even the ultra-dignified U.S. Ambassador Adlai Stevenson was moved to describe it all as a "mad, mad whirl," came about in a routine and little-noticed police arrest on an evening in 1961.

The New York City Vice Squad had been aware of reports of prostitution at the UN, but because of diplomatic immunity and the fact that the United Nations was not physically part of the city, the opportunities for arrests were extremely rare. Moreover, the city police were never able to develop leads that could result in the arrest of the call-girls while in the act of providing their services to non-diplomats.

But the police finally got the lead they were looking for—one of the girls actually was found carrying on beyond the immunity of the UN's gates. The Vice Squad detectives kept the girl under surveillance and at the right moment on the night in question raided an East Side apartment and seized her. A beautiful and shapely blonde, she was booked on a common vice charge. Her paramour, seized in bed with her, was released after promising to testify against her.

Through this girl, and other evidence they gathered, the detectives a short time later arrested Harry Allan Towers as the procurer for the blonde—and a number of other play girls.

From their surveillance, the authorities were able to determine that Towers was the guiding genius of a ring consisting of the fifteen to twenty girls that the CIA told us were involved in the racket. Nearly all of them were foreign born and not too long in the United States.

The spectacularly built blonde taken in the raid turned out to be Maria Novotny. Almost guilelessly she admitted under questioning that she was the niece of Czechoslovakia's President Anton Novotny.

Maria, then nineteen, was held on a morals charge and on a separate count of being a wayward minor.

Towers was held on several counts of procuring, of living off the proceeds of prostitution—in Maria's case alone it amounted to $400 a week, authorities said—and on the more serious charge of importing Maria Novotny into the United States for immoral purposes.

Maria Novotny was placed on probation and Towers' case went before a Federal grand jury because it involved the alleged violation of Federal law—importing an alien into the United States.

The grand jury in short order returned an indictment against the suave international playboy-businessman and he was freed in $10,000 bail to await trial.

Two weeks later, he vanished.

Word of his whereabouts filtered back to the authorities from time to time, placing him variously in London, Prague, and Budapest. But none of the reports was solid, and in any case he was beyond the reach of U.S. officials.

For the most part, the New York City Police Department and the U.S. Attorney's office in New York were content with the status of the case, since with Towers' departure his illegal activities were presumed to have ended.

Then, nearly two years later, the Harry Allan Towers case exploded anew across the headlines of the New York City press with the disclosure that Maria Novotny, Towers' architectural wonder, was connected to the sensational Profumo scandal suddenly rocking Great Britain.

Throughout the Western World at this time, private citizens and public officials at the highest level were intensely absorbed in the almost unbelievable revelations emanating from London.

Tempers flew and sides were quickly drawn as the first accusations were made and hotly denied that War Minister John Profumo was involved in an affair of sorts with a young model and aspiring actress named Christine Keeler.

And when Profumo subsequently admitted his relationship to Christine, the cauldron boiled even more furiously, for Britain found herself with the juiciest sort of scandal to savor, and the entire affair placed in doubt so vital a subject as the nation's security.

The security question was raised by Christine's international appetite for men. By her own admission, Christine Keeler had been sleeping, almost simultaneously, with Soviet diplomat Eugene Ivanov and with Profumo, and in Parliament, in the press, and in every pub in the crowded little island millions were asking the same question:

Did Christine Keeler entice secret information from Profumo and pass it on to Ivanov?

Both Profumo and Christine Keeler insisted there had been no breach of British security, but during the long investigation and the great national debate on the issue enough emerged of a perverse and repulsive nature to cast a pall of shame over much of the country, and to bring about, however fairly or unfairly, the downfall of Sir Harold Macmillan's Government.

It was during that crimson period that the names of Mandy Rice Davies, Christine Keeler, and the tragic Stephen Ward, who later committed suicide, burst into the consciousness of the world.

And it was during that time, too, that Maria Novotny emerged anew.

Investigators checking into Eugene Ivanov's background discovered that he had been intimate with Maria after meeting her at a London cocktail party in 1960, a year before she came to America as part of Harry Towers' stable of UN call-girls.

This disclosure triggered new investigations of the Harry Towers case both in Washington and New York. The new probes took on greater urgency when, almost at the same time, word reached New York in June, 1963, that Towers was in Prague and was being given the VIP treatment by none other than Maria's uncle, President Novotny.

And furthermore—that he was socializing with the infamous Martha Dodd Stern and her husband Alfred!

In New York, U.S. Attorney Robert M. Morgenthau Jr. reopened the two-year-old Towers case to determine if there had been any violation of national security.

And in Washington, New York's Republican Senator Kenneth B. Keating moved along parallel lines to submit the case to Congressional probers on the Senate Internal Security Subcommittee.

Keating, a member of the powerful subcommittee, was not only concerned with a possible security breakdown but with the way the entire Towers case had been handled in 1961.

"It is incredible," he said, "that this international mystery man should have been allowed to escape from the United States while under indictment on vice charges."

As official U.S. concern about security deepened, the Immigration and Naturalization Service, the FBI, and the CIA all launched separate inquiries to co-extend what Morgenthau and Keating were already doing.

Yet despite the intensive probes, the two most important witnesses were safely beyond reach. After fleeing New York and forfeiting his $10,000 bail, Towers went first to Copenhagen, then to Moscow for an extended stay, then to Budapest, and finally to Prague.

And Maria, violating her own probation, took on an assumed name and with a forged passport fled to London where she settled down as Mariella Dibbens, wife of Hod Dibbens, an antique dealer twice her age.

In a newspaper interview she gave during the height of the Profumo scandal—reporters particularly wanted to know details about the celebrated London party she had hosted at which a member of a titled family served guests in the role of a slave, wearing nothing more than a mask and an apron—Maria admitted she had slept with Ivanov before his recall to Moscow in December, 1962.

But she said she had quarreled with him over political matters and emphasized that "certainly I was not knowingly part of any blackmailing or spying organization."

However, asked if she thought Harry Towers was a Communist agent, Maria replied, "My own view was that he was, but not in the accepted sense." She refused to discuss Towers further.

Although perhaps the most notorious of the UN good-time girls, Maria Novotny was far from being the only one suspected of trading sex for secrets.

The reopening of the Novotny-Towers case cast a bright spotlight on call-girl activities at the UN. Probers moved in on the rapidly mushrooming vice scandal and uncovered a number of other playmates linked to Towers' ring.

Chief player in the cast was a voluptuous Yugoslavian girl who had been granted political asylum in the United States after leaving Castro's Cuba. The girl arrived in New York City on May 19, 1960, and went to work as an instructor at an East Side school for prospective debutantes.

But probers on the second go-round found out about her connection with the old Towers vice ring and exposed her—as the madame of the UN play-girls. She promptly lost her job with the school. A short time later she skipped town.

Morgenthau's investigators also tracked down another charming international lady—an employe at the UN, it turned out, who doubled as a pleasure girl for Towers. A Peruvian, the girl had worked at the United Nations until 1962 as an interpreter and secretary. She, too, disappeared when the investigation waxed hot.

A secret Government report obtained by James D. Horan, Assistant Managing Editor, and Dom Frasca, reporter, of the *New York Journal-American,* gave an extensive rundown on the activities of these two girls. The information, gleaned from a witness and quoted by the investigator in his official report, went like this:

> He [the witness] explained it was his impression that the Yugoslavian girl controlled the Peruvian girl as well as other girls . . .
>   He stated that Miss ——— provided him with several names of girls. These girls were provided for the express purpose of prostitution with persons at the UN. . . .

The report showed that the Yugoslavian girl, the madame of Towers' ring, was born on September 9, 1932, and that she went from her native land to Cuba in February, 1955, on tour as a singer.

Eventually she applied for Cuban citizenship, but changed her mind finally and came to the United States.

"The subject then sought and was granted political asylum in the United States in order to be able to work here," the report stated.

A further aspect of the investigation was the discovery that another alien party-girl of the Towers ring had a globe-trotting Russian deliver a recording she had made from New York to an unnamed person in Hungary. When questioned about this delivery by Immigration agents, the girl said simply, "It was a message for my mother."

Though lacking jurisdiction, Immigration nevertheless took steps to stop—or at least censor—such records being sent behind the Iron Curtain. But she never attempted it again.

"We don't care how innocent this girl's message might have been," an Immigration man said. "It's the shocking potential of espionage that shakes us up."

Also a subject of the investigation was the movements of still another European call-girl who assertedly provided UN personnel in New York with her favors. This girl was detected making two trips a year to Berne, Switzerland, where it was found a "contact" would hand over to her $10,000 in currency each time.

In what was described as "a reversal of usual call-girl tactics," the prostitute was bringing the money back to New York and delivering it to "a person or persons unknown."

The suspicion among CIA and FBI agents was that the money was being handed over to a member of the Soviet Delegation to the UN.

Perhaps no case involving kiss-and-collect girls brought more prominence to the problem of prostitution at the UN than the arrest on June 20, 1963, of Mrs. Evelyn "Yvonne" Davis, an attractive thirty-three-year-old brunet possessed of some exceptional physical proportions.

Yvonne, as everyone called her, had unrestricted entry to the UN with a temporary press card that had been issued to her on the basis of her claim that she was a correspondent for the *Filipino American News,* a monthly paper with offices at 202 West 40th Street in Manhattan.

During her comings and goings, observers of the UN scene noted that she soon became a jolly and familiar figure in the lounge where the diplomats relax—and that she often brought along a retinue of jolly girlfriends. It was further noted that while Yvonne no doubt had the ability to compose journalistic prose, she wasn't very active as a writer.

Actually, Yvonne had other interests, too. Up in Suite 1047 of the Shelton Towers Hotel at 525 Lexington Avenue, at 49th Street, Yvonne maintained an office of sorts equipped with market charts, investment tomes, an executive desk, a dictaphone, a typewriter—and a comfortable bed.

She justified the presence of all this equipment with a listing in the phonebook as Shareholders Research Inc. And she further validated the setup by registering herself with the Securities and Exchange Commission as an investment broker.

Yvonne became an outstanding inspirational example to her sex when the Greater New York Citizens Forum conferred its "Brains and Beauty" citation upon her. Moreover, the *American Banner,*

an austere journal, nominated her as the "Prettiest Stockholder."
That last honor accrued to Yvonne because of her consistent
attendance at the annual stockholders meetings of such giants of
American enterprise as U.S. Steel, Corn Exchange Bank, Guaran-
ty Trust, Irving Trust, Chase Manhattan, Chemical Corn, and
others.

It always seemed that when Yvonne attended the meetings, she
had to raise some kind of hell. That attracted the attention not
only of the staid bulls and bears of Wall Street, but also on occasion the man on the street, who read about Yvonne's antics in the
local press.

For one reason or another, Yvonne came to the attention of
Police Commissioner Michael Murphy's Confidential Squad one
day early in June of 1963 and it was decided she would bear some
watching. The information ultimately accumulated on Yvonne
went into a report and what it showed wasn't exactly what one ex-
pects to find in the Dow Jones averages.

Plainclothes Patrolman Donald Smith, of the Confidential
Squad, was then assigned to verify whether, as suspected, Yvonne
was extending her services into other areas beside journalism and
finance. The department had heard reports that when the market
was depressed Yvonne also worked as a public stenographer,
among other things.

His voice more like a wolf than a bear, Patrolman Smith phoned
Yvonne at the Shelton Towers and wondered if she could do
some typing for him. Yvonne, police said, immediately quoted her
rates: a minimum of $20 for twenty pages, and at least $50 for fifty pages.

Yvonne wasn't giving discount rates even on the big jobs. In
fact, if the assignment were involved, she said the account might
even have to take her out to dinner.

At 3:25 on the afternoon of June 20th, a Thursday, Patrolman
Smith went up to Yvonne's. He said that after a brief conversation he settled on the $20 "typing" job and that Yvonne prompt-
ly disrobed and walked around the room. Smith then pulled out
his badge and arrested her.

In Women's Court the following week, Patrolman Smith testified at Yvonne's trial on charges of offering to commit lewd and
indecent acts, and prostitution.

Some of Yvonne's background came out at the trial—she was

born in Holland, the daughter of a Dutch doctor; she had spent most of her childhood in Maryland and the District of Columbia, and had taken courses in business administration and psychology at George Washington University.

She was also a divorcee, she revealed, explaining:

"I've been pretty lucky in the market—not too lucky in love."

It also came out in court that Yvonne had been arrested in Los Angeles back in 1951 for "offering," although she did not specify what. She paid a $25 fine at that time.

Yvonne was convicted but the mercy of the court prevailed. Judge Abraham M. Roth gave her thirty days, but suspended sentence when she agreed to stick to all her other activities except the one that had brought her before the bar of justice. She agreed.

Yvonne's arrest and the resultant purple publicity in the newspapers prompted Secretary General U Thant to command an investigation of his "relevant department," as he put it. Thant didn't specify what department was "relevant" to the embarrassing situation but it was later learned that his own police force, headed by Frank M. Begley, chief of Buildings Management Service, which is the overseer of UN safety and security, had begun the UN's self-investigation.

Thant felt the heat of the scandal on June 28th when a Vietnamese correspondent for *La Vérité de Cambodia* and *L'Echo de Pnumpeth*, addressed him about the situation. The journalist, Tran Van Ky, declared:

"Mr. Secretary General, I think that you must have been informed by your OPI [Office of Public Information] about the stories published on the front pages of some New York newspapers concerning the investigation made by the FBI on certain female activities . . . "

His face contorted by perplexity, Thant interrupted.

"What kind of activities? What was that word?"

"Certain female activities among delegations inside the UN Headquarters," Tran Van Ky shot back.

"Yesterday a newspaper with the widest circulation carried another story that I read with a deep feeling of shame, a shame that I am sure is shared by my colleagues, a story of an accredited United Nations woman correspondent arrested for prostitution.

"There is now such an atmosphere of suspicion in the delegates' lounge, North and South, that some delegates and members of the press corps do not want to invite some of their distinguished female guests to the second floor."

Then the correspondent put it right up to Thant.

"Could you tell us now or perhaps at a later date what steps you intend to take, as an investigation committee, for example, to look into the matter?"

Still committed to surprise and shock, Thant replied simply:

"This particular matter was brought to my attention yesterday and I immediately asked the head of the relevant department to examine the case and submit a comprehensive report. So far, I have not received the report. I expect to have one today. For the moment, I am not in a position to indicate what line of action I propose to take."

The Secretary General also was asked why the FBI had been permitted to investigate inside the UN. U Thant replied somberly:

"I have no indication of FBI involvement at the United Nations."

Actually, the FBI had looked into Yvonne Davis' case for one primary reason—to determine whether there was any possible connection with espionage activity. It found none. But it did not cross the boundary of First Avenue into the UN to find out. The agents did their investigating on the outside.

Almost at once after the Davis case there was a noticeable tightening of security at the UN. Guards cracked down on every pretty woman who walked into the building—even those employed there.

One young secretary, usually even-tempered, was almost in a tantrum when a guard asked her for identification. She spilled half the contents of a big purse before she found her card.

"After all these years here," she protested.

"Can't help it, ma'am," the guard apologized. "I'm new here. I don't know you, and I have my orders."

Another pretty secretary who usually dropped into the delegates' lounge for a cocktail after work, went straight down to the main floor.

"Aren't you stopping for a martini?" inquired a reporter who knew the girl.

"No, I'm not. I feel too self-conscious in the lounge now. All those men looking at you, and you know just what they're wondering."

But the prostitution activities alone were not what had the UN officials in a dither. The odors wafting from the Profumo case in London brought all-too-real portents regarding security to the forefront.

The revelations about Harry Towers, Maria Novotny, the Yugoslavian and Hungarian girls, and all the other stinging episodes of sex at the UN, launched a general public concern about the extent to which the "ladies of the corridors" might have been involved in espionage.

In Washington the chagrin stemming from the revelations in New York was further reflected by Representative H. R. Gross (Republican-Iowa), a senior member of the House Foreign Affairs Committee.

"I am shocked at this situation," he declared. "I think my committee should look into the situation. The UN has been a spawning ground for spies and just about everything else.

"Using V-girls as spies adds another twist . . . and the United States is footing most of the bill."

The Congressman wondered what Ambassador Stevenson had to say now—now that the facts were better known about the girls' activities at the global headquarters. Stevenson had been questioned by the committee a month before about the "girls of the corridor" and he had denied knowing of their existence.

With a deep blush, Stevenson had parried with Congressman Gross during a hearing on proposed changes in the UN Participation Act. Gross, self-appointed watchdog over Government spending, started a digression from the subject being discussed, Stevenson's plea for a housing allowance for U.S. delegates to the UN. Stevenson had said the money was needed to offset entertainment expenses "in New York, the most expensive city in the world."

Gross cited a recent magazine article that painted the UN as a "dazzling, frenetic, an exotic social whirl."

"What about those ladies of the corridor that we hear so much about?" Gross demanded to know.

"That's an aspect of the work with which I'm not familiar," Stevenson retorted with a laugh.

But Stevenson did concede that the UN social whirl is "excessive." He said that he himself was invited to three or four affairs a day, but could find time to attend only one or two.

"The burden of being the host nation puts an added load not only on myself but the entire U.S. delegation."

Stevenson suggested to the committee that it give the twenty-man U.S. Delegation a housing allowance so members would have the facilities to entertain at home. Stevenson further suggested a budget of $50,000 to $60,000 a year for such purposes.

Meanwhile, on June 30th, with only a few days to dig into the revelations about call-girl activities, the probers reported back to Thant, who then revealed the findings through a spokesman:

"Rumors of a call-girl ring being operated are unfounded as far as the Secretariat is concerned.

"However, we cannot speak for the many delegations in the UN. The delegations hold parties outside the control of the Secretariat."

Thant had more or less indicated his helplessness as Secretary General to cope with such activities at the UN.

Normally, men who avail themselves of the pleasures provided by call-girls, are merely satisfying a natural desire, a bit of harmless fun, as many would concede. But in the case of diplomats there is always the danger of a spy trap, as both fiction and fact have told us repeatedly.

It's no secret at the UN that mingled with the serious and dedicated diplomats there are a number of gay blades who have no hesitancy in letting it be known that they have a fancy for fast women. Few of these harbor any qualms about bringing their shapely companions to the UN and parading them around the lounges and corridors.

Over the years there have been striking blonds, stunning brunets, and glamorous redheads who have cavorted around the UN with seeming immunity despite the rule that visitors are not permitted to promenade about the premises.

Yet these women have attained a sort of immunity, a carte blanche to come and go as they please, because they have been sanctioned for admittance by their diplomatically accredited "sugar daddies." That privilege leaves the guards and security officials powerless to crack down, for such action would only prompt the diplomat to raise a howl with the Secretary General.

It isn't the UN's business either to pry into the private activities of diplomats or their girlfriends. But it does make things rough for the security force trying to spot the dames who don't have any business there—the ones who are soliciting.

It has been an open secret at the UN that a few diplomats and staff employes maintain love nests in apartments around town. The risk of entrapment by espionage operatives is considered somewhat greater for these playboys, for no one can be certain who the kept woman is or what she is really up to.

The very location of the United Nations in the heart of a great city that harbors more entertainment activity than any metropolis in the world creates a climate that can easily tempt a man to gravitate into the "mad, mad whirl" Ambassador Stevenson described.

The establishment of the United Nations on First Avenue has given real estate values a tremendous boost and where once stood old-law tenements and decrepit lofts, there are now magnificent, towering new apartments and glass-walled business buildings.

One of the more beguiling attractions in many of these new structures is the formal cocktail lounge, generally with its entrance at street level. Many of these places on the perimeter of United Nations Plaza have become the hunting ground for callgirls out looking to connect with a free-spending diplomat or playboy with UN accreditation. One needs little imagination to guess what happens once they meet.

The call-girl snaring a diplomat who winds up with his shoes under her bed for the night is no danger to the security of any nation. The danger comes only when a play-for-pay girl is out for bigger stakes, such as those the authorities believe the Harry Allan Towers ring was after.

What makes it all so frightening is that we don't know precisely what connection there really was between Towers and his ladies of pleasure—and the Soviet Union.

Chapter 18

The Chicago Adventurer
Who Gave U.S. Passports to the USSR

All the training the KGB gives its candidates for espionage would be as worthless as a Siberian snowflake if they were not properly equipped upon graduation as agents with one of the most important tools of their trade—a passport.

To the KGB, a valid United States passport, and an identity to go with it, is worth considerably more than its weight in gold. For with that combination, any agent who has been thoroughly oriented in the nature and habits of Americans and taught to speak, to think, and to act like a native of this country, can be inserted into the United States as a spy—and we'd never know it.

We are dealing now with the "master" or "illegal" spy, who is dispatched here to work, independently of "legal" conspirators, from a cell or command post as inconspicuous as an export firm or as innocent as the small shop of an antique dealer. His most vital concern must be to conceal his identity at all costs, and the U.S. passport is his principal means of proving who he really isn't.

When the KGB inserts an agent into the United States, he arrives with a carefully memorized *legend*—a highly refined and totally detailed story—of his identity and background. In most instances, these stories fit the names and family histories of real Americans. The authorities say they have no way of determining just how many Soviet agents are operating in this country today with forged passports and the borrowed identities of legitimate U.S. citizens.

The FBI has had far less success in unmasking "illegal" spies because of the very nature of their modus operandi. The "legal" spy is easier to spot because he is usually an accredited diplomat or consular clerk assigned to the United Nations or the Soviet Embassy in Washington. His identity is known and he can be watched—as the FBI often does.

The classic example of the "illegal" spy was Colonel Rudolph Ivanovich Abel of the Soviet Military Intelligence, who was arrested by the FBI in 1957 after long years of espionage activity behind the facade of a small photography business in Brooklyn and the highly effective pose of his assumed name, Emil R. Goldfus.

He was unmasked only because a fellow Soviet spy, Reino Hayhanen, had too much to drink and blurted out the truth about the seemingly innocuous Brooklyn photographer. Hayhanen himself had entered the United States on October 21, 1952, under the name of Eugene Maki, an American born in Idaho in 1919 who as a child was taken by his parents to live in their native Estonia. Hayhanen entered the United States with a valid American passport that had been issued to "Eugene Maki."

Besides buttressing the activities of the "legal" spies, the main function of "illegal" agents is to be prepared to take over the subversive machinery in event of war or any other emergency that would precipitate a severing of diplomatic relations—and a thorough housecleaning of "legal" spies.

Therefore, possession of a U.S. passport is truly something the Russians desire. Even if they are not prepared to send one of their spies over on a stolen or misappropriated passport, mere possession of the document would be extremely valuable, for it would give the KGB samples of our special inks, distinctive watermarked papers, and the latest signatures used on such valid documents that provide the wherewithal to cross our borders. With a sample passport, they could even forge their own!

With this knowledge very much in their awareness, FBI agents in Chicago had more than a mere passing interest in a report that reached them a few days before Christmas of 1962 . . .

"Hey, I think I've been a party to a fraud," the voice came over the telephone to one of the agents in the FBI's Chicago office. "Some guy had me take out a passport on the promise that he was going to get me a job in South America . . . I also gave him $5. And you know what—I haven't seen him since."

In and of itself the report did not alarm the agent—until the caller mentioned that at least a dozen other persons had also taken out passports and paid the man $5 apiece on his word that he would obtain employment for them with a construction firm in Bogota, Colombia.

The agent made arrangements to meet the informant at his home in Joliet, about thirty-five miles southwest of Chicago and the seat of Will County.

At two o'clock on the afternoon of December 23rd, the agent was ushered into a modestly furnished one-family dwelling and shown to an armchair in the living room. The G-man sat down and listened to the same story he had heard on the phone. But in far greater detail.

"I saw an ad in the Joliet paper sometime last month," the man, a construction worker, began. "It told about a construction company looking for people to work on a project in South America, and it invited anybody who was interested to meet a representative of the firm in a room in the Hotel Woodruff . . . "

When he went there, the man said, he found others in the room being "interviewed" by a tall, balding, mustached "hiring agent" who identified himself as Mr. Meyer.

"He told us that the first order of business was for us to obtain passports. None of us had passports, so he told us to apply for them at the State Department office in Chicago. He said that once they were issued, we were to bring them back to him so he could complete arrangements for our jobs in Bogota. We were going to get free transportation down there and free lodgings, he told us."

The man went on to tell the FBI agent that he was issued his passport some three weeks later and that he brought the document back to Meyer at the Woodruff.

"I saw some of the other guys who were with me that first day," the informant went on to say. "Meyer took the passports and also collected $5 from each of us. He said the money was to pay for getting us visas for Colombia."

But none of the applicants for the jobs in Latin America heard from Meyer after he took their passports and cash. As the FBI agent would learn later, some of the victims of the conspiracy had phoned or written to the State Department asking what happened to their passports—and to Mr. Meyer.

The information the FBI agent gathered from this informant helped launch an immediate investigation, which quickly led to the files of the State Department in Chicago and a trackdown of all persons who had taken out passports in the preceding month. The search was greatly facilitated because applications must list the country or countries a person requesting a passport proposes to visit. Agents found fifteen applications that listed Bogota, Colombia, as a destination—and they immediately sought those persons for questioning.

One was the man who had tipped off the FBI about the scheme. The other fourteen all agreed with the details of the informant's account of how they had been conned by the man who called himself Meyer.

The search for Meyer had been under way long before the interviews with his victims were completed. Agents went in search of the accused confidence man within two hours after the G-man had spoken to the informant in his Joliet home.

Their first step was to check the hotel registration, which turned up the name of Paul Carl Meyer with a Chicago address.

Before many more hours passed, the G-men had determined that Paul Carl Meyer was a real person—and obviously the man who had made off with the fifteen passports. But they had no immediate clue as to Meyer's whereabouts. They did not yet know that their quarry was well out of their reach—three thousand miles away in Madrid, Spain.

They learned where Meyer was only after they had concluded a thorough investigation into his background and movements which shaped this portrait of the twenty-two-year-old Chicago-born son of a maintenance worker:

He had attended Chicago public schools and Maine East High

School in suburban Park Ridge, which he quit in 1957 after his junior year. An examination of school records showed that he was a D student or, as the dean of students put it, "just an average boy of slightly below average performance."

Further investigation revealed that Meyer had gone to live in Ecuador in 1961 and apparently prospected for minerals. When he returned to Chicago in 1962, he told friends and relatives that he had also taught English in a Quito school.

And the FBI men also were told that Meyer had fallen in love with an Ecuadorian girl and planned to marry her as soon as he was able to "scrape some money together."

The fifteen passports, the FBI concluded, might provide Meyer with just the nest-egg he was looking for—especially if he could sell them to someone who really treasured proprietorship of so many valid and valuable passports. Like, say, the Russians . . .

What heightened the FBI's suspicions that those passports might indeed be headed toward a Soviet destination was the report in early January from Central Intelligence Agency sources in Madrid, indicating that Meyer had been there in late December. Further investigation showed that he had used his passport to identify himself when he took a room in a hotel in the city, and that he also showed the passport when he cashed travelers checks there.

But the CIA always seemed to be one small step behind Meyer. By the time they had traced him to Madrid, Meyer had taken off for West Berlin. And when our intelligence sleuths pursued his trail to the West German capital, the only trace of him that they found was the evidence that he had showed his U.S. passport once again to cash travelers checks.

The CIA agents lost Meyer's scent at a checkpoint on the Berlin Wall. They had no recourse but to conclude that Meyer had crossed into the Communist zone—and that those passports were on their way into Soviet hands.

That was the last the CIA and the FBI would hear about Meyer for several months. The next time the authorities became aware of his whereabouts was on June 7, 1963, when to their utter amazement Meyer walked into the CIA offices in Washington, identified himself, and said he was prepared to "give you a full confession."

Meyer began by saying that he had decided that the only way he could raise enough money to marry his sweetheart in Ecuador was to obtain U.S. passports in the manner he did and sell them to the Russians.

Everything went off like clockwork, Meyer told his CIA listeners, until he crossed into East Berlin and made his way to the Soviet Embassy.

"Do you know what they told me when I offered to sell them the passports?" Meyer said. "They laughed at me and tried to convince me that they were worthless."

Although they insisted the passports had no value, the Russians tried to talk Meyer into turning them over to them.

"They said I could get into a lot of trouble if I was caught with them," Meyer related. But he refused to do so.

While at the Embassy, Meyer said he was propositioned to become a spy for the Russians. The way they put it to him, Meyer explained, was:

"We want you to cooperate with us concerning political secrets."

"I had no subversive motives and I had no intention of becoming a spy," Meyer went on. "All I wanted was to make some money so I could marry my fiancee."

But if he spied, the Russians told Meyer, he would have his money to wed his sweetheart. For espionage, the Soviets were willing to pay. Perhaps he might earn as much as 2,000 marks ($500) if he did his job well.

What kind of espionage did the Soviets want him to perform in East Berlin? Meyer wanted to know.

Not East Berlin, they told him. West Berlin was where they wanted him to serve. The target, they made it clear to Meyer, was the United States Mission.

What kind of secrets where the Russians looking for?

No reply to that question. First, he was told, he'd have to undergo training in an East Berlin spy school.

Meyer said he was taken to an apartment in the city and after a few lessons was given a camera disguised as a portable radio, which he was also taught to operate.

Then came his assignment.

Go to West Berlin and develop a friendship with an American

girl employed in the American Mission. Once Meyer and the girl were on good terms, she was to take him into the mission where he would photograph the interior of the building—and also any documents he might find.

Meyer followed those orders, but not, he said, in precisely the manner the Soviets had outlined. He found that he couldn't become friendly with the girl they had selected.

"But I got to know another one," he confessed. "Yet I wasn't able to get anywhere when it came to taking pictures of documents."

After he reported his failure to the Soviets in East Berlin, Meyer said, they gave him a new assignment. Now he was to target in on a West German girl employed in the British Mission. But the method he was directed to employ was slightly different from the approach they had mapped for the unproductive conspiracy with the American girl.

"They told me that I was to blackmail the West German girl," Meyer asserted.

Evidently the Russians had something on their intended victim—that she maintained two apartments, one for conducting an illicit romance.

When Meyer approached the girl and, following orders, told her that Communist agents knew about her clandestine love nest, she capitulated to his demands for secret British documents. She promised to deliver them to Meyer.

But, Meyer insisted, the documents never changed hands because the place where they had agreed to make contact was too crowded.

"I swear I never delivered a single document of any kind to the Russians," Meyer said.

Now the CIA wanted to know what had become of the passports Meyer had offered to sell at the Soviet Embassy.

"They took them," Meyer said. "They convinced me finally that it was too risky for me to have them and that the best thing I could do was to turn them over to them. And that's what I did."

How much did they pay him, Meyer was asked?

"Nothing for the passports," Meyer assured the CIA. But he admitted that he was compensated with the $500 they had promised to pay him for his work as a spy. Meyer said he received the money piecemeal over the ten weeks that he engaged in subversion.

There was one last question that the CIA had to ask of Meyer—why did he decide to make a clean breast of his role in espionage?

"Because I thought it was my duty to do so," he replied.

The CIA then turned Meyer over to the FBI in Washington and he repeated his story without any significant variations during a lengthy interrogation by the G-men.

Officially it was now a Justice Department case. And the logical next step that should have been taken was to place Paul Carl Meyer under FBI arrest, bring him to Chicago, and have the United States Attorney seek an indictment for fraud and violations of the passport laws, as well as espionage.

But no such thing happened. Paul Carl Meyer walked out of the FBI offices in the Justice Department Building into the bright afternoon sunshine of that June day in 1963—a free man.

A month later, Meyer answered the Chicago Draft Board's callup and went into the Army as a private. At about that time, too, he sent for his sweetheart, Yolanda, in Ecuador and they were married. In September of that year, Yolanda announced to her husband that she was going to have a baby.

Almost a year to the day after he began his Army service, Mrs. Meyer presented her husband with a daughter, Lucia. Within a matter of weeks, the Army handed Meyer an honorable discharge at Fort Knox, Kentucky, for "dependency reasons" and allowed him to return to his wife and baby.

Meyer settled down with his family in a small furnished flat on Addison Street near Cicero Avenue in Chicago and got a job as a truck driver for a Northwest Side newspaper distribution agency. And for the next six months, Meyer continued to live what seemed like a normal, routine existence.

But it wasn't all that normal and routine in the absolute sense, for everywhere Meyer went—he was shadowed. The FBI maintained a twenty-four hour vigil over him from the day he was returned to civilian status and went to live in Chicago. Late in the afternoon of February 1, 1965, they observed Meyer and his wife carrying their belongings out of the apartment building and loading them into their car.

They trailed them through heavy rush-hour traffic to a modest two-story stucco dwelling at 4031 North Pulaski Road and watched the couple carry their possessions into the house. It was an innocent adventure—all the Meyers had done was to move to a new and better apartment.

Paul Carl Meyer was still living a normal and routine life and he was looking forward to an even more promising future now that he had moved his family into more commodious accommodations.

But time was running out on his freedom. That very afternoon, as he settled into his new apartment, a Federal grand jury in Chicago returned a four-count indictment of violating a Federal law that prohibits the use or delivery of passports to persons other than those to whom they were issued. Meyer was specifically accused by the jury of delivering the fifteen passports to "representatives of the Soviet Union in East Berlin sometime in February, 1963."

The indictment was handed up to Judge Julius J. Hoffman in Federal District Court and a warrant for Meyer's arrest was issued immediately. An FBI agent—one of the several G-men who had been trailing Meyer over the past year—was sent to take him in custody.

But the agent met some unexpected resistance from a most improbable barrier—Meyer's new landlady, Mrs. Joseph Ernst.

"I didn't want to let him in even though he showed me his credentials," Mrs. Ernst explained later. "I thought they might be phony. So he left his card and I was to call back. I never did."

Mrs. Ernst said that she had taken a liking to Meyer and his wife from the moment she first set eyes on them when they responded to her want ad in a Chicago newspaper for the $95-a-month second-floor apartment. She said she had listened to their tale of woe about needing an apartment desperately and consented to let them move in even before the gas could be turned on in Chicago's subzero weather.

"Their baby was sick yesterday and I helped the mother take care of the little girl since they didn't have their gas on yet. My husband and I figured that if nobody gives them a break they won't get started. Her husband seemed so nice and polite . . . "

But Mrs. Ernst and her husband apparently weren't the only

persons who felt Paul Carl Meyer deserved to be given a *break*. The FBI had given Meyer what appeared to have all the earmarks of a *break* when they turned him away after he confessed his role in the passport fraud and his involvement in attempted espionage against the U.S. Mission in West Berlin. He was left unmolested—but not unwatched—for some twenty months. He was given the opportunity to fulfill his commitment to the draft, to marry the girl he loved, and to start a family.

But it wasn't because the FBI had a soft heart for Paul Carl Meyer that he was allowed such unprecedented freedom. Not at all. The FBI had decided to play a cat-and-mouse game with Meyer in the expectation that he might again try to obtain passports for delivery to the Russians—or even engage in espionage activity in this country.

But Meyer had walked the straight and narrow for every day of his twenty months of freedom. When the FBI decided further surveillance of the suspect was unlikely to yield any new shades of subversion, the case was turned over to D. Arthur Connelly, chief of the Criminal Division of the U.S. Attorney's office in Chicago.

That decision was made in Washington by U.S. Attorney General Nicholas R. de Katzenbach.

Connelly took the case to the grand jury and asked for an indictment against Meyer only on the passport fraud. The prosecutor made no effort to prefer charges against the suspect for espionage. The mystery of why the Government declined to seek prosecution on such charges lingers to this day, and the questions that were raised in the wake of the headlines the case created still cry for answers.

Meyer admitted he had conspired with the Soviets to photograph the U.S. Mission and whatever documents he might have found there. Though he insisted that no overt act of espionage had been committed, the mere fact that he had agreed to work as a spy for the Soviet Union—and was paid for services rendered—constituted a clear-cut act of subversion.

CIA agents are known to have spoken with the American girl whom Meyer had singled out to help him gain access to the U.S. Mission. But there was no indication of what she told them and her identity was never disclosed.

In any event, Meyer was indicted for illegal possession and distribution of U.S. passports—and the FBI couldn't take the defendant into custody because of a balky landlady.

The problem was solved the next afternoon when Deputy United States Marshals Robert A. Phillips and Robert E. Cauley went to the residence on Chicago's Northwest Side and ran into Meyer on the front porch just as he was leaving for some shopping in the supermarket.

He appeared stunned when Phillips and Cauley told him he was under arrest.

"Please let me tell my wife," he begged the marshals. They accompanied him upstairs and he explained to Yolanda in Spanish what was happening. She became hysterical and the marshals had to stand by patiently until Meyer calmed her down.

Then Meyer was driven to the Federal District Court and brought before Judge Hoffman for arraignment. The four-count indictment was read in court and no plea was taken from Meyer until he had time to obtain an attorney. The judge set bail of $2,500 and when Meyer was unable to make arrangements immediately to post the bond, he was ordered jailed.

Meanwhile, well-timed simultaneous announcements of Meyer's arrest were made in Chicago by U.S. Attorney Edward V. Hanrahan and in Washington by Attorney General Katzenbach. Both pronouncements were masterpieces of brevity and classics of understatement.

"The passports were real and they were issued to real people," declared Katzenbach after a bare-bones explanation of the counts in the indictment. But he would not say how Meyer had obtained the passports or how he delivered them to the Russians.

"The indictment stems from an extensive investigation conducted by the FBI," Katzenbach went on to say, making no mention of the fact that Meyer had turned himself in to the CIA more than twenty months before. If the Attorney General had let that cat out of the bag, how would he explain why it took all that time to indict Meyer—without revealing that the FBI had purposely allowed him his freedom so they could keep him under surveillance?

There was a similar paucity of information from Hanrahan in Chicago, who stood before reporters and said:

"The passports had been delivered to apparently some kind of an installation in East Berlin. Our investigators here have no information beyond that on the circumstances under which the passports had been delivered."

It is inconceivable that the U.S. Attorney, who had obtained the indictment against Meyer on the strength of his detailed confession to the CIA and FBI, could face newsmen and tell them so little about a case that was already clearly spelled out in the indictment, very much a public record.

Hanrahan was asked a series of questions and his responses, each of them, were paragons of insignificancy.

"Were Meyer's motives political?" a reporter for the *Chicago Sun-Times* asked.

"I don't know what his politics are," replied Hanrahan noncommittally.

"Was he paid for the passports?" a newsman from the *Chicago Daily News* wanted to know.

"The Government doesn't know whether Meyer was paid for the passports," the prosecutor responded. He made no mention of the fact that Meyer, in his confessions, had denied ever receiving compensation for the passports.

"Is Meyer a Communist?" asked a reporter for the *Chicago Tribune*.

"I don't know whether he was a Communist or a Communist sympathizer," Hanrahan said.

But the U.S. Attorney did volunteer one significant bit of information.

"Meyer was a sole entrepreneur," said Hanrahan. "There is no indication of an espionage ring involved."

It wasn't until the next day that the real story came out—and it tumbled from the lips of the very man accused of disposing of the passports to the Soviet Union.

"No, I didn't sell the passports," Meyer said as he left Federal Court following his arraignment and release in $2,500 bond. "I gave them to them for nothing."

Then came this eye-opening statement from Meyer:

"They didn't arrest me. They didn't know anything about what I had done until I went to the CIA and the FBI and told them the whole story . . . "

Earlier, in court, Meyer's attorney, Raymond L. Suekoff, an old family friend, went before the bench and told Judge Hoffman that Meyer had gone voluntarily to the CIA and FBI in Washington "the day after he returned from Europe and made a full disclosure of all the information that is in this indictment."

Suekoff also let it be known that his client was allowed his freedom after his confession, that he served in the Army for a year, and that he had settled down to domestic tranquility for some seven months before the Government finally decided to nail him on the passport charges.

Among those in court that day was Meyer's father, Edward, who commented:

"Paul is a good boy but always has been an adventurer. He was a Boy Scout, too, and a good one."

Suekoff added:

"Paul realizes he made a very serious mistake. I think he is a good subject for probation. He has a wife and child. I have known his family for ten years and never have known him to be in trouble before."

But still there was no answer to the key questions in the case:

• Why was Meyer turned away by the FBI after he had confessed his role in the passport scandal?
• Why was he permitted to serve in the Army?
• Why did it take the Government twenty months to bring about his indictment?

But the biggest question of all—why Meyer wasn't charged with espionage because of his service as a Soviet spy—was not raised until twenty-three days later. That was on February 3rd, when he appeared in court for sentencing on his guilty plea to the passport charges.

Judge Hoffman was the first to stand up to the Government's seemingly kid-glove treatment of Meyer and to call the shots the way he saw them.

"I read the FBI's statement and I wondered if there should not have been an additional count on the indictment of a much more serious nature," he said.

Hoffman, of course, was referring to Meyer's admitted role as a paid spy for the ten weeks he spent in Germany, hopscotching between East and West Berlin in his efforts to gather information for the Russians from the United States and British Missions.

The judge's statement had been precipitated by an impassioned plea from Suekoff for leniency for his client, inasmuch as he had come forward and made a clean breast of his involvement with the Kremlin in subversive activities.

"He had no subversive motives," Suekoff had said. "He was merely trying to get money to marry the girl he loved in Ecuador."

Suekoff suggested to the court that Meyer should be released on probation.

But the judge said he couldn't be that lenient.

"I must assume I am dealing with a dangerous man," Hoffman stated. "He engaged in a dangerous plot, dealing with an enemy of our country—an enemy as recent as the morning paper."

The judge refused to consider Suekoff's view that Meyer had engaged in a "childish prank" and, still insisting that the Government should have clobbered him with more serious charges, proceeded to pass sentence.

He gave Meyer a total of two years to serve in jail, a term that in no way reflected the judge's seeming concern and his own characterization of the defendant as a "dangerous man."

Hoffman had the law on his side. He could have thrown the book at Meyer and sentenced him to a total of twenty years in prison and levied a fine of $8,000. But the court invoked only a tenth of the sentence it could have imposed and none of the monetary penalties that were within its province to assess.

Nothing in the case made sense even though it had now been disposed of in court. Only what Prosecutor Connelly, the chief of the Criminal Division, had to say after Meyer had been led away in handcuffs to begin serving his sentence appeared to shape an outline of logic.

"The Government," said Connelly, "is satisfied that Meyer did not supply the Russians with any important information. If we weren't satisfied on that point, we would have indicted him for espionage, which carries the death penalty . . . "

Then, finally and at last, Connelly told reporters the details of the case from its inception—how Meyer recruited the fifteen Chicago-area residents for jobs in Bogota, got them to apply for passports that they turned over to him, and his flight to Spain, then Berlin where he hooked up with the Russians, worked for them as a spy, turned over the passports to them, and finally came home to make a clean breast of it with the authorities.

Through his own investigation since the case was wrapped up in 1965, the author has learned why the FBI released Meyer after his confession to them. The reasons have already been spelled out in this narrative—the FBI wanted to discover whether Meyer was still involved in espionage.

But there are still a number of unanswered questions, chief of which is why Meyer was let off the hook for espionage.

Yet that is the name of the game. We find the Government repeatedly coddling spies on both sides of an espionage conspiracy—our traitors and their subverters.

It is significant to note, in this year of 1973, that not one of the more than two hundred Soviet and Iron Curtain-country spies who have been arrested or accused of espionage is lodged in any of our jails. None ever spent any time worth mentioning in prison.

And less than a half-dozen of our own conspirators are behind bars today.

For all the millions upon millions of dollars that have been budgeted year in and year out by the FBI in the war against espionage, for all the thousands of man-hours spent in pursuit of spies, and for all the remarkable solutions rendered by the G-men in cracking so many hundreds of cases of subversion—we show a pitiful record when it comes to punishing the people who have committed treason against this country.

Top (*left to right*): William E. Dodd, U.S. Ambassador to Nazi Germany; millionaire Alfred K. Stern, son-in-law of Ambassador Dodd; Martha Dodd, Stern's wife and Ambassador Dodd's daughter. Martha and Alfred cushioned their flight from the U.S. with over $1,250,000.

Below (*left to right*): The late J. Edgar Hoover, FBI chief; Peter and Helen Kroger, in reality Morris and Lona Cohen. Their true identities were unmasked by the author.

Top (*left to right*): George and Jane Foster Zlatovski. He was an OSS lieutenant and she wheedled vital secrets; Lavrenti Beria, the Kremlin's dreaded secret police chief.

Below (*left to right*): Mark Zborowski, Harvard researcher and sometime Soviet Secret Police agent; Paul C. Meyer, passport king of Chicago.

Left: U Thant, former UN Secretary General.

ght: L. Patrick Gray III, former Acting rector of the FBI.

Top: Sergei M. Kudryavtsev, head of Moscow's spy ring in Canada.
Center: Embassy of the USSR, Washington, D.C.
Below: V. I. Markelov, who escaped punishment for his spy activities.

Top (*left to right*): Jack and Myra Soble, Red spies extraordinary; Harry Alan Towers, TV executive and alleged procurer. Below (*left to right*): Leonard J. Stafford and Ulysses L. Harris, the sergeants who goofed as spies.

Left: Maria Novotny, the beautiful niece of the President of Czechoslovakia; Right: (with hat), Dr. Robert Soblen, who cheated justice with an overdose of drugs.

Part III

The Kremlin Coup that Ranged from the Bronx to Old Bailey

Chapter 19

From a Football Field to Nuclear Sub Espionage

It didn't seem to be such a big story when Great Britain arrested five Red spies and charged them with the theft of key United States-NATO atomic-submarine defense secrets. After all, the stage for that drama appeared to be three thousand miles across the Atlantic. Here at home we had so many other stories to command our attention that the goings-on in London were being handled as routine news.

That's the way matters stood just after midnight on Thursday, February 9, 1961, in the City Room of the *New York Journal-American*. The office was aglow in a brilliant bath of fluorescent light and everyone on the midnight shift—reporters and rewrite men, copy editors, makeup men, copy boys—was on the job. I was there, too. I was Night City Editor.

As always, everyone plowed into the first order of business—drinking coffee brewed on a portable electric stove by our copy chief, Israel "Ko" Kohansov, who had won many Hearst Newspaper awards for headline writing, but could never take a prize for the gook he percolated and passed off as coffee.

The second order of business was to read the morning papers. Rewrite men, copy editors, and others on the staff read the news in the *Daily News, Mirror, Times,* and *Herald-Tribune,* as well as several suburban papers from Long Island and New Jersey, to know what was going on and be better prepared to handle our own stories for the *Journal-American's* first edition, which hit the street at 9 A.M. as the first of New York's evening newspapers off the press.

The big news that morning was in the *Daily News*—a first-class scoop. Its big black Page-One headline blared: "Marilyn Monroe a Mental Patient."

"Why the hell didn't you know about this story?" roared the Night Managing Editor, Edwin C. Stein. He was yelling at me.

And since Stein was my boss, I couldn't engage him in vocal combat. I had to return a proper, well-fashioned, civil reply: "Nuts!"

Stein was trying to get my goat because I'd just finished the manuscript for my new book on the screen's sex goddess, the biography, *Marilyn Monroe: Her Own Story,* a tome based on many interviews and, most memorably, a very, very long walk that Marilyn took with me through Central Park—alone. So, as her biographer, as the guy who was supposed to know Marilyn Monroe inside-out, it seemed it should have been my business to have gotten the story about her confinement to a New York psychiatric clinic.

But then again, one must consider the slogan of the *Daily News:* "All it takes is talent."

And that talent has made the *News* America's largest-circulation newspaper. On the *J-A* we had talent too—perhaps reflected best in the Audit Bureau of Circulation figures that showed we sold one-third the number of copies of the *News'* two-million-plus daily output.

Something like an hour went by after my encounter with Stein and the *Journal-American's* lobster trick was in full swing. By now I had laced into the mountain of stories before me and thrown them to the rewrite battery—John Pascal was working on Marilyn Monroe, trying to develop a new angle; Don Flynn was writing about the big cleanup after the city's seventeen-inch snowfall; Dan Foley was doing the bit about a library official in

West Orange, New Jersey, who had delinquent borrowers dumped in the clink for failing to return their books; Steve Pelletiere was on a teenage scientist who stole deadly strychnine sulphate from a Long Island high school and brought it home to conduct experiments in his basement lab; and Cy Egan was nailing down the story of an advertising executive who threw a roomful of furniture to the street from a Brooklyn hotel window, got tossed in the psycho ward, escaped, and was finally collared in Las Vegas.

So, who had time to mess with a British spy drama—or, at the moment, what seemed like one.

While all this was going on, I was on the phone talking to my old high school teacher.

Strange?

The staff thought so, too, when they heard the announcement from the switchboard jockey, Bobby Bernstein:

"Hey, George, there's a guy on the phone who says he's your old high school teacher and has gotta talk to you right away."

"Ha!" bellowed Stein, the Night Managing Editor. "He wants to take you back to class and teach you how not to get scooped on your own stories."

I picked up the phone and began to talk with Matthew Chambers, my old teacher at James Monroe High School in the Bronx. After a brief exchange of amenities, he said in a voice trembling with urgency, "George, did you see the pictures of those British spies in the newspapers?"

"You mean those five who stole the submarine secrets?"

"Yes, yes—but I'm talking about only two of them—the Krogers. Do you know who they are?"

"You know I was never very bright in school," I jibed. "Why don't you give me the answer?"

"Okay, I'll tell you. That guy's no more John Kroger than you are. And his wife's name isn't Helen . . . I'm going to tell you who they really are . . . "

Suddenly a tingle of excitement brushed me. I straightened up in my chair and waited tensely. I sensed a story in the making—but how big that story would be by the time we went to press was beyond my immediate imagination as I listened to the man who had been my teacher back in 1939.

"Remember our undefeated football team of 1927?" he continued. "It was before your time, but you couldn't have forgotten the team because it was one of the best we ever had. And the fullback on the team—a hell of a fullback—was Morris "Unc" Cohen, a big strapping fellow with lots of beef and muscle. Remember?"

I said I didn't remember. The only thing about 1927 that I remembered was celebrating my seventh birthday on Thanksgiving Day by smoking my first cigar—then vomiting all over my turkey dinner.

"All right, so your memory doesn't reach that far back. But mine does and I'm telling you right here and now that the Kroger they've arrested in London as a spy for stealing those naval secrets—that's Morris Cohen!"

In the newspaper business you learn to take sensational stories in stride. When a reporter phones in from Brooklyn and says, "A jetliner with seventy passengers just crashed into a row of tenements," you leap to your feet. You grab the two-way radio and shout to all reporter-photographer teams in *Journal-American* radio cars to go to the scene. You scream at rewrite men to phone the police, to call residents in nearby stores and houses for eyewitness stories even before your reporters get there, and you get someone to write the bulletin for a fast replate extra. You attend to hundreds of other details, all in a matter of minutes.

But there is one sobering fact you always face on a big-breaking news story—you don't have it alone. Every paper in town is going to have it. What's left for you is the challenge to do a better job of coverage than the opposition—to get more details, more color, better written stories, more pictures. You rarely experience the real taste of victory on a story, as the *Daily News* did when it broke the news of Marilyn Monroe's confinement in the hospital. The *News* had that one alone and it was the most triumphant paper in town that morning of February 9th.

But now, as I listened to my old teacher, I was gripped by the exhilarating possibility of a personal scoop in the daily journalistic rat race of the Big Town.

"How sure are you that Kroger and Cohen are the same person?" I asked.

"Absolutely certain," he answered. "I spotted their pictures the other day. I recognized Cohen. He's changed—lost a lot of weight, his hair is gray, his face is drawn. But it's still 'Unc,' no matter how you look at him. And his wife, Lona, next to him, clinches it.

She has changed, not as much. They're the ones. No question about it."

Then he added: "And the others are just as positive as I am that they're the Cohens . . . No doubt about it."

"The others?" I burst out. "Who besides you recognized them?"

All at once I was locked in a cold sweat born of the twin torments that attend every classic scoop. First, there is agony in knowing your story isn't worth a hoot unless you can back it up. Without confirmation you can't publish the story. One man's say-so that Kroger is Cohen is not enough. It could be a case of mistaken identity.

But my ex-teacher said there were others who could back him up. I would find out who they were. If they could substantiate the Kroger-Cohen link, forcefully and convincingly, a good part of the battle would be won. But I would have to check further with one stronger authority—the Federal Bureau of Investigation.

But there still was the anxiety, which would continue until the *Journal-American* and the opposition evening papers were out, and I could see with my own eyes that they didn't have the story, too.

"Who are the others?" I inquired apprehensively, hoping one of them wouldn't be a reporter on the *World-Telegram & Sun* or the *Post.*

"One is 'Doc' Weidman," Chambers told me. He was referring to Joseph "Doc" Weidman, who had coached the '27 team and many Monroe High elevens afterward. Recently he had become athletic director and swimming coach (Chambers was Monroe's swim coach) at another Bronx high school, DeWitt Clinton.

"Another is Al Siegal, who was a teammate of Cohen's," Chambers went on. "You can find Al in the phone book. He lives in the Parkchester housing development in the Bronx, owns a delicatessen there."

He volunteered several other names, including those of some teachers, a few retired by now, others still teaching. Some had been my teachers.

"How do you know these people have all recognized Cohen in the pictures?"

"We all spotted the pictures and called up each other about it. And we've all notified the FBI . . . "

All of the persons who had recognized Cohen and spoken to each other about him, had communicated with the FBI in New York and related their suspicions that the former football player was the spy Peter J. Kroger, he repeated.

"Has the FBI done anything about it?" I asked.

"Yes, they are doing something—but I don't know what. I do know they sent agents around to James Monroe High, about five years ago, to talk with Cohen's old teachers and get a line on him since graduation. The G-men questioned dozens of Cohen's former classmates and teachers. No one was told then what Cohen was suspected of being mixed up in, but the agents did say their investigation was in connection with communism."

I asked what Chambers could tell me about Cohen's background—the background that had led from the Bronx to Great Britain and charges that he, along with his wife, were Soviet spies. He filled me in.

It was an incredible story which, briefly, showed that Cohen had been a Communist sympathizer since the mid-thirties. During the Spanish Civil War, Cohen joined the Lincoln Brigade and fought against Franco's forces. Sometime in 1938 he returned to New York. He was seen at Monroe High alumni and letter-club functions on and off for a number of years and even taught public school in the city for a while. He had earned his degree at a Southern college—no one seemed certain which one—and later attended high school affairs, mostly in the forties. At these functions he seemed to be a loner. He didn't mingle much, spoke little. After 1951 or 1952, my ex-teacher said, Morris Cohen and his wife Lona, whose real name was Leontina Petka, dropped out of sight.

"We haven't seen Cohen since," Chambers added, "except now—in the pictures that show him as a spy."

I thanked my old teacher profusely for calling me and said goodbye. As I put down the receiver, I turned to Night Managing Editor Stein. He saw the expression on my face and knew I had got some kind of big news tip.

"Can we lead the paper with it?" Stein growled. He had heard bits and pieces of my conversation and the mention of spying, so he had an idea what we had been talking about.

I asked Ed for a conference. We went off to a quiet part of the office to talk. I filled him in. When I had related everything my teacher had told me, Stein's face, too, wore a look of incredulity.

"You've got one of the great stories of the year in your hands," Stein told me, "but I don't dare print it. Not in its present form."

Stein was one hundred percent correct. At the moment we only had a foot in the door of a great scoop. There would have to be considerable legwork on the story before we could break it—and even then we'd be taking an awful chance.

"Suppose," Stein asked, "Cohen should suddenly turn up in Newark or Detroit, after our story is out? Do you know he could walk into the *Journal* building and take over the paper, lock, stock, and presses? We'd be working for him—if he'd hire us."

Of course, he was referring to libel. Even if the teachers and old teammates swore on a stack of Bibles that Kroger was Cohen, that would be no defense against a suit if the real Cohen turned up somewhere else and was not the British spy.

"I'll put everybody to work on it right now," I told Stein. "I'll check with the FBI myself. We'll nail this down."

"Do you know what time it is?" Stein asked.

"It's 2:25 A.M. and everyone we want to talk with is asleep," I conceded. "But we're going to wake them up . . . "

"And while you're at it," Stein cracked, "wake up J. Edgar Hoover and have him sign a sworn affidavit—it's about the only way I can convince the publisher that he won't be out of a job in. the morning when this story busts."

So we went to work. I threw the first assignment to Don Vandergrift, an Assistant City Editor who was a gifted digging reporter. He was to talk with "Doc" Weidman and a couple of the other teachers.

Larry Nathanson, another dogged newshound (he now works with me on the *New York Post*), got another list of names to check on the phone.

Fred Shapiro, who'd scrape the bottom of the Marianas Trench to get a story, was to call Scotland Yard in London and ask if they knew Kroger had another name—like Cohen, for instance.

Meanwhile, I sent for the clips from the morgue on the British spy case and began to read up on it. It was nearly 5:15 A.M. before I had finished brushing up on the London reports—for, don't forget, we were still putting out a newspaper with other news and I had to handle a raft of other stories. Generally there are anywhere from eighty to a hundred stories processed through the City

Desk for the first edition. Not all of them would get into the paper, but each one constituted news and had to be covered. The news editor generally decided which of the least important were to be left out because of space limitations.

I learned the following from my survey of the spy case:

Peter J. Kroger and his wife, Helen, were seized at their home in Ruislip, a suburban town outside London, where they ran a bookstore. The store was near the huge U.S. Third Air Force headquarters base. When or how the Krogers made it to England was as much a mystery to me then as the story of the arrest, announced February 5, 1961. It had been handled by Scotland Yard in guarded fashion.

On the previous afternoon, a Saturday, Scotland Yard Detective Chief Superintendent George Gordon "Moonraker" Smith saw Henry Frederick Houghton and Ethel Elizabeth Gee, both Admiralty civil servants, leave Waterloo Station and approach the Old Victoria Theater to meet a businessman, Gordon Arnold Lonsdale. When Miss Gee handed Lonsdale a small shopping basket containing two parcels, Superintendent Smith placed them under arrest. Later, on Saturday night, the Krogers were taken into custody.

At their hearing in Bow Street Magistrate's Court, Scotland Yard's counter-espionage police unit charged the five with stealing Great Britain's antisubmarine research secrets, developed initially by the United States, and passing them to a foreign power—unquestionably the Soviet Union. That was all I could find out—then.

In the meantime, my reporters returned with the results of their phone calls. Each reporter had hit paydirt—everyone contacted from the list of names supplied by my former teacher confirmed that Peter Kroger was Morris Cohen, and provided details that substantially matched those given me earlier by Chambers. But the call to London was a dead end. Scotland Yard absolutely refused comment. There was only one alternative. Call the FBI, as I had planned.

I phoned the New York office. The agent on duty couldn't comment. He advised me to call later and speak with the Agent-in-Charge. But I couldn't wait—I wanted to break the story in the first edition, and I had only until 6 A.M. to pin down the facts and write them up. So I woke up the boss of the New York FBI, Harvey G. Foster, at his home. I expected him to blast me, but he didn't.

He listened patiently to what I had to say about my investigation into Cohen. I told him everything pointed to the likelihood that Cohen really was the British spy, Kroger. Did he know that?

In light of what was to be revealed later, it was an absurd question. Foster not only knew about Cohen, but knew a great deal more about his connections and activities in espionage right here in the United States.

But we wouldn't hear about that until much later. At the moment, Foster could only adhere to FBI policy. He could merely offer the standard reply: "No comment."

"Tell me this," I said to Foster. "If I print the story—will you deny it?"

"Not if it's true and you have your facts straight."

"Do I have the facts?"

"No comment."

"How about if I wake up Hoover?" I asked. "Do you think he'd set me straight? I've got a reporter in Washington who can reach him."

"He might set you straight, but it won't be on this story."

In desperation, I said to Foster. "Okay, I'm going to print the story. Do you want to tell me now not to? You could save me a multimillion-dollar libel suit."

"You know I can't tell you what to print, nor what not to print," he said. "You are the editor—you've got to make that decision."

I was really up against it. I could see Foster wasn't going to yield. Nor was I going to catch him in an unguarded moment when he might drop a hint that the story was all right. So I was no better off after my talk with the FBI's New York chief.

I went into a hurried conference with Stein. I told him what Foster had said.

"Did he deny that Cohen was Kroger?" Stein asked.

"No," I replied, "he merely said no comment."

"Well," Stein put in, "you know the FBI has investigated Cohen—you've gotten that information from highly reputable citizens. You've told all this to Foster and he's refused to comment. Don't you think that if this whole thing is untrue, if the FBI has never investigated Cohen, you would have got an outright denial of it from Foster?"

I told Stein I had no doubt of that. If the FBI had never heard of Cohen, I would have been told so.

"I think you've got a story," Stein said. "Write it and we'll let the lawyers decide on the libel aspects."

I went to the typewriter and batted out the story in something like fifty-five minutes. Meanwhile, Stein had the headline written, two eight-column lines in 140-point type:

BRITISH-HELD RED SPY FORMER N.Y. GRID STAR

Then, at 7 A.M., I called Larry Brock, a Hearst attorney, at his home and read him the story. His comment:

"If your facts are right, you've got nothing to worry about."

That was small consolation. Suppose my facts weren't correct? Suppose everyone who saw Kroger's pictures in the paper was wrong? Suppose Kroger wasn't Cohen?

The last vestige of doubt was removed from my mind when one of my reporters called me from the Bronx and said, "If this Kroger isn't Cohen, I'll turn in my press card."

That was Seymour "Cy" Spector. I had roused him out of bed at four o'clock that morning, had him come into the office, take a picture of Kroger from our files (an Associated Press glossy, not a newspaper reproduction), and bring it up to the home of one of Cohen's old classmates.

"The picture in the 1927 high school yearbook and the photo you gave me," Spector said, "are of the same person. Everything matches—the shape of the eyes, the folds of the lids, the contour of the eyebrows, the nose, the dimples, and the shape of the lips and the mouth—even the ears and chin. Kroger is Cohen."

Spector was highly qualified to speak. He was the *Journal-American*'s camera columnist. I weighed in with all the facts to Stein.

"We'll go with it," Stein said, swallowing an ulcer pill and washing it down with a swig of Kohansov's demon brew that was alleged to be coffee.

And we went to press.

The story, which was copyrighted—so that our opposition, the *World-Telegram & Sun* and the *Post*, would have to credit the *J-A* when they lifted it from our pages—started like this:

One of the five members of a British spy ring who stole key NATO naval secrets is a native New Yorker who was a star football player at James Monroe High School in the Bronx.

The *New York Journal-American* learned today that the spy, Peter J. Kroger, a white-thatched, slender man of 50, is Morris "Unc" Cohen—whose trail has been followed by the FBI for years.

The story created a sensation. It triggered a torrent of phone calls to the FBI from the city's other six papers, reporters descended on Agent Harvey Foster's office, demanding to know whether the *Journal-American* story was authentic. There was no immediate comment. Evidently Foster had to wait for a ruling from Washington on whether anything could be said.

At the office, I was swamped with calls. The New York offices of the *London Daily Mail*, the *Express*, and the *Telegraph* called me. They wanted all the additional information I could furnish.

"This story has rocked Fleet Street and our editors are querying us. Their attitude is that we should have had it, you know," said one of the reporters. Evidently the AP and UPI had flashed the news to London before the English correspondents based in New York had a chance to see the *J-A*'s scoop.

"The whole spy case has caused a storm in Britain and, of course, any thing that can be reported on the principals involved is wanted desperately over there. The whole island is shaken up—it's our worst blunder since the Fuchs case. Our Government is most embarrassed, rather."

Indeed the spy case had shaken up Her Majesty's Government. It was the worst penetration of Britain's security system since Klaus Fuchs gave the atom-bomb secrets to Russia. It triggered some top-secret correspondence between Prime Minister Macmillan and President Kennedy, and similar communications from Lord Carrington, First Lord of the Admiralty, to Admiral Arleigh Burke, U.S. Chief of Naval Operations.

What was the case all about?

Chapter 20

How the FBI Put the Heat on "Unc"

It was a very complicated case with five chief characters, each playing separate and distinct roles in espionage . . .

Let us begin with Gordon Arnold Lonsdale. At thirty-five, Lonsdale had a wife and children in Moscow, but he accepted the fact that his country came first. He belonged to a new generation of crack Soviet agents who were being trained at that very moment—and even right now—in a fantastic "school for spies" in Moscow.

In this school, Lonsdale was taught a complete catechism of Western history and habits. He attended classes in English, geography, the theater, and the capitalistic system. He learned to dress, talk, and order food in the manner of the West. He was taught the names of political leaders, business tycoons, and entertainment and movie idols. And he received courses in spy techniques, photography, microfilming, and radio communication.

After more than a year's coaching in the school for spies, Lonsdale was sent to a specially built "American town" near Winnitz, in the South Ukraine, the heart of the USSR. Here not a word of Russian is spoken. Here Lonsdale could have his hair cut in a Western-style barber shop, he could buy gas at a garage that looked like a petrol station in Britain, and he could buy Western drinks in the bars. With the rest of the class of new-generation spies, he viewed American and British films, listened to pop records, and studied Western newspapers. He perfected a Canadian accent. And, not overlooking a single detail, his masters made him develop a taste for chewing gum.

Only one vital point was overlooked in this fantastic operation—and it was to unmask him in the end. The most brilliant spy system ever known had made every arrangement to fix Lonsdale up with a passport and send him to England, handing him the identity of a Canadian boy with a Finnish mother, born among the shanties of Cobalt, a silver-mining ghost town in Ontario.

The Russians had reached back twenty-two years to pluck this dossier from the files of the real Lonsdale, who had been taken back to Finland by his mother in 1932, when the boy was eight years old.

But one vital point was overlooked and it was to help brand their star graduate an impostor in the year 1961. The point, discovered by a Canadian Mountie searching for clues along the frozen northern rim of Ontario, was that the real Lonsdale had been circumcised soon after his birth.

The phony Lonsdale was not!

With that clue everything fell in place. It climaxed the end of a fantastic trail that had spanned the world, touching the United States, New Zealand, Austria, Canada, and finally Great Britain, leading to the arrest near London's Old Vic Theater and to the spy team's downfall.

The trail was picked up by tall, broad-shouldered Corporal Jack Carroll of the Royal Canadian Mounted Police. On a day in 1960, Carroll stepped from a British Viscount onto a snow-covered landing strip in northern Ontario with an urgent, but rather simple set of instructions in his pocket:

"Please check Gordon Arnold Lonsdale, issued Canadian passport Toronto, December, 1954, now espionage suspect."

The message was from Scotland Yard Superintendent Smith.

Carroll's investigation showed him that a Gordon Lonsdale had been born on August 27, 1924, in the derelict silver-mining town of

Cobalt. His father was a two-fisted miner named Archie Lonsdale, a descendant of a British family that had emigrated to Canada two centuries previously. His mother was Olga Elina Bous, a Finnish girl who married Archie two years after she moved to Canada with her parents.

The marriage was not a happy one and it ended when the lovely Olga left her husband and sailed, with her eight-year-old son Gordon, for Finland—and right out of this spy story. Where the real Gordon Lonsdale was in 1961—or even today—is a complete mystery.

Now let us move on to November, 1954. We are in Vancouver, British Columbia. A Russian grain ship is docking at the pier. Who is that coming down the gangplank? It's a man calling himself Gordon Lonsdale.

This is Gordon Lonsdale, full-fledged graduate of that incredible Russian school for spies in the Ukraine, coming into Vancouver as if he owned the city.

And why not?

As he begins prowling round the streets of this Western metropolis he feels strangely at home, this man from Moscow. Everything is the way his masters at spy school told him it would be.

He took a taxi to a rooming house in Burnaby Street; a month later he moved into a more comfortable suite in Pendrill Street, which cost him $15 a week. Lonsdale was in no great rush. His instructions at the Moscow headquarters of the brilliant GRU, the Soviet naval, army, and aviation espionage organization, had been made quite clear: Settle in as a Canadian citizen, get a passport, and catch the liner *America* for England in the spring.

Lonsdale was wearing a smart new worsted suit with narrow lapels and no cuffs. He was highly pleased with the Jacques Fath necktie he wore. The mirror on the door of his furnished room on Pendrill Street showed a chunky man, five feet eight, with thick, dark hair, crinkly gray eyes above high, wide cheekbones, a face the shade of tanned leather. He had powerful shoulders, slightly hunched. His head was lowered like a boxer's.

He delighted in making a success of himself with Western women. They fell for him like a sack of wet potatoes. He was Beau Brummell in every sense of the word.

So, the long arm of Soviet espionage had reached back twenty-two years to create a new Gordon Lonsdale. Meanwhile, he applied for a passport. His reason: To study Chinese at London University. The document was issued.

With two months to kill before his new spy life in Britain was scheduled to begin, Lonsdale went to Toronto and spent his time frequenting bars and clubs—and making time with the women. Strangely, for a man who claimed to be the son of a former miner, Lonsdale had no money problems. With funds that flowed into his hands from a mysterious source in Switzerland, his bank balance hovered around $7,000—standing in readiness to finance his trip to Britain.

On March 3, 1955, the "student" Lonsdale boarded the *America* and sailed for Southampton. At Waterloo Station in London, he hailed a porter. For the moment, the business at hand was not espionage. That would come later. He wanted to dally a bit with those good-looking British babes. If things went according to the schedule laid down by his Soviet masters, an agent would contact him with instructions in a fortnight.

Now let us look at the Krogers . . .

Here is where my investigation into the background of the Cohens drops into place in the espionage story that rocked London.

It was a dossier I compiled over the next eighteen hours following my exclusive story that told who the Krogers really were. In something like two hours after the *Journal-American* hit the street, the FBI in Washington confirmed my disclosure. In its official announcement, the FBI said it already had notified Scotland Yard of the true identity of the Krogers and confirmed it with fingerprints.

I learned that Morris Cohen was one of the highest ranking Soviet agents in the United States before the FBI began to close the net on Communist espionage in the early 1950s. Cohen had worked in close liaison with Colonel Rudolph Ivanovich Abel, the military man who became the most important Soviet spy ever captured in this country.

The FBI was first attracted by Cohen and his wife in 1950. Leontina, or Lona, as she preferred to be called, was born in

205

Adams, Massachusetts, July 11, 1913, the daughter of Ladislaus and Mary Petka, a Polish couple. They moved to Utica, then New York City, where Lona wed Morris "Unc" Cohen after a marriage license was taken out in Manhattan's Municipal Building on July 31, 1941.

The FBI's initial suspicion of Cohen followed the arrest in London of Dr. Klaus Fuchs, in February, 1950, and his confession to spying for the Russians.

Fuchs, a British atomic scientist, admitted he was engaged in espionage for the Soviet Union while assigned to the Los Alamos project, where the A-bomb was developed. Fuchs implicated Harry Gold as co-conspirator and Gold, in turn, fingered David Greenglass. Julius and Ethel Rosenberg were in the same Red cell.

With the heat on them, Rosenberg urged Greenglass, who was his brother-in-law, to flee the country. Greenglass refused and was subsequently arrested. Then came the Rosenbergs' turn to topple into the FBI net that was spread for them.

Even before the Rosenbergs were executed in Sing Sing Prison's electric chair at Ossining, New York, the Soviets had designated Morris and Lona Cohen to be their successors!

They came into the roles with a solid background of Communist activity . . .

After his graduation from James Monroe High, Cohen attended Mississippi State College and the University of Illinois, where he earned a B.S. degree.

Afterward, he served in the Red-tinged Lincoln Brigade in Spain and on his return to the United States he put his name on a Communist Party application; then he met Lona, a fellow worshiper of the Reds.

One day Cohen showed up at the headquarters hall of the Waiters Union, on West 36th Street, paid his dues, and got a union card. But he had no intention of slinging hash or waiting on tables. The Reds were making a bid to take over labor unions and Cohen's job was to sign up waiters into the party.

Then came the war. Cohen got a job first with the Soviet employment agency ANTOR, in New York, and later left his job to join the Army, serving at U.S. bases in Europe for the next three years, until 1945. His bride got a job in a munitions plant.

After the war, Cohen returned to America and melted into the everyday routine like a hundred-million other Americans—but with one notable difference—he was a Soviet agent, as was his wife.

And during this period, incredible as it sounds, Cohen taught at Public School 86 in Manhattan.

A Red spy was teaching New York City school kids!

Suddenly one day, without even the formality of a resignation, Cohen dropped out of his teaching post and vanished, along with his wife. To friends and neighbors, to some of his old teachers, like Joe "Doc" Weidman, his former football coach, Cohen said he was heading for Hollywood, to take a job as a screen writer.

The FBI later tried to pick up that trail. It questioned the studios—20th Century-Fox, Metro-Goldwyn-Mayer, RKO, and others. No one had heard of Morris Cohen. Even the Screen Writers Guild, in which any screen writer of any consequence must hold membership, had no record of Cohen.

How did the FBI get wind of Cohen and his complicity in the spy ring?

With the arrest of the Rosenbergs, Lona Cohen was one of the many Red followers who went to work as co-director of the "Fund to Save the Rosenbergs" (from execution). She and her husband were pulled in for questioning by the FBI. The FBI did not like the answers it got from Morris and Lona. It investigated further.

It learned that the apartment Morris and Lona Cohen occupied in New York was being paid for by the Rosenbergs. It learned further, that after the Rosenbergs had been arrested, Colonel Abel, a new top Soviet agent then, was paying for the Cohens' flat.

The FBI dug deeper. It found that Cohen and his wife were about to be given a large sum of money to finance new large-scale espionage activities in what was to be an extension of the bold conspiracy that led to the theft of our atomic secrets by the Rosenbergs.

The plot, which was to see the Cohens take over where the Rosenbergs had left off, was replete with all the trappings of classic fictional spy stories.

It involved code names, false identities, furtive meetings on street corners, restaurants, and subway platforms, and numerous other espionage devices that characterize the modus operandi of Communist spy activity around the world.

But now, with the hot breath of the FBI blowing on them, the Cohens could no longer serve the Soviets in their espionage plans—it was too dangerous. So, in the winter of 1950–51, Morris and Lona got their instructions and vanished overnight.

They fled only days—possibly only a few hours—before the G-men were ready to close in on them.

And their trail was lost for the time being . . .

Chapter 21

But It's Scotland Yard that Finishes the Job

What happened to Morris "Unc" Cohen and his wife, Lona, after they fled New York?

The answer didn't come until ten years later—after we had revealed in the *Journal-American* that Peter and Helen Kroger were really the Cohens from the Bronx—when the FBI and Scotland Yard finally filled in the vacuum of that decade spanning their seemingly total vanishment.

Morris and Lona made their way to New Zealand, lived there four years, then traveled to Vienna and obtained passports. The Cohens had forwarded forged birth certificates and a 1943 marriage license naming them Peter and Helen Kroger, citizens of New Zealand. That document fooled everyone. The passports were issued and they moved on to London—to begin six years of espionage activity.

When they arrived, they had barely heard of a gray and windswept piece of the English coast called Portland. And of a balding, middle-aged man named Henry Frederick Houghton, a clerk in the Underwater Detection Center at Portland, whose window overlooked the turbulent English Channel, where frigates and a crop of bright yellow helicopters were testing out top-secret asdic and sonar equipment just shipped from the United States and being installed in NATO warships.

From his window, Houghton watched the copters flying in threes, in set patterns, over the water. At preset times, they would winch down their sonar buoys, instruments which transmit and receive electrical impulses that ping off the side of a submerged submarine.

At about this time, the naval scientists were beginning to perfect the "sniffer" apparatus, designed to smell out a submarine by sucking up its unseen diesel fumes.

Moscow was intensely interested in these defense developments and had alerted its spy system in the United States to concentrate "at all costs" on the theft of these secrets. But the extreme security that ringed U.S. bases where such equipment was being installed compelled the Kremlin to target in on the installations in England.

Houghton was picked for the role in the beginning. There was good reason why Houghton was eminently qualified for this dangerous assignment.

Houghton was an Englishman. He was born in a terraced house in Ashfield Street, a working-class area of Lincoln, a cathedral city. But life was unexciting there and at sixteen he had joined the Royal Navy for adventure, serving with distinction in Malta and in the Murmansk convoys during the war. In 1945 he retired with the impressive rank of Master-at-Arms, the senior rating on the lower deck and a post that headed the ship's police.

Houghton went to work for the Admiralty and after five years was assigned to the staff of Captain Nigel Austen in Warsaw, to handle his correspondence, organize official visits, and act as the captain's confidential secretary. Henry Houghton enjoyed this new-found prestige. But inside, he was envious—even bitter—at the superior dash cut by the senior diplomatic staff.

So it was not surprising that he was flattered by the attentions suddenly coming his way from a collection of English-speaking Poles who sought out his company.

At least two of them were Z-2 agents. The Z-2 is the Polish Military Intelligence Organization assigned to subvert Western Embassy staffs by tossing parties for them, introducing them to women, showering them with expensive gifts, and—if necessary—employing a bit of blackmail to win them over.

Others of the coterie of new-found friends Houghton enjoyed in Warsaw were black marketeers, and they were successful in persuading the Englishman to supply them with precious drugs and foods that could not be obtained in Poland.

Houghton's wife, Peggy, timidly questioned him about this.

"I'm handling deals in streptomycin and penicillin," he explained. "The Poles can't get this stuff for love or money. We're going to be rich soon—very rich."

Peggy Houghton soon found evidence that the deals went deeper. While clearing a cupboard, she stumbled onto confidential Embassy papers. Henry became furious, violent. After an Embassy dinner, he shoved Peggy against a parapet, fracturing her leg.

Now Houghton began to drink heavily, his mysterious contacts became more numerous, his violence toward Peggy more severe. Twice she had to paint makeup over a blackened eye.

Halfway through his three-year tour of duty, Houghton was summoned by Captain Austen. The reports of friends and colleagues were laid before Houghton. They had built up an impressive and a damaging dossier against him, enumerating his extravagances, his domestic rows, his strange friends. There was only one thing to be done. Captain Austen told Houghton. Henry was ordered home.

It was one of the worst disgraces an Embassy employe could suffer. Yet despite the label of "unreliable," Houghton returned to London to find himself upgraded by the Admiralty to the permanent rank of Civil Servant. He was posted to an office in the huge building at Portland, whose windows overlooked the secret sonar tests in the English Channel. It was a made-to-order assignment for Houghton, for before he had left Poland his friends had gotten to him. They threatened him with exposure on his drug deals, and they threatened him with beatings. They ordered him to serve in London and he was forced to agree. He was promised lavish pay.

The year was 1953 and the jubilant message went out to Moscow from Commander Igor Amosow, the Soviet Navy Liaison Officer at Z-2's Radio Headquarters at Walez, Poland:

"Contact established."

Moscow had at last achieved the seemingly impossible. It had established a means of penetrating the banks of barbed wire and the photopass system at the top-secret Portland base. Orders began to spill out from Moscow—orders for Houghton.

At Portland, which in 1953 was only one of several antisub research centers in Britain, activity ran a normal week—from 8:30 A.M. Monday to 5:18 P.M. Friday. Then the scientists, office staffs, and security section closed down.

On those weekends, Houghton would borrow the secret and confidential documents Moscow had asked for. He would bring them home to his white thatched cottage in Weymouth. Some he would photograph himself, others he took to clandestine meetings with Russians and Poles, contacts he knew only as "Nikki" and "John." But always as faithfully as he borrowed, so would he return the secrets to their files at 8:30 Monday morning.

The files were not the only attraction for Houghton in that year of 1953. Next door to his office worked smartly dressed Ethel Elizabeth "Bunty" Gee. The demure daughter of a blacksmith and a trusted Admiralty servant, Miss Gee was employed in the drawing-office records section. "Bunty" lived with her aged mother, her Uncle Jack, and her Aunt Bessie in Hambro Road, Portland. She was engaged to a young carpenter in a nearby town.

But the engagement was broken off—Bunty suddenly fell for Henry Houghton like the bow anchor of a frigate. They played badminton to begin with. Nights they went pub crawling. When Houghton found himself in a pincer—remember he had a wife—he'd break his date with Bunty and she'd stay home stitching away at petit point.

But Portland is a rather closely knit community where rumors have a nasty way of getting around. Peggy Houghton heard them. She also found a carelessly dropped love letter from Henry to Bunty. There followed an angry street scene. But it wasn't between Peggy and Henry, because Peggy had already had her fill of violence at Houghton's hands. She went at it with Bunty. It ended with the spinster telling Mrs. Houghton, "Mind your own business! If you can't hold onto your man, you deserve to lose him!"

Peggy Houghton decided she'd had enough. After twenty-three years of marriage, she walked out on Henry in May, 1958. Cruelty was given as the reason in the divorce action.

But even before the divorce, returning now to 1955, Houghton

brazenly had asked Miss Gee to marry him. It was a safe suggestion since he knew Bunty could not leave her aged relatives, whom
she supported. But on those weekends when he would make off
with the Portland secrets, Houghton would team up with Bunty
and live with her as man and wife in London.

Houghton's partnership with Bunty Gee was necessary to the
master plan set down by Moscow. Houghton had been transferred after a while to a less-secret port-repair unit and his access
to the top-secret files was lost. But Miss Gee, who still worked
among the drawings and pamphlets in the buff folders with the
bold red diagonal crosses, marked "Top Secret Material," could
take up where Houghton left off.

Thousands of details on dockyard and harbor installations,
Royal Navy equipment and methods, and data on personnel
poured out to Houghton and through him into the hands of
Russia. Even the preliminary data on Britain's first atomic sub-
marine, the *Dreadnought*, built with information supplied by the
United States, went the same route. In the event of war with
Russia, Western ships would be at the mercy of the very sub-
marines they were determinedly trying to hunt down!

Now let us return to Gordon Lonsdale and Peter and Helen
Kroger, né Morris and Lona Cohen, and see how their paths all
crossed each other's and Henry Houghton's—to form one of the
most fantastic partnerships in espionage ever uncovered.

Following his arrival in London, Lonsdale went his merry way
with his design to gather a clutch of beautiful women. He smoked
hard, lived hard, drank hard. But he never got drunk. He was a
supremely conscientious and diligent spy. Women found him hard
to resist. He had charm and he spoke with a carefully cultivated,
fascinating North American accent. He took his women to the
Savoy cocktail bar, to romantic candle-lit restaurants, or through
beautiful preserves like Windsor Great Park, with one arm
around a mink, the other in a grip on the steering wheel of his
flashy Studebaker.

The women he dallied with were from the Continent, in London
on a holiday, on business, or to work. He hunted at the Overseas
Visitor's Club and had his pick of another crop of beauties. One
was a lovely redhead, who is now a hostess for a Greek shipping
line. He lived with her at Barons Court. Then he moved and took
up with a beauty from Rieka in northern Yugoslavia, whom he

persuaded to give up her role as a kitchen maid in the nurses' hostel in Guilford Street and take up with him.

The Krogers, or Cohens, meanwhile, were settling down in their new home at 45 Cranley Drive, Ruislip—the last house on a dead-end road. The home was perfect for the front that Kroger was to set up as a book dealer. But it was more perfect in other ways. Helen Kroger discovered the house early in 1956, when she went house-hunting, while Peter remained behind in their furnished flat in London. When she got home one afternoon she enthused:

"I've found just the place we need. It has everything—even a trap door in the kitchen floor! The previous owner was a police sergeant who fancied a wine cellar and started to build it. But he never got beyond fixing the trap door and hollowing out a space. It's just what we'll need . . ."

It was indeed just what the Krogers needed. The hollowed-out space was ideal for concealing the radio transmitter and receiver, the size of a portable typewriter, which had been brought over piecemeal in a Soviet diplomatic bag to the Russian Embassy in London.

The Krogers paid 4,200 pounds for their dream home—a home Moscow was to christen "Station Okhotra," after a Russian river.

So the Krogers, who until then had been receiving their instructions from a Russian Embassy contact, could now deal directly with Moscow via shortwave from their new home.

Their work began. Kroger was the spy paymaster and communications expert, working behind his bookstore front. He had had some experience in the States with books. Having worked briefly in a New York bookstore, this background suited him admirably. His wife became the mastermind behind an intricate job of microfilming British secrets—the secrets stolen by Henry Houghton.

Lonsdale was the courier. His instructions were to take the stolen secrets from Houghton and deliver them to the Krogers, who in turn would transmit them to Moscow in several different ways.

No one suspected. By day, Kroger was a genteel bookstore operator; his wife distributed kindness with an automatic precision that completely masked her sinister mission as a servant of the Kremlin. She saved bones for the little dog Trilby across the street. She would baby-sit for busy mothers, bring flowers to ailing neighbors.

At night, in the safety of their home, the Krogers let down their false front and busily engaged themselves in the task of reducing secret documents to the size of a pinhead, using expensive Soviet microfilm equipment.

The microdots would be concealed beneath postage stamps and in the mass of type in preselected lines in Kroger's books, which were mailed to the Continent, to Africa, and even to North and South America, following various devious routes to Moscow. Something like three-quarters of the information supplied by Lonsdale and other couriers was sent by microdot in book parcels. The rest went by their powerful radio directly to Moscow, flashed from the bungalow by way of aerial coils strung over the apple tree in the high-walled back garden.

The transmitting procedure was in itself spectacular. First the Krogers taped their messages in Morse code, fed them into the transmitter and, by means of an automatic attachment that speeded up transmission, the dot-dashes flashed over the apple tree at the rate of six hundred words a minute. There was hardly any danger of detection by British Radio Intelligence because they were never on the air long enough for radio direction-finders to obtain a fix on the clandestine radio transmitter.

Instructions from Moscow came back the same way—indirectly through microdots concealed in book catalogues, but also in high-speed Morse code twice a month to Station Okhotra.

One such message that arrived from Moscow was a personal one for Lonsdale. It was from his wife, Galyusha. The Moscow hierarchy sent word that a meeting had been arranged for Lonsdale with his wife in Prague. It was inevitable that the Soviet brass would arrange the meeting, for Galyusha had become increasingly angry with her husband. In letters she had been sending him in microdots through the Soviet espionage system reaching Kroger, Galyusha complained bitterly. She had heard about her husband's gay escapades with the women of London and she was furious. She wanted him home. Of course, Moscow would not agree. So the meeting between Gordon and Galyusha was a compromise all around.

After the meeting in Prague, at which nothing but more bitterness evolved, Lonsdale went back to Britain. Incidentally, let the record show that Lonsdale, as all good spies must, had a legitimate front. With funds that poured regularly to him from a Swiss bank, Lonsdale set himself up as a business speculator. He bought chewing gum machines and jukeboxes. He also financed a car security lock and even became a director of three companies.

But there was one thing Lonsdale did that was to prove his undoing and the undoing of the entire spy network. The Moscow school for spies had overlooked one human emotion, failed to provide for it in their syllabus of espionage. That was the emotion of loneliness—and the master spy, Lonsdale, couldn't help feeling lonely at times, even with his string of girlfriends. He had to have someone with whom he could talk freely and at ease. Only one such person could safely fill the bill—Helen Kroger.

So Lonsdale started to trek out to the Krogers'. He'd sit with Helen and discuss, among other things, his complaining wife. Understanding Helen Kroger would sympathize with him. It was all very cozy.

But it was a bad error of judgment on Lonsdale's part—and on that of the Krogers for allowing it. By making direct contact with the spy center, Lonsdale had violated Rule Number One.

How fatal this contact was to prove was demonstrated finally in January of 1960. It had a curious beginning. It started as an apparent vendetta against the chief photographer of the underwater weapons establishment at Portland. Anonymous letters began to arrive labeling the photographer a "filthy Jew," and claiming he was using Admiralty photographic equipment for personal gain—which he was not doing. The letters were signed with swastikas.

The photographer reported the matter to the Portland naval constabulary, which took up the case for investigation. It got nowhere trying to trace the origin of the letters.

When investigators questioned the photographer he told them:

"I haven't an enemy in the world—except perhaps Harry Houghton. For some reason he doesn't like me."

The men of the Dorset Criminal Investigation Division began to watch Houghton, whose greedy hands by now were beavering away at naval secrets at an increasing tempo. His movements puzzled Dorset CID and they reported their suspicions to Scotland Yard.

At the same time, Russian trawlers, bristling with antennae, began appearing in the English Channel whenever underwater weapons equipment was being secretly tested. The Admiralty knew someone was tipping off the Soviets. But Houghton was not yet dovetailed into the plot. He had come under official scrutiny only because of the poison-pen letters, with which, ironically enough, he actually had no connection.

Houghton by now had become the "top traitor" in Soviet spy activities against Britain because Her Majesty's Government had decided to concentrate the country's entire underwater research and development in one central location—Portland.

Almost simultaneously, the FBI in Washington had forwarded to Britain and its counter-espionage corps information it had recently gathered—the revelations of Colonel Pawel Monat, former senior officer of the Polish Military Intelligence, who fled to the West in November, 1959. For virtually a year, Colonel Monat had sat down with the FBI and explained the methods and achievements of the Polish Z-2 in Britain and elsewhere.

The FBI flashed the following message to M.I.5, Britain's military intelligence unit:

"Spy ring operating in British naval base, name unknown."

Prime Minister Macmillan ordered an investigation. He demanded top priority for the trackdown of the ring.

Scotland Yard chief George Gordon Smith, nicknamed "Moonraker," took a car to Harrods department store in Knightsbridge, and from there went on foot to the secret headquarters of M.I.5's chief. The two men conferred over the puzzling aspects of the facts in hand.

Could the message from Washington be linked with the clerk being investigated—the lowly clerk named Houghton, who led the high life?

They sent for Houghton's file. Then the two men launched an operation of unprecedented dimensions. Almost one hundred counter-espionage agents were thrown into the probe.

A squad of undercover operatives, some posing as young honeymooning couples, some as more elderly types, moved to Portland and nearby Weymouth, taking lodgings in hotels, frequenting the pubs. Their job: To put the M.I.5 microscope on the activities of Henry Houghton and the girl so often seen in his company, Elizabeth "Bunty" Gee. Their every movement was watched, every conversation was either overheard and recorded or picked up by tiny microphones and pocket tape-recorders.

For weeks the shadow of M.I.5 hovered over Houghton and Gee. Instructions were not to alert Houghton or Miss Gee, for it was vital to trap the masterminds of the spy ring, whoever they were.

Finally one day, unaware he was being watched, Houghton led secret service men to a meeting with Lonsdale, taking tea with him in the gray marbled quiet of Weymouth's Cumberland Hotel. Then he and Bunty caught a tube train from Marble Arch to Waterloo, blissfully unaware that behind them sat two M.I.5 men, who got up at Waterloo and followed the two suspects into grimy Waterloo Road where the couple linked up with a man in a blue gabardine raincoat.

The M.I.5 agents watched as Houghton handed the stranger a blue-gray carrier bag he had carried with him from Weymouth.

The M.I.5 men did not know the stranger in the blue raincoat, but they split up—one pursued Houghton and Miss Gee; the other followed the new suspect. In time, the counter-espionage agent established his quarry's identity—Gordon Lonsdale. The trail led always to Ruislip, but always Lonsdale was able to give the M.I.5 tails the slip so that they never got closer than within a few blocks of Station Okhotra—the Krogers' home.

But Lonsdale eventually slipped up. He was spotted by an M.I.5 agent driving a blue Ford Consul. The license number was noted and checked. It was Mrs. Kroger's car.

Before another day passed, Cranley Drive and its environs had a new roadsweeper, manned by a new man—an M.I.5 agent. There was a new insurance salesman going door-to-door on the block. And a team of telephone linemen appeared in Cranley Drive, making repairs to wires that had nothing wrong with them. A ruddy-faced young man even came to the Krogers' door and offered to do their gardening.

Another agent knocked at the door of a semidetached house on the corner of Courtfield Gardens, which overlooked the white-thatched-bungalow spy center. He asked the help of the housewife and her husband. They were close friends of the Krogers. The urgency and importance of the M.I.5 request was impressed on the couple and they were sworn to secrecy.

The next day the M.I.5 moved agents into their home. From the back bedroom, relays of agents trained powerful binoculars on the heavily barred front door of Station Okhotra.

But the vigil yielded little. Although Lonsdale and the two Admiralty servants, Houghton and Bunty Gee, were established beyond doubt as Soviet spies, the M.I.5 agents could get nothing on the Krogers—but their suspicions were kept alive by the periodic visits there of Lonsdale.

Then one night, Scotland Yard's "Moonraker" Smith himself came calling on the Krogers. Peter Kroger answered the door and came face to face with the jovial Superintendent of Scotland Yard's Special Branch. A big friendly smile creased Smith's face that evening of January 7, 1961.

"Sorry to trouble you, sir," he began mildly. He nodded towards his companion, Chief Inspector Ferguson Smith. "We are police officers, making inquiries about recent burglaries in this area. May we have a word with you?"

"Why, sure, come on in," replied Kroger. He could not have suspected the two police officers of being spy catchers, anymore than he might have suspected two detectives from New York's police force paying a visit to his one-time apartment on East 181st Street in the Bronx.

The approach was innocent enough. Kroger said he would give any information the investigators wanted—certainly it would be to his advantage to help catch any burglars prowling in the neighborhood. Two had already broken into his house. (He had no way of knowing, of course, that the "burglars" were M.I.5 agents!)

Kroger stepped back and ushered the two Saturday-night callers into his spy nest. They scraped and stamped the mud off their feet respectfully on the coconut-fiber mat and entered the living room. It was a warm, comfortable home. Outwardly the two officers could see nothing unusual. Helen Kroger, with an apron over her dress, added a homey touch as she came out of the kitchen, her hands damp with dishwater, to see who the visitors were.

"We're actually from the Special Branch," Superintendent Smith then informed the couple.

The words fell like crushing hammer blows. Now the Krogers

knew the jig was up. They knew that Special Branch, like the FBI, did not investigate a neighborhood burglary, but much bigger matters.

"By the way," the friendly Scotland Yard chief said in his Wiltshire accent, "your friend won't be coming to see you tonight. He's been unavoidably detained."

Lonsdale had come to the end of the road earlier that day, and so had Henry Houghton and Elizabeth "Bunty" Gee.

The action had started early in the afternoon as Houghton and Bunty sped to London by train. Relays of M.I.5 men and women were hot on their trail then, having picked it up at Weymouth. Houghton was carrying his blue bag—and the counter-espionage agents now had a good idea what was inside: Photographs of the *Dreadnought!*

It was time to take them. "Moonraker" Smith alerted the chief of M.I.5, who grabbed a phone and murmured simply, "Ivan."

That was the signal for the M.I.5 agents to move in, and rapidly the word was flashed to a score of British Secret Service operatives.

At 3:20 P.M. when Houghton and Elizabeth Gee walked through the ticket barrier at Waterloo's Platform 14, they were in the grip of a fantastic invisible net. Dozens of eyes were peering at them, yet they never suspected. The girl selling flags, the porter lugging a suitcase, bystanders in street and working clothes—all were M.I.5 agents. All were watching.

Outside, Special Branch men were at the wheels of commercial vans, a simulated taxi, and even a millionaire-style Jaguar. Their engines were idling, ready to roll at a given signal.

For seventy tense, pulsating minutes the cat-and-mouse game was played with unrelenting precision and nerve.

"Two threepennies, please," said Houghton as he bought bus tickets to Walworth for himself and Bunty Gee.

"Two threepennies, please," repeated the M.I.5 girl in the flowered headscarf right behind them. Her companion was a youth.

At their destination in Walworth, Houghton and Elizabeth Gee idled in the busy East Street marketplace, buying small items and shoving them into a small shopping basket on top of a canister containing the photo of the *Dreadnought*—and other secret photographs.

Agent U, accompanied by Agent X, who had ridden the bus with the spies, dutifully made purchases on behalf of the British Government. They spent sparingly—just 4 shillings and 9 pence—for a plastic towel holder and a friction-drive toy fire engine.

The counter-espionage agents, the girl-boy team, followed Houghton and Miss Gee back on another bus, back to Waterloo.

At almost that very moment, Gordon Lonsdale was leaving his office in Wardour Street. Woman Agent X observed his movements as he crossed over to get into his stone-and-blue Studebaker, license ULA 61, Agent X dropped her newspaper. It signaled a Q-car taxi—and Lonsdale had company on his journey to Waterloo, where he would rendezvous with Houghton and Gee.

It was 4:30 P.M., outside the Old Victoria Theater. Inside, the curtain was about to fall on the matinee performance of *A Midsummer Night's Dream*.

The curtain also fell outside. It fell quickly, unfalteringly, as "Moonraker" Smith swooped down on the three spies on the sidewalk in front of Old Vic—just as Miss Gee handed Lonsdale the shopping basket.

"I say there," came the dramatic line spoken in the rich Wiltshire accent by "Moonraker" as he patted Lonsdale on the back, "Scotland Yard for you, boy."

Then, as "Moonraker" Smith and his namesake hurried on to complete the roundup with the arrest of the Krogers, agents hastened to Lonsdale's and Houghton's and Elizabeth Gee's flats. At Miss Gee's digs they found $13,291 in cash and savings bonds, and two hundred photos of top-secret naval pamphlets on antisubmarine warfare.

At Houghton's, $1,800 in a paint can.

At Lonsdale's, the counter-espionage teams found an interesting number of tools of the spy trade—including a flashlight, which seemed quite ordinary until it was taken apart and one of the batteries was found to be hollow and filled with pieces of paper.

But that was a minor find compared with the haul "Moonraker" Smith uncovered at the Krogers' place. The trap door was quickly found, once the linoleum was turned up in the kitchen. In the earthen hiding place the transmitter was uncovered in its metal container.

Additionally, as other agents moved into the house and began to search the premises, they discovered a cigaret lighter, a present from Lonsdale, which was fashioned with a false bottom that stocked paper used by Russian intelligence.

There also was a hip flask, filled with a powder to help visual reading of Morse on a tape recorder. And there were tins of talcum that did not contain talcum but had false bottoms and cavities that held pieces of paper and a microdot reader, resembling a small telescope. And there was $6,000 in U.S. twenty-dollar bills, plus 2,613 one-dollar bills, and $2,030 in U.S. travelers checks and some British travelers checks.

The five Soviet spies were locked up, after their hearing in Bow Street Magistrate's Court. In jail, while awaiting their trial in famed Old Bailey, Lonsdale insisted on his innocence. He was not a Russian, not a spy, but a Canadian emigré, he asserted. Then came his final unmasking—with a physical examination in the jail infirmary!

The prison doctors referred to the information filed by Canadian Mountie Corporal Jack Carroll, who had talked with a country doctor in far away Cobalt, Ontario. The doctor had remembered after all those years the little boy who was Gordon Lonsdale. He checked his records. And his records showed that the little boy had been circumcised.

It was a physical characteristic the prisoner going by the name of Lonsdale could not hide—and he was trapped. Obviously he was not the real Gordon Lonsdale.

Chapter 22

In the Dock at Old Bailey

The trial in Old Bailey, world-famed hall of justice, was about to get under way when another blow of sizable dimensions befell two of the accused spies.

Scotland Yard had begun, after its initial find of spy equipment in the Kroger house, a plank-by-plank search of the residence. It took two days to find some additional items, like money in the ceiling, and nine more days to complete the search. And the most important item from a long-term counter-espionage point of view, strangely enough, was a silver locket, hidden in the living room wall. Inside the locket was a picture of three children.

Who were those children?

No one seemed to know—but the search went on, both in England by Scotland Yard and M.I.5, and in the United States by the FBI. For it seemed then that those children, fantastic as it may sound, might have had an important place in the lives and operations of the spy couple known as Peter and Helen Kroger.

Peter and Helen Kroger refused to say who the children were. They also refused to admit they were anyone other than the persons they pretended to be. There was no way to extract from them the identity of the youngsters.

But fingerprints on file in Scotland Yard, which had been sent to Great Britain several years earlier during the sensational arrest of Russian master-spy Abel, were waiting for comparison tests. They were the fingerprints of Morris "Unc" Cohen and his wife, Lona.

They were compared with the Krogers' prints—and they matched.

The world, of course, did not yet know this, or that the Cohens and the Krogers were one and the same couple.

That was to be my own personal scoop—a scoop of which I'm very proud.

But there must have been considerably greater pride for Scotland Yard Superintendent Smith and his assistants and the members of Great Britain's finely trained M.I.5 unit as they sat in Old Bailey on Wednesday, March 23, 1961, and listened to the sentences meted out to the quintet of spies, after a swift trial and conviction.

Lord Parker, the Lord Chief Justice, asked Lonsdale to face the bench and hear his sentence read. A smile creased Lonsdale's face after hearing his counsel plead with the court for mercy, with the alibi: "At least it can be said of this man that he was not a traitor to his own country."

But the tone of Lord Parker's voice and the words it carried quickly dimmed the smile and Lonsdale grimaced. A gasp broke the silence of the packed court.

"You are clearly a professional spy. . . . It is a dangerous career and one in which you should be prepared—and no doubt are prepared—to suffer if you are caught. I sentence you to twenty-five years in jail."

Then came the Krogers' turn.

"You were both in this up to the hilt. You are both professional spies, and the only distinction between the two of you and Lonsdale, if I am right, is that yours was not the directing mind and that you are a little older. I sentence each of you to twenty years."

Kroger staggered backwards in the dock, his brow creased in pain at the prospect of a near-lifetime of separation from his wife after twenty years of marriage.

Two wardens gripped his arms, but he broke away to reach out and touch his wife's sleeve.

All through the trial, Kroger, formerly Cohen, the old footballer from James Monroe High in the Bronx, now a long way from home, was sentimentally soft, kind, solicitous to his wife. Every day when they came into court, he was careful to see his wife seated before he took his own seat next to her.

Now, as sentence was passed, Kroger was hurried from the dock.

Then it was his wife's turn to leave, to be led to jail to spend the next twenty years of her life.

Lord Parker next turned to Houghton.

"I have considered long what to do with you. You are, however, now fifty-six, and a not very young fifty-six, and it is against all our principles that a sentence should be given which might entail your dying in prison.

"But for that, I would give you a longer sentence. In all the circumstances, I think the proper sentence for you is fifteen years imprisonment."

And now the last of the five, Houghton's paramour and partner in espionage, had her turn to hear herself sentenced.

"I have reluctantly come to the conclusion," said the Lord Chief Justice, "that I cannot distinguish between you and Houghton. I am quite unable to think it possible you did what you did out of some blind infatuation for Houghton. Indeed, having heard you and watched you, I am inclined to think yours was the stronger character of the two.

"I think you acted for greed. The sentence on you is the same as that on Houghton—fifteen years' imprisonment."

The Attorney General, who had prosecuted the case, then raised the question with the court about costs. He said the expense ran to 5,100 pounds.

The five prisoners were brought back into the dock and Lord Parker told them:

"An application has been made that you pay the costs of this prosecution. My order is that Gee, Houghton, and Lonsdale should each pay 1,000 pounds toward the costs of the prosecution, and the Krogers jointly 1,000 pounds."

There was no fear that the five spies would have to split rocks in prison to pay off the debt. None whatsoever, for they had ample funds among them. When arrested their total wealth added up to nearly 11,000 pounds, or more than $30,000.

The Russians had thought of everything—even the money their spies would need for the cost of their prosecution when they got caught.

Chapter 23

The Army Sergeants Who Goofed as Spies

It could have turned into a Keystone Cops comedy-scenario. But it didn't because the two uniformed patrolmen of the Freeport Village police on Long Island weren't exactly types to play the funny characters who cavorted across the screen in the days of silent movies. Those Freeport cops were on their toes when they spotted the 1966 Ford station wagon cruising suspiciously along community streets—and they were doing their jobs when they pulled the driver over to the curb on North Bergen Place.

"License and registration, please," said one of the patrolmen, casting a searching eye at the other four occupants of the vehicle.

Instead of his driver's credentials, the man behind the wheel flashed an identification card. The patrolman snapped back.

"We're on a case," the driver snorted impatiently.

The policeman grinned sheepishly. "Okay, sir," he rasped, "sorry about that."

The patrolman strolled back to the police cruiser and murmured to his partner, "I wonder who they're after. That's Army Counter-Intelligence."

The station wagon pulled away and headed for a preassigned destination on the Sunrise Highway near the Long Island Railroad station. Cruising in the same area were four other cars, all late-model sedans, bearing sixteen FBI agents.

Their assignment was to shadow a tall, broad-shouldered, muscular black man with a modified Fu Manchu mustache who was arriving on the 8:07 P.M. train out of Pennsylvania Station in Manhattan. They had been dispatched to Freeport to begin tying together the loose ends on one of the year's most scintillating spy dramas.

A few blocks away on West Merrick Road, more radio-equipped FBI cruisers were coursing slowly along the busy street keeping a 1965 green Rambler sedan in their sights. The car, bearing two occupants, had diplomatic license plates that an earlier check through the Motor Vehicle Bureau found to have been issued to the Byelorussian Mission at the UN.

The driver appeared to be desperately searching for a place to park on the crowded street.

The Rambler had been followed to Freeport from twenty miles away—the Soviet Delegation headquarters on East 67th Street—and the agents tailing the car had every reason to believe the man sitting beside the driver was heading for a rendezvous with the black man making his way out to the Island on the train.

Their paths had crossed before on numerous occasions and at various locales. The beginning ranged back to a day fourteen months before the night of May 27, 1967, when the leading characters and supporting actors in this spy saga were converging climactically on Freeport.

The first recorded date was July 3, 1966, when Army Warrant Officer Willie Fletcher, stationed at the Strategic Communications Command Facility in Suitland, Maryland, just outside Washington, was invited with his family to spend the Fourth of July holiday in Neptune, New Jersey.

The invitation had been proffered by another soldier at Suitland, thirty-one-year-old Staff Sergeant Leonard J. Safford, a career man who had eleven years of Army service under his belt and was then serving as administrative supervisor at the Strategic Communications Command Facility.

Their destination was an unpretentious Cape Cod dwelling in Neptune where another enlisted man, thirty-seven-year-old Sergeant First Class Ullyses L. Harris, made his home with his family. A fourteen-year soldier, Harris, like Fletcher and Safford, had Top-Secret clearance for his work with the Signal Corps at Fort Monmouth, New Jersey.

Harris and Safford had previously served together in various other military installations and the men, with their families, often visited each others' homes over the years.

Fletcher had never met Harris before and his acquaintanceship with Safford had evolved out of their duty together at the sensitive Army installation in Suitland. As a warrant officer, Fletcher not only shared Top-Secret clearance with Safford, but through his broader supervisory duties also commanded far greater access to official military and defense material that flowed through the facility.

There was no other consideration in Fletcher's mind when Harris asked him to visit his old buddy than that it was a purely social outing. But it wasn't many hours after arriving in Neptune, following a festive backyard barbecue enjoyed by the men, their wives, and the children, that the true purpose of the visit surfaced.

Fletcher became astonishingly aware of that ulterior motive when Safford nudged him at the picnic table to follow him off to a corner of the yard for a whispered conversation with Harris. Their host came to the point with dispatch. He eyed Fletcher with a shrewd gaze and rubbed his chin thoughtfully.

"You handle some pretty important stuff down there in Maryland, I hear," Harris said in a tone that almost at once mirrored conspiratorial shadings.

Fletcher nodded politely. He wasn't yet clear as to what Harris was driving at.

"Lenny has clearance also," Harris said. He could smell something coming in Harris' overly blunt approach.

"Well, what I'm trying to say is that you have access to classified material that Lenny can't get to," Harris said in a silky whisper. "You know what I'm driving at?"

"No, not really," Fletcher said flatly. He gazed at Harris with rueful bewilderment. He was almost sorry that he had brought his family to Neptune for the holiday. What's going on here? he asked himself.

"Look, Willie," Harris said softly. "You need money. You got a family and lots of expenses. Army pay ain't so good, right?"

"I get along," Fletcher replied in a tone that offered no apology for the remunerations and benefits the Army gives its warrant officers.

But suddenly Fletcher seemed to suffer a resiliency in his stand against Harris' approaches. The wheels in his mind had been spinning.

"Just what are you aiming at, Ullyses?" he asked in a voice all at once condescending.

Harris' thick lips curled into a half-smile.

"What I want to know is can you, maybe, gather some of that confidential data down at Suitland and bring it off the base?"

Harris' voice trailed off as he eyed Fletcher with a fixed stare, his face somber with seeming anxiety for a favorable response.

It was a bewildering moment for Fletcher. He had no doubt anymore about what Harris was aiming for. It was plain and simple. The tall, wide-shouldered bruiser with the miniature Fu Manchu mustache was asking his visitor in so many words to gather classified information and sell it.

Could there be any doubt to the reader who the ultimate purchaser would be?

So far as Fletcher was concerned, the situation was highly suspicious. He was reasonably convinced that Harris—and no less so his companion on the trip to Neptune, Leonard Safford—were engaged in illegal activity.

The thought that it might be espionage did not elude him. The silhouette of probable conspiracy was more than a vague outline now despite the little that had been said thus far.

"What if I can bring classified material off the base?" Fletcher asked quietly. "What's the pitch?"

Harris smiled, pleased. He reflected his satisfaction at Fletcher's response. He had reached him. This was not the time to go into detail. Fletcher seemed approachable—and that was all Harris had to hear for now. He was not prepared to go beyond the initial approach just made. His goal was achieved. He had felt out Fletcher and had found him responsive.

"We'll talk some more another time," Harris said carefully. He

clutched Fletcher and Safford by the arm and escorted them back
to the picnic table where their wives had been sitting and chat-
ting.

There was no further discussion on the topic Harris had
brought up. The rest of the afternoon was spent in the pleasantness of a social gathering, and at seven o'clock that evening the
visitors piled into Safford's car for the drive back to Maryland.

In the weeks that followed, Fletcher and Safford saw each other
frequently at the Strategic Communications Command Facility
but said little about the matter broached by Harris. From time to
time, Fletcher queried Safford about his friend's overture.

"I could use that extra money that Ullyses was talking about,"
Fletcher said at one point. "When are we going to hear from him?"

"Just sit tight," Safford replied. "We'll get word pretty soon."

Then in early September, Safford approached Fletcher.

"Ullyses is coming to Washington in a few days," he said ex-
citedly. "He says he is going to try and work something out with
you."

Fletcher seemed puzzled.

"Just with me?" he frowned. "What about you?"

"I'm in it, too," Safford said slowly. "But it's you he wants to
talk to."

Fletcher tried to pump more information out of the sergeant
but received only vague responses. Safford either didn't know
much about Harris' plans—or was reluctant to discuss them with
the warrant officer. Fletcher suspected the latter was a more accurate barometer of the situation.

On the Labor Day weekend, Harris came to Washington and
met Safford and Fletcher at the Jefferson Memorial.

"Everything is starting to work out swell," Harris advised his
listeners. "We'll have something cooking in a few weeks and we're
all going to make a lot of loot out of the deal."

Harris didn't dwell on specifics. But he left little doubt as to
what the "deal" would be.

"It's very important," Harris said in a firm voice to Fletcher,
"that you begin to figure how to smuggle classified information
off the base. You know the place better than Willie or I know it. If
you can't bring the stuff itself out, maybe you could photograph
it. But one way or another, you got to let me know how it's going
to be done."

The triumvirate in the developing conspiracy parted company

at the memorial and Fletcher did not see Harris again until the following February. But he heard from him on at least four other occasions, each time on the phone. Each time Harris prodded Fletcher about his progress in developing the plan for getting the information off the base, and each time Fletcher added a refinement or two to his previous evaluation of how he could best smuggle secrets out of the facility in Suitland.

In one of their last conversations in December, Fletcher informed Harris that he was fairly confident material could be taken off the base "without too much risk of getting caught."

Harris was delighted to hear that Fletcher had made so much progress.

"I'll get back to you very soon," he said. "I think we're in business."

But Harris wasn't only keeping in touch with Fletcher. He made periodic calls to Safford as well. And in one of those longline linkups between Neptune and Safford's home in Chillum, Maryland, instructions were laid down for a specific assignment.

Harris told Safford that he wanted photographs made of the Army Traffic Command Facility at Roslyn, Virginia, just across the Potomac from the nation's capital.

Safford proceeded immediately to delegate that task to a soldier, Robert A. Cook. The assignment was made without Fletcher being involved or even apprised of that clandestine compact.

Not until February 10, 1967, did Fletcher's role in the conspiracy crystalize to any appreciable dimension. Then it stiffened dramatically into an unmistakable configuration of subversion with an involvement that thoroughly astonished the unbelieving warrant officer.

He was summoned to a rendezvous with Harris and Safford in the Fairfax Restaurant in southeast Washington, where the three GI's feasted on a sumptuous and scrumptious meal which cost them not a red cent. Yet *red* was the color of the money that paid for the gastronomic goodies—for the person who picked up the tab was none other than Nikolai Fedorovich Popov, a First Secretary at the Soviet Embassy.

During the meal, Fletcher seemed to be the focus of Popov's remarks. The diplomat, a round-faced, blue-eyed blonde of average height who seemed to be in his middle thirties, affected a habit of twitching his left nostril nervously when he spoke. His tone was an unvarying spurious basso, even when he was ordering appetizers and entrees from the waiter.

Fletcher couldn't help but feel that Popov was parading all the characteristics of the classic fictional spy of literature, movies, and television.

"I understand you are in a position to provide confidential information that is routed through the Strategic Communications Command," Popov said slowly, enunciating carefully in a clipped British accent that did not camouflage the viscous syllables of the diplomat's native Russian.

"That's right," Fletcher answered briskly. "What do you propose?"

Popov proceeded to outline a plan that appeared to have been mapped thoroughly beforehand and which evoked no surprise from either Harris or Safford. They seemed to be familiar with its details as though they had been briefed earlier.

"You will have no further contact with me until I let you know," Popov said with a secret sort of smile. "You will make arrangements with Ullyses and Lenny about delivering the material to them. They will get it to me. It is for safety reasons, you understand . . . "

Fletcher nodded. He understood.

Over the next four months, Fletcher delivered batches of documents to Safford but none to Harris, who had his own espionage duties to perform from his sensitive post at Fort Monmouth. He was too busy to be involved in the Maryland espionage operation for the time being.

As a loner, Safford proved to be an exceptionally proficient courier, receiving the material from Fletcher and bringing it to Popov. The sergeant and the Soviet diplomat found three locales where it was both convenient and safe to meet and pass the military documents. These were the Fairfax Restaurant, the Hillandale Shopping Center in Hillandale, Maryland, and another Maryland site, the Palmer Park Shopping Center in Palmer.

After Safford delivered a batch of documents to Popov at the Palmer Park Center in mid-April, the Soviet spy advised the sergeant that a meeting with Harris was urgently needed.

"There has been a change in plans," Popov said firmly. "You and Ullyses are going to deal with a new contact."

The Russian then informed Safford that arrangements had been made with Harris to meet at his home in Neptune to finalize the switch in contacts.

The next day, Safford and Popov, driving in separate cars, went to Harris' place and found a burly, middle-aged, dark-haired man with a slight mustache seated in a comfortable wingback armchair in the living room.

As Popov entered the room, the man rose to his feet quickly and embraced the visitor.

"My dear Nikolai," he said, bubbling with excitement. "How wonderful to see you."

Popov handed the introduction to Safford.

"This is Anatoly," he smiled. "He is your new contact."

The man introduced to Safford was Anatoly Tikhorovich Kiryev, a counselor of the Soviet Mission at the UN.

"You will receive further instructions about when you will meet Anatoly," Popov said.

Back in Washington after that brief meeting, Popov sent word through Safford to Fletcher that he was to meet the Embassy official on the sidewalk under the marquee of the fashionable Mayflower Hotel at eight o'clock on the night of April 22nd. Fletcher parked his car on a nearby side street and walked to his meeting with the Russian. A few minutes after he arrived at the hotel entrance, he spotted Popov coming toward him. He was carrying a small parcel.

Popov shook hands with Fletcher. The Russian's nostrils twitched as he spoke with the soldier.

"I have in this package instructions for you and Ullyses," he said tersely. "Follow them. There is nothing more I have to tell you."

He handed the brown-paper-wrapped package to Fletcher, then turned and walked away at a brisk pace. Fletcher took the parcel back to the Strategic Communications Command Facility in Suitland and entered an office over whose door the sign read: "Military Intelligence Officer."

As he had been doing from the very morning following his return from the first visit to Harris' home in Neptune, Warrant Officer Fletcher was reporting his dealings with the spy ring to Military Intelligence. All the material bearing on military secrets that he delivered from the base to the Russians had been provided by the Army's intelligence people.

Unknown to Harris, Safford, and the other conspirators, Willie Fletcher was a counterspy!

When the parcel was opened, it was found to be an ordinary cigar box. Inside were two sets of instructions—one for Fletcher, the other for Harris. Fletcher's orders were relatively routine. He was to continue delivering secrets he filched from the military installation to Safford who, instead of bringing them to Popov, was to pass them to Harris.

Then, in turn, Harris was to get them into Kiryev's hands.

The date of May 27th was designated in the instructions for the first delivery under that new routine. Harris was to turn over the information he received to Kiryev in front of the Packard Shoe Store at 8A West Merrick Road in Freeport.

The instructions were explicit—Harris was to take the 8:07 train to Freeport, take the stairs to the street, make his way to North Bergen Place, and pretend to make a call from an outdoor phone booth on the grounds of the Big Apple Supermarket. That procedure was dictated so as to enable Harris to observe the scene and determine whether he was being followed or watched.

When Harris arrived in Freeport that night he had no idea that he was being watched—nor that FBI agents were preserving his entire routine on movie film.

After Harris left the phone booth, the sixteen agents in the four cars and the five Army Counter-Intelligence sleuths in the station wagon continued to keep him under constant surveillance. They tailed him as he walked to the Savoy Inn at 108 West Merrick Road and stood outside the tavern for four minutes—just as the instructions had told him to do.

The agents also observed their quarry glancing at a piece of paper with frequent regularity. He was reading the instructions on his itinerary.

As he started for his ultimate destination, where he was due to arrive at 9:15 P.M., other agents, who'd been keeping tabs on the green Rambler from the Byelorussian Mission, saw the driver park the car and observed the man beside him glancing anxiously up and down the sidewalk.

By 9:14 P.M. Harris had made his way along West Merrick Road from the Savoy Inn and was within fifty feet of the shoe store.

The man in the passenger seat of the Rambler spotted him finally and got out of the car. As Harris neared him, the man took quick steps toward the soldier and greeted him with a vigorous handshake.

Then the two began to walk along the street. They went about one hundred feet when suddenly their watchers observed them shaking hands again. The man then walked back to the car and was driven away immediately. Harris strolled back to the station and caught a train back to New York.

The man who had rendezvoused with Harris was no stranger to him. They had met before at Harris' house. He was none other than Anatoly Kiryev. And as the FBI would learn later, the man who served as his driver was Vladimir Makhatin, who was employed as a chauffeur with the Byelorussian Mission.

Makhatin returned Kiryev to the Soviet Mission in Manhattan. Harris went home to Neptune.

After other meetings that were observed by Army Intelligence officers and FBI agents in and around the Washington area, the Army on August 4th made a surprising move with a man who figured as a prime suspect in espionage. They transferred Harris to duty with a long-line communications unit—in Korea.

This strategy was employed to ferret out other possible conspirators in the spy network. Harris, a valuable cog in the espionage web, had been taken out of action, and the authorities wanted to determine who, if anybody, would become his replacement.

But after four months, during which Government agents failed to unearth any additional parties to the conspiracy, the Defense Department was advised that the time had come to close the ring on the spies.

Harris was arrested at his post in Korea and whisked back to the United States on August 24th.

Just as the plane which brought him back was touching down at Andrews Air Force Base, Army Intelligence agents were knocking on Safford's door in Chillum.

With the two arrests, the Defense Department made a public announcement of the conspiracy and let it be known that the two sergeants were being held in custody for court-martial.

But no action was contemplated against Popov or Kiryev. The

Russians had already flown the coop. Their missions had returned the two diplomats to Moscow barely days before the Government moved in on the conspirators. The suspicion to this day is that the Russians had gotten drift of the investigation and decided to spare Popov and Kiryev the embarrassment of being declared persona non grata by the State Department and ordered out of the country in disgrace.

For Safford and Harris, the next one hundred days were extremely lonely as they waited for a military tribunal to hear their cases. They were confined to solitary confinement in a wing of the stockade at Fort Belvoir, Virginia, known as "Little Alcatraz."

On December 5th, Safford was brought before a seven-member court-martial panel headed by Colonel Marcello W. Bordley Jr. The defendant was flanked by two Army lawyers, who advised the tribunal that their client was prepared to plead guilty. But they depicted Safford as a man who had toiled as a spy to earn extra money for his family—while all the time scheming to foil the Russians.

Yet there was no evidence to convince the court that Safford had done anything to thwart the conspiracy. And he was compelled to admit that he had received $1,000 from Popov in payment for services rendered as an espionage agent.

Safford also pleaded guilty to another charge that had nothing to do with subversion—theft of a $24,076 Treasury check from the Air Products and Chemical Inc. firm in Blandensburg, Maryland.

After listening to the pleas, the panel went into its deliberations to arrive at a sentence. Twenty-five minutes later, they summoned Safford before them and Colonel Bordley announced the verdict:

Twenty-five years at hard labor and a dishonorable discharge from the Army!

A week later, on December 12th, the panel convened again for the court-martial of Sergeant Ullyses Harris, who stood on his insistence that he was not guilty.

The evidence against him mounted quickly.

Warrant Officer Willie Fletcher testified about his role in the conspiracy as a counterspy. He started with the day he went with his family to Harris' home.

"He asked me if I had access to any classified material," the witness said. "I understood it to mean whether I would gather classified information and sell it. I decided to play along and see what I could learn—and I reported it to Army Intelligence."

Fletcher went on to testify as to the methods he employed in delivering "material furnished me by military intelligence" at a "drop" designated by Popov, as well as the information he passed to Safford, the instructions he received from Popov in the cigar box, and other details of the conspiracy.

Then Army Counter-Intelligence and FBI agents who had maintained the surveillance over Harris' Freeport meeting with Kiryev paraded to the stand. They told of their intensive observations along West Merrick Road and the rendezvous of the soldier and Russian in front of the shoe store.

None of the witnesses testified at the public portion of the court-martial about whether or not they had seen Harris pass anything to Kiryev. Because so much testimony and evidence hinged on national security, the tribunal held closed-court sessions at which, it was learned, photostatic copies of the documents delivered to the Russians and other Top-Secret papers were introduced in evidence.

Dozens of photos of the Freeport meeting were also shown to the court, which led observers to remark that the *secret* rendezvous was one of the most photographed events on Long Island.

The tribunal returned a guilty verdict against Harris. The sentence:

Seven years at hard labor and a dishonorable discharge.

That was three years less than the maximum that could have been imposed.

But as in every case of espionage the real culprits—the Kremlin spies who generate subversion—were once more beyond the reach of justice.

The sergeants who goofed as spies were punished severely, yet the very men who instigated and nourished the conspiracy were home free.

The cloak of diplomatic immunity, which shields such foreign agents, had prevented the authorities from seizing Kiryev and Popov when their Government was dispatching them back to the Soviet Union.

Not that it would have made a particle of difference if the Russians were detained. For there isn't a single case on record over all the years of Soviet espionage in this country of any Kremlin diplomat being brought to trial.

It's only foolish Americans, like Safford, Harris, and those others who sold their country down the river for a few bucks, who have paid the high penalty for crimes committed against our national security.

Chapter 24

How Not to Steal the Grumman F-14 Airplane Secrets

"A Soviet citizen employed as a translator at the United Nations was indicted by a Federal grand jury today on charges of acting as an illegal Soviet agent in this country and espionage in obtaining plans for a new Navy fighter . . . "

This was the opening paragraph of a Department of Justice press release issued Thursday, February 17, 1972. It was another exercise in frustration.

The indicted Soviet citizen was Valeriy Ivanovich Markelov, a mild-mannered, fair-skinned thirty-two-year-old Russian who was charged in the first count of the indictment with obtaining "documents connected with the national defense relating to the design of the Grumman F-14 aircraft for the use and benefit of the Soviet Union."

The second count accused Markelov of acting as "an agent of the Soviet Government in this country without notifying the Secretary of State." The State Department statement went on to explain that "such notification is required of individuals who are not diplomatic or consular officers or attachés."

The press release was one of the most incredibly stupid statements that could have been made by the State Department. Yet such pronouncements have been made repeatedly and without letup over the years in tandem with the expulsion of every Soviet spy caught committing espionage against the United States.

One would have to assume the State Department looks upon Russians as some sort of idiots in expecting them to follow the absurd demand that they register their spies in Washington before embarking on a program of subversion in this country.

Has anyone ever heard of a spy walking into the State Department, laying his credentials on the desk, and declaring, "I'm here to register as an agent of the Soviet Union"?

That isn't the way the spies we've written about thus far have operated—and Valeriy Ivanovich Markelov's methods did not reflect any radical departure from the modus operandi of the espionage agents who preceded him in this country.

Like many of the others, Markelov was reaching for the impossible dream. He was after the plans of the F-14, nicknamed the Tomcat, which is slated to become the next generation of Navy carrier-based interceptors.

The supersonic Tomcat, which will replace the current F-4, was chosen over the controversial F-111, also known as the TFX, after the latter was determined to be too large and heavy for use as an interceptor.

What makes the F-14 unique is that it will be the first operational aircraft with swing-wing capability. This feature enables the pilot to pull the wings back almost parallel to the fuselage to attain unheard of speeds—speeds that are still classified.

The plane is also said to be capable of spotting an enemy aircraft at distances of two hundred miles with its radar, and to have the potential to destroy the other craft with its rockets.

It is difficult to determine precisely when Markelov first heard about the F-14 or when the Soviet Union became interested in the plans. But the Russians are voracious readers of newspapers and magazines, and it was no secret that the Grumman Aerospace Corporation in Bethpage, Long Island, had been awarded a $5-billion contract to build 313 of the aircraft. Grumman had also built the famed F-4U Corsair, one of the best fighter planes of World War II, and had produced the Lunar Extravehicular Module (LEM), the spidery-looking spaceship that landed our astronauts on the moon.

One of the last places Markelov would be expected to be found was at an engineers' conference, since his duties at the Russian Translation Section of the UN called on him to revise first drafts prepared by other translators on scientific and technical material.

But there he was big as life on that balmy afternoon of October 15, 1970, hobnobbing with the engineers at their convocation in a midtown Manhattan hotel. Out of all the engineers Markelov met that day, none appeared to hold his interest as much as the man we shall call Frank Prushkin.

What undoubtedly attracted Markelov to his quarry was that Prushkin was a design engineer employed by Grumman—on the F-14 project!

It wasn't much of a strain for Markelov to open a line of communication with Prushkin, who happened to be of Russian descent. But that wasn't the principal plateau of their compatibility. Markelov also happened to be a graduate engineer.

Before going to work at the UN in November, 1967, under a five-year $18,500-a-year contract, Markelov had spent ten years at the Bauman Higher Technical School in Moscow. He majored there in mechanical engineering, and then served at the institution from 1963 to 1966 as a researcher in industrial technology and patent matters.

With his knowledge of engineering established, the Soviet espionage network recruited Markelov for duty as a spy in the United States. His mission would require him to work under the cover of a translator's post at the UN—and Markelov was sent to a school for translators for a year before being dispatched to New York to begin his role in espionage.

Now, at last, after three years of seeming non-achievement (and we say that only because the FBI is not aware of any espionage activity in that period), Markelov made his big move at the engineers' conference.

"We should get together for drinks and dinner," suggested Markelov after a brief conversation with Prushkin. "There is so much that we can discuss. I am very impressed with your work on that new airplane . . . I would like to hear more about it . . . "

Prushkin appeared amenable to the suggestion and gave his home phone number to Markelov, who jotted it down in a small address book.

"You live on Long Island, I see," Markelov observed. That wasn't difficult to figure out since Prushkin's area code was 516. "Perhaps I can meet you out there and it will save you the trip into the city," the translator went on benevolently.

Prushkin acknowledged that it was all right with him if Markelov wanted to make the wearying trek out to the Island.

"Call me whenever you decide," Prushkin said briefly as he shook hands with the Soviet spy.

His meeting with Markelov didn't dwell heavily on Prushkin's mind after that day, for the entire conversation had been brief and relatively inconsequential.

Thus when his phone rang on Sunday night, December 2, 1970, and he heard Markelov's voice, Prushkin was somewhat surprised. He had almost forgotten about the Russian's offer to take him to dinner.

"Will you be free tomorrow night?" Markelov wanted to know.

"Fine with me," Prushkin responded. "Where shall we meet?"

Markelov suggested the Marcpiere, a restaurant on Route 110 in Melville, which was about a fifteen-minute drive from the engineer's home.

"They have an excellent continental cuisine," Markelov said. "And the drinks are superb."

Prushkin agreed to meet Markelov there and the next night at eight o'clock found his host waiting for him in the foyer next to the hatcheck room. The two men were escorted to a table and in less time than the waiter needed to bring them their cocktails, Markelov had laid his cards on the table.

"Very frankly," Markelov said, drawing in a deep breath, "I have a proposition to make to you. I would like you to provide me with information and data on the F-14 . . . "

His words trailed off and in the silence that ensued, Markelov studied the stunned expression on Prushkin's face.

"There will be big money for you," Markelov said, shifting restlessly as he sensed Prushkin's shock.

"But I could lose my job . . . I could go to jail if I'm caught doing that . . . " the engineer stammered.

"Nothing will happen to you," the Russian said with an air of confidence. "It will be done in such a way that not even you will suspect that you are doing anything wrong."

Markelov burst out laughing. He apparently enjoyed the humor in his own remark.

By the time the main course was over and dessert was served, Markelov had Prushkin convinced that the plans for the F-14 could be removed from Grumman—and those that couldn't might be photostated or photographed with relative ease.

"But now is not the time to discuss that phase of our project," Markelov said. "First I would like you to deliver the preliminary information that I have requested . . . "

That included brochures, literature, photographs, and unclassified general specifications on the F-14 that were available at Grumman for general distribution to the press. Markelov said he wanted these documents "to orient myself with the kind of plane that this Tomcat is."

That was how it all began . . .

Over the next fourteen months, Markelov, who received the initial delivery of material he had requested, made increasingly more stringent demands on Prushkin in a plot designed to obtain every last ounce of information on the F-14.

In the beginning, Prushkin delivered material of a classified nature that included design plans of the aircraft, specifications of its power plant, and other data which the engineer told Markelov he was able to filch from the engineering design section at Grumman.

But a point came in the conspiracy when the Russian made even more pressing requirements of Prushkin, for information the engineer said he could not deliver.

"There is only one of a kind of such material," Prushkin explained. "There is no way I can make copies of it."

But Markelov had a solution when he learned that Prushkin could smuggle some of the data out of the plant overnight without great risk of getting caught, provided he returned the documents in the morning. Markelov supplied the engineer with a portable copying machine with instructions in its use.

"Make the copies at your home at night," he told Prushkin.

By the fall of 1971, Markelov began asking for material that Prushkin told him was Top-Secret and kept "under lock and key."

"It must be signed for when it's taken out," Prushkin explained. "And it must be returned before the end of the day. There is no way I can bring it out of the plant or even photostat it."

Markelov solved that problem, too. On November 1st, he provided Prushkin with a thirty-five-millimeter camera.

"Take pictures of the documents at the plant and give me the undeveloped film," the Soviet spy told the American.

What had become one of Markelov's most ambitious objectives from almost the outset of the conspiracy was gathering information concerning the causes that led to the crash of an F-14 during one of the early test flights over Long Island, on December 30, 1970.

"I must learn everything about what went wrong with the plane," Markelov told Prushkin.

What occurred in that mishap was that two of the plane's three hydraulic systems failed as William H. Muller, chief test pilot for the F-14, and Robert K. Smyth, chief test pilot for Grumman, were bringing the plane in for a landing at Calverton in eastern Long Island. The plane was barely two hundred feet off the ground when it became uncontrollable. Muller, who was at the controls at the time, and Smyth ejected themselves to safety.

The $17-million-dollar plane took a stiff nose dive after the pilots abandoned it and it crashed in flames.

Documents pertaining to the inquiry into the crash also were provided from time to time for Markelov, who since that encounter in the Marcpiere Restaurant until the night of Monday, February 14, 1972, had met the Grumman engineer on ten other occasions in restaurants on Long Island to receive classified information and make fresh demands for additional data.

Now, on the night of February 14th, Prushkin again was to deliver a role of film and several documents he had promised to put into Markelov's hands. They rendezvoused in the Wah Lum Chinese Restaurant on East Main Street in Patchogue.

"You have been doing a magnificent job," Markelov praised Prushkin over dinner. "We are delighted with the wealth of material you have given us."

As he had done on numerous other occasions, Markelov handed an envelope to Prushkin.

"There is another $100," Markelov smiled. Then he raised his cup of tea in a toast. "May our association continue as well as it has gone . . . "

It was not to be. For at 8:40 P.M., just as Markelov and Prushkin stepped out to the sidewalk, a half-dozen FBI agents led by John F. Coughlin leaped from the shadows and surrounded the astonished Russian translator.

"You are under arrest," Coughlin said. "Now I want to advise you about your rights. Before asking you any questions, you should understand that you have the right to remain silent and that any statement you do make may be used against you in court. Also, you have the right to talk to an attorney before answering any questions or to have an attorney present at any time. If you cannot afford an attorney, one will be furnished to you if you wish. And you have the right to remain silent until you have had the opportunity to consult with one . . . "

The agent who read Markelov his rights and the other G-men couldn't understand a word of his reply. Though Markelov spoke fluent English, his response was in Russian.

Markelov was bundled into a sedan and driven to the FBI offices, where the routine of arrest did not seem to disturb him in the least bit.

The tall, stocky Russian, garbed in a brown, fur-lined suburban coat and Tyrolean-style brown fedora, showed only the slightest annoyance by closing his eyes as he was led handcuffed into the building past reporters, photographers, and television camera crews, who had been alerted in advance about the arrest.

The news media had been notified by two sources—the U.S. Attorney's office in Brooklyn, which has jurisdiction over the Eastern District, comprising Kings, Queens, Nassau, and Suffolk counties on Long Island, and by the FBI in New York.

John J. Malone, the Bureau's Regional Director and Agent-in-Charge, told newsmen:

"Markelov had eleven separate meetings with the engineer at various restaurants in the New York area and persistently requested confidential data concerning the new plane."

Robert Morse, the U.S. Attorney for the Eastern District, let it be known that the conspiracy was strictly one-sided.

"From the inception of the case," Morse said, "Grumman officials and the engineer directly involved cooperated fully with the FBI . . . "

In other words, after going to dinner with Markelov at the Marcpiere on the night of December 3, 1970, Prushkin immediately informed his superiors at Grumman about the Russian's proposition.

The FBI was notified and Prushkin was advised to "go along with the play all the way." And all the documents he provided Markelov, and those he photostated and photographed over the fourteen months of the conspiracy, were carefully doctored to provide the Russians with the maximum amount of misinformation about the F-14.

Because he had no diplomatic immunity, Markelov was subjected to the treatment of a common criminal. At 11:30 P.M., after FBI agents had tried in vain to question him, the Russian was escorted from the FBI offices with his wrists handcuffed behind him and taken to the Federal House of Detention on West 4th Street.

The next morning, he was led handcuffed into Brooklyn Federal Court, but Judge Max Schiffman was compelled to adjourn arraignment proceedings until the next day because Markelov did not have an attorney. Moreover, he had refused to speak English in the courtroom despite his fluency in the language.

After he was taken back to the Federal lockup, word came up from the Soviet Embassy in Washington that they were assigning an attorney to defend Markelov.

Meanwhile, Nikolai Loginov, Soviet press spokesman at the UN, called Markelov's arrest "a provocation" and suggested that newsmen query the FBI about the meaning of his statement and for further details.

He was referring to the timing of Markelov's arrest—at the exact moment when Congressional hearings were beginning on FBI budget appropriations. The Soviet oracle suggested that the headlines of Markelov's arrest were "staged" to influence approval of a bigger budget for the FBI.

But the FBI was not about to comment. Not that it ever does. But this was one time when you could be certain there'd be no rejoinder to the Russian charge. The Nixon Administration had just begun talking about a possible visit by the President to Moscow in the months ahead. The word that had filtered down from the White House to the Justice Department was "cool it."

Evidently, however, no one told Judge Schiffman about the President's intentions to establish a new cordiality with the

Russians. Schiffman handled the proceedings the way a judge presiding over an accused spy should conduct the case.

He listened to arguments by Leonid Vitorovich Shoherbakov, who had flown in from Washington and stood beside Markelov, and the court also took judicial notice of Aleksei Y. Skotnikov, First Secretary of the Soviet Mission to the UN, who was in court as an observer. But nothing that Shoherbakov and Skotnikov had to say impressed the judge.

He ordered Markelov held in $500,000 bail. And since even the Russians didn't have that kind of loot in their petty cash coffers, Markelov was hauled back to the Federal House of Detention.

The next day, another hearing was held before Judge Schiffman who listened to pleas by Markelov's newly retained attorney, Donald Ruby, for lowering of bail.

"My client would like to be free to move about the New York area and to travel to Washington for conferences with officials of the Soviet Embassy," Ruby said.

Assistant U.S. Attorney Morse told the judge that the Government "didn't wish to make the situation worse" and consented to a lower bail.

Judge Schiffman then decided to reduce the $500,000 bond to a mere $100,000. Within minutes, Soviet Consul Shoherbakov arrived at the courthouse with a Police Department escort. He lugged an attaché case which he opened in court to reveal a glittering array of greenbacks—one bundle of $70,000 in one-hundred-dollar bills, another of $30,000 in fifties.

Before Markelov was released, Judge Schiffman set the ground rules for the prisoner's freedom—he must give the court twenty-four hours notice of his travel plans.

After these proceedings, nothing more was heard about Markelov for weeks. But an investigation by this writer revealed that within days after his arraignment, Markelov moved out of his $300-a-month nineteenth-floor suite in the vintage but still fashionable Hotel Windermere at 666 West End Avenue in Manhattan, where he had been living with his wife and eleven-year-old daughter, both named Nadezhda, and went to stay at the Soviet Mission headquarters.

Then, in a strange move by the Government, permission was granted on May 19th—on the eve of President Nixon's trip to

Moscow—to let Markelov go to Russia, although he was still under $100,000 bail and faced a trial which, if resulting in conviction, could have brought a maximum sentence of ten years in prison and a $10,000 fine.

Both Justice Department officials who were to have prosecuted the case, and spokesmen of the State Department, refused to comment about the move or to admit that it was related to Nixon's visit to the Soviet Union.

Edward J. Boyd, chief of the Criminal Division of the U.S. Attorney's Office, was the only official who had anything to say:

"We have every intention of trying the case. I have not had any dealings with the State Department."

Evidently Boyd hadn't gotten the word yet.

Even Markelov's attorney, Donald Ruby, seemed to know something that Boyd didn't know.

"I don't think I'm at liberty to comment on that," said Ruby with a smile when advised about Boyd's announced determination to prosecute Markelov.

The next time Markelov's case came before the public eye was on August 15th, the day after a super-hush-hush hearing in Brooklyn Federal Court, held at the ungodly hour of 7:30 P.M.—two and one-half hours after court is normally closed. The utmost secrecy surrounded the appearance of Assistant U.S. Attorney Edward J. Boyd before U.S. District Court Judge Mark Constantino. No newsmen were present at the proceeding—because no Fourth Estaters had been informed about it. But they caught up with the story the next day.

The Government's attorney informed the court that "there was nothing specific to be gained" from prosecuting Markelov.

"There is no quid pro quo," Boyd declared. "The decision involves our general relations with the Soviet Union and their restraint in dealing with American citizens."

Did this mean that we could expect a new rapport with the Communists—that instead of being jailed, our citizens and CIA agents caught spying in the Soviet Union would be spared the years of imprisonment in Siberian labor camps meted out to them in the past, and sent home instead?

Had President Nixon and Premier Kosygin worked out a deal whereby we would free each other's spies after they were caught?

249

No answers to these questions were forthcoming.

But Boyd left no doubt that the decision to drop the case against the Russian spy emanated from high up.

"The decision came after consultation between the State Department and the Department of Justice in the belief that it will best serve the national and foreign policy interests of the United States," Boyd told the court.

Judge Constantino then granted the motion for dismissal of the charges lodged against Markelov—and he also ordered the $100,000 bail returned to the Russians.

Though Valeriy Ivanovich Markelov had no diplomatic immunity and could have been prosecuted, he was allowed to escape punishment and return to his homeland.

The case was another exercise in frustration for the FBI. With the vast sums budgeted to the Bureau for its investigations of espionage in this country, and despite its brilliant record of achievement in arrests, the money, hours, and energy spent chasing spies appears to be a wasted effort most of the time. For the FBI's arrest record shapes a glaring contrast with the dismal number of convictions and jailings of Russian spies.

For reasons that it doesn't want to talk about, our Government is willing to forgive and forget subversion perpetrated against this country.

Is it any wonder then that the Soviet Union shows no reluctance—or any letup—in dispatching its spies to the United States?

It's the safest territory in the world for espionage operatives to ply their trade.

INDEX